D0593954

# NINE LIVES

✳

# NINE LIVES

## From Stripper to Schoolteacher: My Year-Long Odyssey in the Workplace

### LYNN SNOWDEN

W. W. NORTON & COMPANY

New York    London

Copyright © 1994 by Lynn Snowden
First Edition
All rights reserved
Printed in the United States of America

Lyrics from "Slave to the Grind" by Skid Row © 1991 Wordiks
Music/New Jersey Underground Music (Bach, Bolan, Snake).

The text of this book is composed in Electra with the display set in
Peignot Demi.
Composition and manufacturing by the Haddon Craftsmen, Inc.
Book Design by Charlotte Staub.

ISBN 0-393-03673-1

W. W. Norton & Company, Inc.,
500 Fifth Avenue, New York, N.Y. 10110
W. W. Norton & Company Ltd.,
10 Coptic Street, London WC1A 1PU

1 2 3 4 5 6 7 8 9 0

*To Jeremy*

All you need to be assured of success in this life is ignorance and confidence.

—MARK TWAIN

# CONTENTS

# Acknowledgments

**M**y thanks and gratitude to Bill Tonelli, David Hirshey, and Will Blythe for getting me started, and to my agent Richard Pine and my editor Starling Lawrence for seeing to it that I finished. My heartfelt thanks to Richard and Star for their terrific advice, thoughts, guidance, encouragement, and that most valuable gift to all writers—faith. The advance helped, too.

This book would not have been possible without the considerable help of the following people: Many thanks to Scott McGhee, who took the enormous leap of faith in hiring me for my first job when the book was only a concept, to Sebastian Bach, Dave "the Snake" Sabo, Scotti Hill, Rachel Bolan, and Rob Affuso for not treating me like a journalist; and to Curt Anthony, for being so patient and kind. Many thanks to Jim Tuthill, Carol Smith, and Ralph Sykes for making sure I got hired as a teacher, and to my lifelong friend Paige Takach, who spared me from hotel living by getting me to housesit for her parents. Thanks also to Johnny LaVoie and Sandy Turner in Las Vegas, who cut through red tape with a chain saw; to Cheryl Lynch for

## ACKNOWLEDGMENTS

her generosity of time, spirit, and clients at Baker Winokur Ryder; and to the fabulous GiO, who taught me many things, not the least of which was how to remove stockings in a memorable way. Special thanks to my great good friend Anne Russell, who has never given me bad advice and who also found a family willing to let me be a mom for a while, and to Steve Radlauer, whose helpful criticism and unflagging humor kept me on track. My thanks and admiration to Nancy Tartt and Kat Hammer, for showing me it's possible to be extremely politically correct and maintain your sense of humor at all times. A million thanks to Mark Wurzel, who did the impossible in finding me a factory job. And to everyone who cannot be named—you know who you are, and thanks very much.

Many thanks, although it's hardly adequate, to my family, who tried not to worry excessively about my personal safety while I was on the road, and whose words of encouragement were greatly appreciated. Most of all, I thank my husband, Jeremy Conway, who really *is* the hardest-working man in show business. I can't count the number of people who are amazed that my husband would "let" me do some of the things in this book. I thank him for not using that word in our marital vocabulary, and for his unwavering belief, support, encouragement, and love.

# Introduction

I suffered my first crisis of identity when I was seven years old. My father was a naval officer, which meant we moved quite often, and for the past two years we had been living in London, England. My brother was old enough to attend the American School in London, but my fate was to be the only American child at the very British George Eliot School. Other than developing a strange habit of referring to my hometown of Virginia Beach, Virginia, as "back where I belong," I seemed to have made the adjustment well.

For my seventh birthday, my parents said I could invite several of my school friends over to our apartment for a party. Shortly after my friends arrived, I barricaded myself in my bedroom and refused to come out. I had been speaking in a British accent at school and an American one at home, but now, with both my school chums and my family looking on, I didn't know how to speak without provoking one of the groups to laughter.

I came out of the bedroom once my family promised not to stare or giggle when I spoke to my friends. Looking back on it now, the reason I was so distressed was not entirely due to performance anxiety over speaking with a foreign accent. I could see for myself that the worst had happened: The identity I had adopted during the day was now my true identity. I really *was* a British schoolgirl who could fake an American accent, not the other way around.

I was relieved to discover that once we moved back to the United States, I became, once again, an American schoolgirl who had a lot of trouble correctly mimicking a British accent.

As an adult, I remain convinced that whether you like it or not, what you do during the day determines who you are at night. The job we perform influences nearly everything about our lives: where we live, how we dress and style our hair, when we sleep, whom we have as friends—perhaps even what accent we have, the kind of language we use. It determines our status or lack thereof in the community, it fuels how others see us, and how we see ourselves. As much as we may love and depend upon our families, the workplace is where we spend, for better or worse, the overwhelming majority of our waking hours in our lifetime.

Knowing this, and recognizing my chameleon ability to change according to my surroundings, I wondered what would occur if I took on nine vastly different jobs in the space of a year. Presuming that my "core" identity would remain exactly the same, I was interested in how it would feel to know that people were treating me differently because of what I did for a living, not because of who I am as a person. I know that most of us respond to a stereotypical image—all accountants are dull, all doctors are smart—rather than to the person to whom we are being introduced.

I experienced this phenomenon of the workplace when I worked as a fashion model for three years. Before settling into a career as a free-lance journalist for magazines, I worked as a photographer's assistant after graduating college, which led to someone suggesting that I should model. After I signed with an agency, I resisted picturing myself as a "real model": one of those creatures who are stupid beyond belief, but have an uncanny ability to look good wearing only eyeliner, who know exactly how to stand at all times, and who can saunter down Fifth Avenue in faded jeans and a knapsack looking like they're in designer clothes. I thought that in my case, modeling would be something I would do during the day to earn money. I had forgotten all about my experiences in England.

I was surprised to see that it took only a few photo sessions for me to start striding down Fifth Avenue in faded jeans, with the right knapsack and—most important—the attitude that made people start asking me, "Are you a model?" The attitude you pick up from work is what makes people on the street see you differently. I didn't become any more attractive. I just became a model.

Of course, once I became a model, I deeply resented being thought of as someone who is stupid beyond belief, possessing only a talent for looking good in eyeliner. We tend to believe that all stereotypes are based in truth except for the one that applies to us.

With this in mind, I was interested in selecting professions that have very strong stereotypical images. Not only do we have preconceptions about the sort of person who works in certain jobs, there is an accompanying belief that we also know exactly what each of those jobs entails. I wanted to examine persistent myths about jobs, the people in them, and women in the workplace in general.

While making my list of likely careers for this book, I received suggestions from family, friends, and co-workers. Since I wanted to limit my selections to interesting jobs that didn't require highly specialized training, ideas such as "a lawyer" and "a cop" were immediately ruled out. George Plimpton has already played football for the Lions, so that was out too, and even if I wanted to follow in Gloria Steinem's footsteps by working undercover as a Playboy Bunny, the era of Playboy Clubs has thankfully passed. One friend suggested that I try to become a bodybuilder and compete on the television show *American Gladiator*. One viewing of the show convinced me that, given my skinny build, this was an impossible goal. I briefly entertained the thought of becoming a jockey until I found out I'm too tall.

With these limitations in mind, I aimed for the widest mix possible, in both the types of jobs and their geographical locations. I wanted to enter these worlds as a kind of "Everywoman" character, and work with the people who inhabit them daily. I was interested in male-dominated fields, female-dominated fields, high pay, low pay, volunteer, blue collar, white collar, highly reputable to downright sleazy.

I also chose the jobs for their contrasting value. How differently would I feel if I were a high school teacher or a roadie with a heavy metal band? What would be the reaction when people heard I counsel rape victims or if I said I work with celebrities? What's harder, factory work or housework? Where would I notice more sexual harassment—as a cocktail waitress or as a stripper? Where is the power in working in a uniform, a business suit, or nothing at all? Which jobs would be the most lucrative, the most fun, the most demanding, the most demeaning? And more important, could someone like me, who is basically unqualified for any of these positions, even get hired in today's economy?

I spent a year answering these and many other questions, and the results are in the pages that follow. This last question, however—usually in the form of "Why would they hire *you?*"—was raised by friends and strangers alike every time I had to look for another job. I tried not to let it get to me, but it was something I had to ask myself from time to time.

I have not always approached job hunting in the appropriately humble frame of mind. When I was eighteen, I lied in order to get hired as a waitress, and said I had worked elsewhere. My mother asked how I was going to fake this "previous experience" on the job. "I've eaten in a lot of restaurants," I said. Rather than admit this excellent recommendation to my new employer, I knew it was better to lie on my application. I learned this when I was turned down for a job at a Foto-Mat, where I would have had to sit in a tiny booth in a mall parking lot. The manager said he couldn't hire me because I "didn't have any experience."

"My brother once locked me in a steamer trunk for half an hour," I said. "Does that count?" I also learned most employers do not appreciate sarcasm in a job interview.

But getting back to that persistent question "Why would anyone hire me?" I was sufficiently worried about this to ask an attorney if it's illegal to lie on a job application—at the time, it was my sole job-hunting technique. I discovered it's only a criminal offense to lie on a federal job application, but most applications warn employees that providing false information is grounds for dismissal. In my case, I thought I could afford to take that chance, but unfortunately, in today's economy, you need to do more to get a job than simply scrawl a few phony places of business in the section for "previous places of employment." A year's worth of experience as an underqualified worker with no applicable experience led to the formation of what I call my Five Basic Rules of Successful Job Hunting:

*Rule 1.* Never contemplate how unlikely it is that you'll be hired. It's a self-fulfilling prophecy, like worrying about surviving the plane crash when you discover there's engine trouble. Just concentrate on flying.

*Rule 2.* Getting the job is far more difficult than anything you'll be required to do once you're hired. You won't have any problem living up to the employer's high expectations of your job skills if he or she liked you in the interview. A reasonably observant person can learn almost any job in three days.

*Rule 3.* Never worry that your lack of qualifications will be an issue. This may actually help, since your dearth of experience keeps you blissfully unaware of exactly what you're letting yourself in for. This allows you to maintain a cheerful attitude during a job interview, something an employer is always impressed with when hiring someone for what is actually a horrible position.

*Rule 4.* Ask your friends for help. It can't hurt. They might know someone who can give you a job, or they might know someone who knows someone who can.

*Rule 5.* When all else fails, offer to work for no salary. If you're already unemployed, it's not as if you're taking a drop in pay, and once they see you in action, most employers will eventually arrange for you to move into a paying job. If they turn out to be cheap ungrateful bastards, you can always quit. You'll at least come out with something for your résumé and valuable on-the-job experience. This comes in handy if Rule 3 doesn't seem to be working out.

Trust me on this. I got hired nine times last year.

# NINE LIVES

❋

# 1

# Sex and Drugs and Rock and Roll: How to Make Explosives, Stage-Dive, and Live Happily in Filth

How do you pack to go on the road with a heavy metal band when you're told to travel light? I call a girlfriend of mine for last-minute advice. She's a graphics artist for television and has never traveled with a band, but she happens to be home, so she qualifies as an expert. I tell her I've already got tiny travel bottles for all my creams and moisturizers but I have one overriding anxiety.

"We're traveling by bus," I explain. "Not the whole time, but until we get to hotels. But you know there's one bathroom on a bus, right? A small little thing? How am I going to share a bathroom on a bus with eleven other guys? I take about fifteen minutes to wash my face at the end of the day! What if I cause a mutiny or something?" My husband is away on business and I'm desperate for reassurance.

She laughs. "You think these heavy metal guys don't spend a lot of time in the bathroom? With their big hair and all the eyeliner? Are you kidding? I bet there's a whole bus devoted to hair care." This thought cheers me up.

*"Maybe I can ride on that bus," I say.*

*"Yeah, say you want to ride on the beauty bus, or whatever they call it," she says, before wishing me luck. I hang up and stuff my hair dryer in with my jeans, and decide also to jam in a tube of mascara and some eyeliner. I look at my watch and see I have fifteen minutes before I have to leave for the airport. I study the contents of my small suitcase. After some hesitation, I throw in my favorite summer dress on the off chance I'll need to look nice. It's time to go and I'm scared to death. My heart is pounding.*

*I check again for my plane ticket and turn off the lights in the apartment. I see a small pocket flashlight lying on top of the stereo. On an impulse, I grab it and stick it in my purse. I'm a little afraid of the dark, so I thought it might come in handy.*

I wipe my watch crystal with my hand, a gesture that succeeds only in making it dirtier. I don't need to know what time it is, since I've just been told the band will be coming on-stage in about ten minutes, but old habits die hard. I look out at the audience, and I know what they're feeling. I've been one of the thousands of teenagers who are anxiously, feverishly, and noisily awaiting the start of a rock concert. On rare occasions, I had a good seat on the floor or I worked my way forward to be one of the hundreds in the crush up front, and I've often been one of the unlucky ones way in the back holding a pair of binoculars. But I've never been up on the stage at a time like this.

Then again, it's different now—I'm working as a roadie, I'm one of the people milling about making last-minute adjust-ments before the band comes on. Because I know so well what it's like to be out there, I can't help but stand on this coveted vantage point with a small bit of smug pride.

I'm one of two pyrotechnicians; we're responsible for the special fire effects that blow up and flame out at key moments during the concert, moments that are timed to emphasize the force and power of the music. Pyrotechnics are standard for, although not exclusive to, heavy metal concerts, and the heavy metal band I work for, Skid Row, is particularly eager for loud, violent displays of firepower.

I put on my safety goggles and crouch down on a ramp. Unscrewing a small bottle of powdered magnesium mixed with potassium nitrate, I pour the entire contents into one of the dozens of iron canisters situated about the stage. Even though the personal danger is fairly minor, this part of the job makes me nervous, since I know what the stuff looks like when it explodes: a long, nearly white, blast of flame. Crablike, I move on to the next canister.

The audience can see at a glance that I'm not a groupie or someone's girlfriend or a backup singer—the three usual occupations of women in the rock world. I'm in a grubby T-shirt and jeans, my hands are filthy, and most important, I'm wearing a giant, laminated "All Access" crew photo I.D. that dangles from a cord around my neck. I can evaluate the audience just as easily: They're thousands of white, suburban teenagers who've traveled to this outdoor arena in Clarkston, Michigan, a city midway between the depressed automotive centers of Flint and Detroit, to see their favorite band. It's the most important night of the year for most of them. I find it strange to realize that I have a job where every single workday involves creating a major event in thousands of people's lives.

The hardcore types are up front, baring their tattoos, shaved heads, and Doc Marten combat boots, as they've bullied their way up to the barricade by some nasty Darwinian process. One guy with a ring through his eyebrow is raising a fist at me. I smile at him. The less aggressive fans in Skid Row T-shirts and cutoff jeans are the next group back. Scattered throughout are the girls wearing tops that slide provocatively down one shoulder. They're easy to spot since they're sitting astride the shoulders of some guy who will no doubt be expecting a meaningful reward for carrying them around this way for the next two hours.

When I look up from my work, audience members shout things at me, something about a backstage pass or a guitar pick. "Get a life," mutters my boss, Curt, in response to the heckling. We gather up the empty bottles of powder and make our way to stage right to the control board. We're among the last to leave the stage, as the explosive powder works best if it's not allowed to settle too much.

While we wait, I look at the giant painted backdrop of the cover of Skid Row's last album, *Slave to the Grind*. The album, their second, entered the music charts at number one, a rare feat reserved for performers whose followers are so devoted that they line up at record stores at dawn on the album's sale date. The kids in the audience lined up for the album, lined up for the concert tickets, and lined up to get into this place. Now the delirium of actually being here, out of a line, away from school, away from parents, away from anyone who is not a member of their particular tribe, is reaching its dizzying peak. The stage lights come on, and we in the crew screw in our earplugs as the restless anticipation of the crowd suddenly finds its voice: a pure animal howl set against the first rushed repetitive guitar riffs that mark the title track of *Slave to the Grind*.

All available hands fly up protectively to our already stoppered ears as the first concussion charges are detonated by Curt seconds later. It sounds like three cannons going off simultaneously, and the music is suddenly the aural equivalent of a train wreck. The drummer, Rob, is joined by the three frantically playing guitarists, Rachel, the guy with a nose ring joined by a chain to an earring, Snake, and Scotti, who run on without missing a note. They're followed by a six-foot-three-inch lean drink of water known as Sebastian Bach (née Bierk), the lead singer, who pauses in his triumphant entrance to acknowledge the screaming crowd. The smoke dissipates and it's clear that nothing went amiss—no one died or got hurt—but the physical sensation of the explosion was just this side of getting kicked by a horse. Curt and I give each other the thumbs-up.

The lyrics of this particular hard-driving anthem speak directly to every kid who fears he'll be stuck working at the Pizza Hut forever: "I won't be the one left behind/ Can't be King of the World/ If you're Slave to the Grind." The audience screams these words, arms outstretched, hands forked in the universal heavy metal salute. The point in a heavy metal concert is not to sit back and enjoy the music but to participate, to be engulfed in the sensory overload of light, heat, and noise. They thrash around, especially in what's known as the mosh pit, the area directly in front of the stage, where the swirling mass of aggressive males effects a rugby scrimmage. The rather tender violence among them is the only acceptable way for them to show one another affection, acceptance, and brotherhood. It also provides a relatively safe outlet for a considerable amount of rage and frustration.

The security guards at the barricade are trying to cope with the number of fans determined to rush over them to get on-stage, so they can dive off it again into the churning mosh pit. The guards, local guys hired for their heft, look dazed and confused, as if they've been clubbed on the back of the head—and they have, if they're standing in front of the enormous columns of speakers. One kid tries to scale a guard as if he's a piece of furniture. He gets as far as landing a foot on the guard's shoulder and one hand up on the stage before he's yanked off by his belt. Like others before him, he's hauled off to the sidelines, and set free in the back of the crowd. It'll take him only about fifteen minutes to fight his way to the front again.

Meanwhile, the roadies who hand off various guitars to the band members—the backline guys—are putting on paper masks in order to cope with the blizzard of dust, ash, and soot raining down from that initial concussion charge. I make my way down into the pit in front of the barricade in time to check out my favorite effects: the fireballs and the short blasts of flame that burn out during "Monkey Business." I notice that bits of plaster from the cement band shell are also raining down, making it look as if it's snowing. Sebastian sees me standing in the pit and, for this unexpected result, gives me an enthusiastic thumbs-up.

I've been doing this for ten days and I can't think of a better line of work: Pyrotechnicians earn upwards of $600 a week plus $28 a day in per-diem money to make things blow up. Of course, the life-style takes some getting used to.

"You don't shit on the bus." This is the extent of my orientation lecture from Todd Mackler, the tour manager, delivered to me ten minutes after I arrive. Mackler, a thirty-year-old from Arizona, has an almost militaristic demeanor, both in his blond crew cut and in his refusal to concentrate on more than one task at a time. "It's a chemical toilet," he explains, "so if you do, everyone will know it, 'cause it stinks to high heaven and makes everyone miserable." As we have one twenty-seven-hour drive on the itinerary, he anticipates my next question. "We stop at truck stops, just tell the driver if you need to stop."

Despite this anxiety-provoking rule, I'm told by my newly introduced busmates that bus tours are infinitely preferable to plane tours. Tour buses have a front lounge, a tiny kitchen, a back lounge, and a windowless area in the middle with twelve bunks. "The bus is your home," says Scott, a deceptively fierce-looking lighting technician. "You have all your stuff on it, you're not always going to the airport or waiting at the airport. You can't really sleep on a plane. But sleeping in your bunk on a bus is great. I never sleep better, not even at home."

I'm also told that yes, there will be "chicks" on the bus occasionally, but only in the back lounge (it has a door that locks), and if someone "wants a chick to share his bunk and spend the night, it has to be voted on by the rest of the bus members."

The tour is a convoy of three semitrailers filled with equipment and staging, two buses filled with the crew, and two comparatively empty buses for the band. I'm relieved to hear that I'm on the same bus as the only other woman on the tour, Toots, the wardrobe mistress. But when Chris Reynolds, the unflappable British production manager, shows me my bunk, the bottom one of a three-tiered stack, accessible by rolling directly from the carpeted floor to the mattress, I'm filled with dread. It was as if a friend was allowing you to crash not on his sofa, but actually under it. "Bottom bunks are a little noisier from the engine, but more stable," he says cheerfully. "There's a lot more sway on top. You'll be fine here. It's like being back in the womb."

My first night in this tiny crawl space begins with a full hour of suppressing feelings of intense claustrophobia. How can such a space be shared with another person unless through demonic possession? With the tiny reading light on, I can see how small the place is; in darkness it seems even smaller. With the curtains open I feel exposed and vulnerable: Mike, the big burly rigger, is literally an arm's length away! I'm surrounded by tattooed, bearded, long-haired men who may or may not be asleep! But with the curtains shut, and the bunk above me only about ten

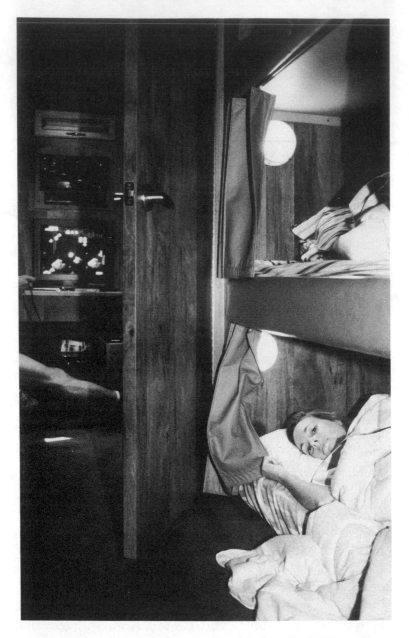

Home, sweet home. Me in my coffin on the bus. (*Leslie Wagner*)

inches away from the tip of my nose, I'm in a coffin: Maybe someone will throw open the lid and drive a stake through my heart.

I sleep fitfully, clutching my pocket flashlight as if it's capable of warding off evil. This is not what I expected at all. I thought we would get on the bus after the concert, and I would then extend the courtesy to my busmates of washing up as quickly as possible in the tiny bathroom. Then we'd nap—or sing songs? play word games? tell the stories of our lives?—until we reached the next town and a hotel. We'd wake up, check in, sleep until noon, shower, and then head down to the arena for a sound check in the afternoon. That's when I thought roadies went to work. After all, how much time could it take to plug in a few amps and hang a backdrop? After a couple of hours of this sort of activity, I thought we'd go back to the hotel, have dinner, trash a hotel room or two, change in time for the concert, and head back out to the arena to enjoy the show. I didn't know roadies erect the entire stage and hang and focus the lights. As a con certgoer, I thought—if I bothered to think about it at all—that that stuff is already there from the previous concert and it's just a matter of moving things around the way you like them.

I see now that the above routine is much closer to rock star than roadie. My confusion may have been compounded from my talks with Scott, the band's manager, who always travels with the band, not the crew. The crew's routine is this: You work all day and sleep on the bus in a coffin.

After a restless night, morning comes all too quickly. There's something singularly unfortunate about being awakened at 9 A.M. by someone yelling "Hey! Wake up!" and then opening your eyes to find that you're not at home but in a bus in the deserted parking lot of an empty arena somewhere in Canada. My tour itinerary is packed away somewhere, and without it I have no clue as to where we are; even worse is the knowledge that any showering to be done will be in some hideous locker room last used by some reeking hockey team. Putting this out of my mind, I grab some coffee from the caterer's table inside, brushing between two roadies loudly arguing over who gets the last box of Apple Jacks.

I sit down to scribble nervous notes about procedure as Curt Anthony (or, as the crew calls him, "Little Timmy," owing to his boyish resemblance to the kid in the Lassie movies) explains my duties. The fact that this thirty-year-old has all of his fingers despite a lifelong interest in blowing things up inspires immediate confidence.

We set up one of the trunklike road cases for a worktable out on the floor of the arena. He patiently teaches me how to rig individual fuses to the canisters and flash pots, which are iron cylinders of various sizes with cable outlets at their bases. An eight-inch-long fuse, a screwdriver, and some tape is required to do this, along with some sort of knack that I don't have, as several minutes go by before I can successfully finish one. The rest of the crew doesn't seem to notice my incompetence, for while they may think they can do everyone else's job, the realm of pyrotechnics remains a dangerous mystery that automatically grants some sort of grudging respect along with a very wide berth.

As frustrating as learning how to fuse canisters is, it's less physically taxing than having to carry the thirty-five fused devices, which weigh anywhere from ten to sixteen pounds apiece, from our little workspace up onto the stage, which has now been erected. A ramp up to the stage from the floor is set up much later in the day, so this exercise includes heaving the unwieldy canisters up a distance of more than five feet onto the stage, and then scrambling indelicately up there myself. I grab them and carry them up the stage stairs to the overhead ramps, a routine no Stairmaster prepared me for. I'm humiliated to discover that I can't carry four canisters without dropping one of them, and carrying two at a time means making endless trips. And so I repeatedly trot back and forth and up and down the stairs, dodging other roadies who are madly dashing about wheeling equipment, barking orders, and belching louder than I had previously thought possible.

By lunchtime, I'm exhausted. The caterers give us sloppy joes, a meal that instantly recalls high school cafeteria fare. "This is prison food," says Lumpy, a roadie who bears more than a passing resemblance to Charles Manson. He tosses his half-eaten, dripping sandwich down in disgust. "And I ought to know."

The afternoon is spent taping small firecrackers to the stair risers, a task I enjoy because I can actually sit down. Curt teaches me how to rig everything together in a mass of plugs, cables, and extension cords that all lead back to his control panel. "Watch," he says, throwing a spool of cable on the floor so it feeds out without tangling, a trick that requires the cable to have been initially wound in alternating directions. I'm giggling with delight over this, as I can't get over what an ingenious trick it is. Why doesn't the public know about this? No more tangled Christmas tree lights, extension cords, or garden hoses! I notice a few roadies are giving me funny looks for laughing at spooled cable. As I obviously need a break, Curt tells me I can go take a shower, something I've been dying to do all day.

Dying to do, that is, until I see the locker room: Wooden pallets on the floor, cigarette butts, dead bugs, and bits of paper litter the large open shower area. There are no mirrors, which may be a good thing under the circumstances. Clutching a change of clothes, my toilet kit, and a small, thin towel I got from our bus, I search for a cleanish part of a wooden bench to set these items down on while I undress. I can't decide if I'm more nervous about the prospect of other roadies bursting in here mid-shower or the prospect of walking around barefoot.

When I get back to work, clean but scarred for life, I tell all the other roadies what they're in for. No one is even remotely concerned. "One time," says Scott, who's been on the road for fifteen years, "there was just a fire hose in the parking lot."

"Yeah," says Mike. "At least it's not some outdoor festival, where there's Port-O-Sans. Try cleanin' up in one of those."

I'm impressed they'd even try. I remember what Todd told me last night about Sebastian's avoidance of soap and water. The band, along with Todd, the bus and truck drivers, and band security, have access to a hotel—and a nice, clean private bathroom—every day. The rest of us get to stay in a hotel only on our days off. "Sebastian went four weeks without showering one time," Todd said with a chuckle. "And this is sweating every night! I have to tape his ankle, and I can tell how long it's been since he's showered by counting the rings of adhesive. Just count the rings, you know?"

While we've been in this arena all day, the members of Skid Row have been hanging around their hotel and are due to arrive at 5:30, for a ten o'clock show. Pantera, a thrash metal band that makes heavy metal sound like easy listening, is touring with us as the warm-up act, and they're due to go on at eight, after the doors open at 7:30. I know this from reading the Xeroxed signs taped up around the dressing rooms backstage. It's near our six o'clock dinner break, so I decide to try and find the production office in the rabbit warren of hallways, as it's where you go to make a free long-distance call or to get a backstage pass for some cute thing you met hanging around outside the bus.

At the moment, the production office is harboring a mostly naked Sebastian Bach, who is, contrary to previous rumors, fresh from a shower, and is just barely wrapped in one of our skimpy white towels and still has shaving cream on his earlobes. He's stunningly good-looking, with streaky blond hair, more than a couple of tattoos, and sultry, almost feminine features. Chris introduces me as Little Timmy's assistant. "Oh yeah, the chick!" he says exuberantly. He enthusiastically shakes my hand while I worry that his towel is slipping. Most business manuals lack a section on how to handle that first meeting with your boss when he's wearing a towel. "Listen," he says, heartily smacking my shoulder, "I want you to blow this fuckin' place up, okay?"

I assure him we will, as I assume that's what pyrotechnicians are supposed to say to everyone except a fire marshal. But when showtime does roll around and everything I worked on during the day actually ignites, explodes, and flames out, I'm completely impressed and unbelievably proud. Even deadpan Curt manages a smile.

When the concert ends at 11:45, it seems as if I first walked into this place about ten years ago rather than only this morning. I'm more than ready for bed and am actually looking forward to the sanctuary of my little coffin, but I'm told that now I have to participate in an unpleasant exercise called "load-out." This is the dismantling of everything it took a day to erect and packing it all into the trucks. A grueling hour later, I'm scrubbing off what soot I can in a trashed women's room, as the locker room is full of showering roadies. After a few stiff drinks on the bus, I crawl doglike into bed, as we speed along into the (presumably) Canadian night.

At 9 A.M., it begins all over again in a different city. Everyone I call asks where I am, and it becomes an embarrassing question. "I don't know," I tell my parents, who seem shocked. I glance around the production office to see if anyone's eavesdropping. "What difference does it make?" I say a bit testily. After all, I'm either in a bus or in an arena—which smells like a giant urinal deodorizing cake—all day and all night; it's not like I'm out sightseeing or sampling the local cuisine. I do notice that my indifference to actual place is not shared by seasoned roadies, as they remember each electrical or structural foible of every arena from previous tours, and, more important, they remember local groupies and drug dealers who must be summoned to the parking lot—if they're not there already, that is, soliciting their wares as we wander to and from the bus throughout the day.

After three days as a roadie, I discover the joys of streamlining all activities, and begin to sleep in my clothes, as this cuts out many unnecessary steps of changing in and out of a nightshirt on the bus. I also see how pointless it is to wash my hands before eating lunch, as I'll only get them dirty later anyway. I begin to see the simple beauty in drinking shots of tequila without bothering with the limes or salt.

Some roadies streamline their laundry routine when they realize that paying to have socks washed is more expensive than the cost of cheap socks bought in bulk. "I wear a pair of socks four days straight and then throw them out," says Ronzo, one of the backline guys who's toured with the band since their beginning five years ago. "After two days, I turn them inside out, so it feels like a fresh pair. Well, *psychologically*," he adds. Lumpy also advocates the socks-in-bulk route, and says he once went through a whole tour with one pair of pants, but now he streamlines his end of the tour packing and shipping hassle by "throwing all the shit out on the last day."

By the fourth day, I discover I don't need two types of moisturizer and it's really enough for me to just brush my teeth before bed. Since I can now fuse canisters nearly as fast as Curt, he teaches me how to make the airburst cluster explosives, the fireworks type of effect at the finale. I nervously tap out powdered magnesium and strontium with tiny aluminum flakes onto four-inch squares of Saran Wrap. Curt carefully gathers the corners and twists it into a tight little package with an electrical squib sticking out of it. Neatness counts with Curt. "Has to be Saran Wrap," he warns me. "It burns without dropping globs of molten plastic the way Handi Wrap does." After we ceremoniously shout "No smoking onstage!" we hang these tiny bundles from the lighting grid.

I take a break and notice that the production office is suddenly filled with roadies, a sure sign of a pending day off, as they're using phones to book tee times at the golf course in the next town. Golf is quite the rock-and-roll sport. "Alice Cooper is a brilliant golfer," Chris tells me. "He played with my father-in-law once, really impressed him."

The next town turns out to be Ottawa, Ontario, and for me, the most memorable and impressive sight is my own spacious hotel room, with a bed that seems as large as a lake and a bathroom so clean you could eat off the floor. There are several large fluffy towels for my own exclusive use, and all the privacy I could ever want. But I eventually tire of lounging about naked in the midst of this heretofore unappreciated luxury, so I call around to find out what everyone is doing. I heard about the last day off, where a few roadies and a couple of the guys in Pantera were under the influence of some hallucinogens, and believed the couch in the hotel lobby was, well, *menacing* them, so they attacked it with a knife. After viewing the carnage, they decided to hide out in a tattoo parlor until their manager could arrange to change hotels. This is why one of the electricians has been rubbing Neosporin into his new tattoo all week.

As the golfing is already under way, and Ottawa apparently lacks notable tattoo parlors, my choices for the afternoon seem to be bowling (Curt and Mike tour with their own bowling balls), basketball at the local YMCA with Snake and some other guys, joining a rather large contingent planning on a day at a strip club, or going along with the few opting for local shopping and drinking. I join this last group, and at the end of the day we all meet up in the hotel bar to compare notes.

"They asked me to leave!" says a very upset Chris Mohr, known as "Mohrshead," who can belch the loudest, longest, and most often of all the roadies, which is no small contest. "This tittie bar! They said, 'No leather jackets!' I was with all them guys with leather jackets, but I took mine off and then they said, 'No sleeveless shirts!' I mean, I'd only been in there about five hours already and had about a million drinks! I don't know why they asked me to leave." He belches, and three businessmen across the room look over. "Fuck," says Mohrshead disgustedly.

The businessmen, and anyone else in the bar not in the rock world, are driven out when some roadies for the Grateful Dead show up and shout greetings to their friends and comrades with Skid Row. The Grateful Dead stadium tour requires part of the crew to travel a few days ahead just to erect the huge stage. Unlike other professions, shop talk among roadies is interesting to outsiders.

"Linda McCartney," says a roadie who's watching the news above the bar. "What a hypocrite!"

"Fuck yeah," says another roadie who's worked on a Wings tour. "There she is in an all-leather outfit, flying around in a private plane, using all that fuel and polluting everything, and she always asks if you're vegetarian! And if you're not, she preaches about how you should be and how wrong it is not to be one! Paul's nice, he doesn't preach, he keeps pretty quiet."

Other nominees for hypocritical behavior include one rocker who participated in a Just Say No concert "and is a total gak head," *gak* being roadie slang for cocaine. Aerosmith and Mötley Crüe are cited for their new intolerance for other people drinking now that they're on the wagon.

"These guys have a problem," says Ronzo about Mötley Crüe. "I don't have a problem." An order for another round of tequila shots is shouted to the bartender, and since it's a day off, limes and salt are requested. "I really don't see why I can't have a drink just because they can't handle it."

"With them, at least it's only that you can't have liquor backstage," points out someone who's toured with Aerosmith. We all gulp down our shots. "If we were sitting here in this bar, on our day off, like we are now, and the Aero-police passed by, we'd be fired."

"The worst tour? Hammer. He figures he's made it this far in the business, he knows everything, so he hires friends, relatives, very few professionals. It's a nightmare."

"He has two buses just with relatives!"

"Yeah, and the buses have Kentucky Fried Chicken all over everything! Seriously! I'm not being racist, KFC is their sponsor!"

"Hey, did you know that Robert Palmer once played fifty-four shows straight? They offered their crew a day off in the middle but they said no, it'd fuck them up too much to break the routine!"

"Gene Simmons is really into fat chicks." A weird hush descends over the bar, as this is absolutely the worst thing that can be said about anyone in the rock world. His public romance with the very thin Cher was, according to this guy, simply a cover for his actual preferences. "The fatter the better," he assures us.

Conversation eventually resumes after that sobering announcement. A guy who recently joined up with the Springsteen tour is mentioned. "Better him than me," says Mike. "A four-hour show? No thanks. It's like workin' a fuckin' opera."

"Some nights it was all I could do to stay awake," says Scott, who's toured with the Boss.

"How's he to work for?"

"Good. Good bonus." This is the little extra sum generally paid, but not always, at the end of a tour.

"I know the guy out with him right now doing his Tele-PrompTer."

*What?!* I practically do a spit take and interrupt for a clarification.

"You didn't know he uses one?" says Mike. "It's for the lyrics."

"Wait a minute," I say, still unable to grasp this startling news. "He wrote the songs, *why can't he remember them?* His fans can remember them!" Suddenly everyone jumps to the Boss's defense.

"Give the guy a break!"

"Yeah, it's a four-hour show!"

"The guy's written maybe four hundred songs! It's just for reference, it's not like he's fuckin' readin' off it the whole time!"

I offer to pay for this round and the bill is passed to me. "Fifty-seven dollars?" I gasp out.

"Sign the bill real sloppy and don't put your room number," Lumpy whispers. "They don't always catch it."

"I once went off the road *in debt* because of my MasterCard bills," says one of the truck drivers. "I drank more than I earned."

I notice Sebastian is waving me over to his side of the bar. "Have you seen Phil's dick?" he says, apparently referring to Phil Anselmo's dick, the guy sitting next to him with the shaved, tattooed head. The angry lead singer of Pantera. "It's fuckin' *huge*, man!" Sebastian says this as if he's talking about the local mall. Phil is smiling ever so modestly. "It's like, fourteen inches!"

Sebastian continues. "I mean, I've got ten inches, you know, *hangin'*. But Phil, whenever he shows his to anyone he says, 'This is nothing! You should see my dad's.' "

"Maybe I'll see it another time," I say. I suspect that this offer of penis exposure may be some bizarre hazing ritual, so I change the subject as nonchalantly as possible. But back at work the next day, I discover that's not the case at all, as Phil's dick is regarded as something of a natural wonder, and is the topic of almost daily conversation.

"You haven't seen it?" says Chris. "God, it's massive!"

"Definitely a baby's arm holding an apple," says Toots.

"Well, they say everything's bigger in Texas."

"Can we please," says Louis, the Vari-Lite techie, "get through just one day without talking about Phil's dick?"

I watch Pantera perform with new interest. But studying Phil onstage, his arrogant, supremely pissed-off posturing and growled vocals only make me wonder: *With a dick like that, what's he so mad about?* I have an urge to make an announcement to the crowd of teenagers who may be feeling inadequate: *See, he's got a big one, and as you can see, it apparently doesn't solve everything.*

I walk out to the bus to find Curt and discover several roadies engrossed in an episode of *Murder, She Wrote*. Noting my shock, one of them lights up a joint and says, "Talk to us about it when you've seen Pantera about a hundred times." To the fans inside, how anyone could be watching Angela Lansbury when they could see Phil Anselmo in the flesh is unfathomable, but the life of a roadie doesn't always mean they tour with bands they like to listen to. For while much is made about the hard life of a touring musician, however long the band tours they eventually go home. The crew members may go from one tour to another and another in their small, overwhelmingly white male world of recommendations and contacts. "I'm home maybe five days a year," says Mike.

"I was gone for sixteen months once, didn't come home at all," says Curt. Todd points out that in the last eighteen months he's hardly been back home to Phoenix, Arizona, but he still managed to meet a woman, get married, and father a baby. "My wife hates me," he says fretfully.

Most roadies aspire to somehow get off the road by the age of forty, and while the idea of being stuck in one place clearly gives them the willies, there are worse concerns. "Doing that nine-to-five thing," sneers Curt, not really meaning the actual work hours but giving up the outlaw status. It's becoming one of "them," a member of the straight world, and consequently gaining "ligger" status, a derogatory roadie term for anyone back-stage at a concert (no doubt proudly waving a VIP pass) who is not actually working. My temporary absence from what I think of as the "real" world prompts me to mention to Sebastian that being a roadie is like being a kid who has run away with the circus.

"Not the circus," he says. "Rock and rollers are the last pirates in the world! We come into a country, we rape, we pillage, we destroy," he laughs uproariously, "and then we leave!" He leans his head back and howls in the manner of a man who will never need a self-help book to get in touch with his masculinity. "Aoo-oow! Long hair! Earrings in our noses! Modern *pirates!*" I realize that this is a much more apt metaphor, as women can join a circus, but there were very few women pirates.

"You know why I got that?" he says, showing me a large, col-orful tattoo on the back of his hand. "It's so I won't ever have to work in fuckin' McDonald's."

This prompts me to ask some co-workers what they'd be doing for a living if they weren't roadies. "I'd be a plumber or an

electrician," says Sarge, who has hair down to the middle of his
back, a goatee, and quite the tattoo collection. I can't imagine
answering the door and feeling comfortable about letting him
in, no matter what the state of my toilet. Mike says, "I'd probably be working in an Off Broadway theater."

"I'd be an electrician, customizing people's homes," says
Ronzo. "That, or owning my own bar."

"I'd be driving a truck, delivering liquor," says Mohrshead,
who's been saved from this fate by knowing Snake, the guitarist,
since he was three.

Of course, the irony in their defiance of straight life is that
underneath the long hair and tattoos, they're actually extremely
professional, highly dedicated workers who have a very low tolerance for slackers. They'd probably be disgusted by the bureaucracy, politics, and rampant incompetence present in most companies. With their willingness to work long hours and their
highly developed skills at crisis management and individual
problem solving, in corporate America they'd be either pain-in-
the-ass workaholics or company vice-presidents.

"You're gonna stage-dive tonight!" Sebastian yells at
me as he runs offstage during a drum solo to sit down, drink
Evian, and spit onto a towel taped to the floor. I'm standing
with Curt at stage right, near the control board. It's my fifth
show, and I've certainly seen plenty of fans stage-dive back into
the crowd, but it wasn't something I'd been meaning to try myself. I look to Curt for advice. He shrugs.

Patrick, the band's security guard who must wade into the
crowd after Sebastian when he stage-dives, yells over the din, "I
wouldn't advise it, but if you're going to do it, tuck your lami-
nate down your shirt or they'll pull it off you. Also, jump from
the center of the stage, it's closer to the barricade and the

In conference with the boss: Sebastian Bach and I share a quiet moment at work. (*Leslie Wagner*)

crowd's more into it there. When you jump," he says, swiveling his torso in demonstration, "turn your body so you're not landing face down, try to land on your side or your back. That way if the crowd doesn't catch you, you're not breaking a fall with your nose and teeth." I nod dumbly, trying not to think about how I'll have to clear eight feet of space just to miss the bouncers and the metal barricade in order to hit the crowd that might not catch me anyway. Well, it's probably no worse than handling explosives. Or riding in a cab in New York City.

Sebastian rushes over and pulls me onstage, and it seems as though I have no choice. I take a big running jump, hoping not to die, dizzy with a rush of adrenaline. I hit the crowd on my side, and am deliriously grateful to discover I've landed on what seems to be a cushion of hands, the impact not nearly as rough as I'd imagined. "Awesome dive!" a guy beneath me yells. I instantly want to do it again as I'm borne aloft and magically moved forward. Once at the barricade, a security guard helps me over, and Sebastian yanks me back up on stage. My legs are wobbly but I'm laughing. The crew is astonished. This is behavior strictly reserved for psycho fans or rock stars, certainly not sensible folks like roadies.

Patrick walks over to me while I'm loading up a road case after the show. "A kid broke his neck stage-diving tonight. Cracked a vertebra."

Chris comes over soon after. "You don't see the kids limping away, after the guards help them out, faces bleeding," he says. "Promise me you won't dive anymore." I shrug, but I know I'll do it again. I liked it too much.

The next night, Sebastian and I hold hands and dive together, and I remember too late how the crowd tends to descend upon him in a complete frenzy. Upon impact, the crowd pulls like a massive vortex, as fans dive over me to scrabble at Sebastian.

Just when I'm about to be trampled underfoot, I see Patrick pushing his way in, extricating the two of us from the crowd as if we're in quicksand—by yanking us forcefully out by our arms. "I've lost hair, skin off my knuckles, my shoes," says Sebastian after the show. "It's fun, but it gets a little crazy."

Stage-diving becomes something I look forward to doing all day. The odds of successful stage-diving increase dramatically if you're a lightweight woman, as there's a built-in incentive for guys to reach up and grab you rather than let you fall. This didn't help Jim, a 250-pound bodyguard whom Sebastian ordered to stage-dive when we played an outdoor concert at the Meadowlands in New Jersey. As he became airborne, the crowd magically parted, and Jim smashed down onto asphalt, seriously bruising himself. "I was hurtin'" was all he'd say about it. We started calling him Moses in honor of his ability to part the sea.

After eleven days on the road, a day off finds me examining my battered body in my hotel room mirror. Thanks to the boot-camp work routine, I do look lean and slightly more muscular, and the scale in the bathroom reports I'm eight pounds lighter. A monstrous bruise with an accompanying scab adorns the side of my right knee, the result of Sebastian's unintentionally violent retrieval of me from the crowd after a stage-dive in Montreal, pulling me up and over the top of a speaker. There are two smaller bruises and scabs on my left shin from cracking into a stair riser on the stage during load-out on two different nights. One red bruise above my right breast, two inches below my clavicle, achieved on impact when stage-diving with Sebastian. One faint purple bruise on my right knee induced by banging into a road case one groggy morning. My left wrist is swollen from a misplaced, overly exuberant high-five from Rob the drummer, and my right-hand knuckle is scabbed from scraping against the inside of a flame projector canister. The last time I was this banged up was when I was nine years old and trying to roller-skate and jump rope at the same time. I also have a blister on my thumb from repeatedly tearing duct tape for the sticks of explosives, and my nails are a complete wreck.

Toots's nails are perfect, as she tends to have a manicure on days off, and she does mostly office work. While Curt meets with a fire marshal one morning, I wander off to find her unpacking the band's dressing-room cases. A six-year tour veteran at twenty-four, Toots (a childhood nickname) went straight from a strict English boarding school to the rock-and-roll life, and while she retains the telltale poise, she admits it takes her a few weeks after a tour to stop saying *fuck* so much. She bravely sniffs at a shirt to see if it should be laundered.

"Rob's very clean," she says, referring to the shirt's owner, "so it's pretty safe." She gathers up Rob's fake leather pants and hands them to a local hire, a runner, to deliver them to a laundromat. "Just wash them, no drying. Bring them back wet." She catches me looking at the photo of Rachel's girlfriend stuck in the mirror in his road case—it's exactly what's tattooed onto his arm. "I think I could recognize everyone in the band just from their smell," she says, as we move on to Sebastian's case, where any sniffing is done with extreme caution.

She gingerly removes the pants that he wore the previous night, black hip-huggers slit up the sides and lashed together with cord. She sniffs them and offers them to me. I cautiously inhale and catch something vaguely familiar, like mildewed carpet and wet Keds sneakers; or maybe Baz (as he's known to friends) is managing to secrete something like bong water, due to the liberal amounts of pot and Evian he consumes, as it doesn't really smell like regular sweat. Toots arranges his pants over a sink and generously sprays them with something called Fresh Again. "I have cases of it," she says. "It kills bacteria and

Lean, mean, and fusing flash pots. Check out the stage diving bruise behind my right knee. (*Curt Anthony*)

odors, works really well." The bottle's label insists it's "better than dry cleaning. Great for uniforms!" She uncaps the bottle and pours some of the liquid directly into the crotch and around the waistband. The soggy pants are then draped on a chair outside in the parking lot to dry out and air, where they will be passed unnoticed by fans intent on hassling us for backstage passes. "That's about all I can do," she says, heading back to the production office. "He won't let me wash anything." In these grungy times, it's not cool to be too clean.

I walk back in time to hear the fire marshal asking Curt to discourage the audience from holding up lit matches or lighters during songs. Yeah, right. We're detonating $850 worth of gunpowder and explosives, and the fire department is worried about a few Bic lighters? Curt later tells me they always ask that, and you have to tell them no, it's impossible. This particular fire marshal didn't want a demonstration of any of the effects, as some do, he just wanted to determine whether they could accidentally trigger the sprinkler system.

By late afternoon, when most of our work is finished, the groupie-mongers among the roadies can get down to what makes touring really worthwhile. At this point, the parking lot has perhaps fifty or a hundred women hanging about in their finest acid-washed denim, hot pants, pink pumps, and lace ensembles and fluffing their big, streaky, heavy metal hair. The girls' hunger for access is so raw that even the most troll-like roadie is flirted with in what can only be called frightening abandon. When not accosting roadies, the girls primp, reapplying pink frosted lipstick and adding yet another coat of mascara.

"If you only knew what Sebastian means to me," says one girl, stopping me in the parking lot. "Is Sebastian nice?" she asks. "I know Rob is supposed to be the teddy bear of the group, the kindest one. Do you know where they're staying? I have one wall with pictures of just Sebastian. Two walls of the whole band, one wall of Mötley Crüe." She pauses to gauge my reaction. "I don't know, maybe you think I'm a stupid idiot or something." She smiles. "You look like Sebastian's sister," she says. "You're so pretty. You could model, do you know that?" I tell her I can't help her with a backstage pass. She asks for my name, and I'm instantly suspicious: She could try to pose as my friend in order to convince someone else to give her a pass. "I can't help you there, either," I say.

This is why certain roadies have aliases "for the chicks," explained one. "So they don't know your real name." It's also an alert to the rest of the crew; if a girl is asking for, say, "Jason," we know that she isn't really a *friend* of his.

I usually try to work in a nap shortly before our dinner break, and I find I'm often rocked to sleep by the gentle movements created by some mutually exploitive coupling in the back lounge. This is most often the work of "Condom Man," our little nickname for one of the more notorious groupie aficionados, who, thank God, practices safe sex—the evidence of which is inevitably left in the back lounge wastepaper basket.

Today I visit the other bus, which is known for its frozen margaritas, as it has a blender, and one roadie I'll call Smooth Dude is delivering his standard speech to two teenaged girls who have accepted his invitation to join him in the air-conditioned inner sanctum of a crew bus. He gets straight down to business. "If you want a backstage pass, there are things," he says, pausing, "you have to do."

"Can't you just give us passes because you're nice?" says one girl, tugging down her miniskirt in a nervous attempt at modesty, her glossy red lips stretched into a well-rehearsed smile.

"Why should we give you backstage passes?" says Smooth Dude, a not unattractive twentysomething guy. He looks at the other roadies on the bus, who nod in agreement. No one has offered the girls a drink. The girls look at me, but I'm sipping my margarita and picking at a scab on my knuckle. "A girl roadie," one of them says. "Cool."

"It's not that easy for us to get passes," says Smooth Dude, changing the subject, "so you have to do something."

"I just wanna meet the band, you know?"

"Show us your tits," says one of the other roadies. When pointed demands for sexual favors are rebuffed, roadies go to Plan B, which is the Polaroiding of Tits. The girls giggle.

"No way!" says one.

"You don't understand what it's like!" says Smooth Dude, reverting to Plan C, which is the Plea for the Pity Fuck. "I have not been with a woman in months! It's no fun doin' it with your hand night after night!" Of course, Smooth Dude had just been with a girl not so different from either one of these only yesterday, which was two days after his girlfriend visited.

"I'm sorry," says one before giggling with her girlfriend.

As Plan D begins with the Silent Treatment, the girls take the hint and get up to leave. "If you leave," announces Smooth Dude, "you can't come back in." This actually works sometimes, where the thought of lost access causes some girls to change their minds and do whatever it takes to stay. Today, however, it doesn't work, and they get off the bus. Smooth Dude looks out the window to see if there are any girls out there who look Most Likely To. "Shit," he murmurs. Of course, the tragedy for these girls is that giving Smooth Dude a sexual favor in exchange for a shot at a sexual favor with the band will result in a backstage pass with his initials on it. This signifies to crew and band alike that these girls are spoiled goods, and they'll be avoided like the proverbial plague.

Not everyone indulges in this sort of behavior and, surprisingly, quite a few are absolutely faithful to their wives or girl-friends. "Me and my girlfriend just broke up," says Ronzo. "She told me I was making her squeeze her emotions into a two-week period. Well, those two weeks in the summer are the best two weeks!" He shakes his head. "If I met someone nice on the road that would be great, but they usually just want something off you. Tickets, backstage passes, dick. To meet the band. There are some guys who are really into that, and don't care, and for a few years I was the same way, but after waking up next to some-one and I didn't even know their name . . ."

This is when Todd chimes in with, "I think it was when you woke up next to Lumpy."

Ronzo laughs. "I can't really explain it," he says, "but there has to be emotion there now."

Groupies seem more pervasive and annoying on our days off, as they follow us into the elevators, they sit near us in the restau-rant and in the bar, desperately eavesdropping, sending wait-resses over with notes and, very, very occasionally, drinks. We see some faces over and over, girls who follow us from city to city, causing us to wonder how they can afford to do it, and why on earth they would even want to. While the guys have utter scorn for these women so willing to sell themselves, they've ac-cepted me as one of their own, a hardworking member of the battalion. I'm expected and allowed to just do my job; no one patronizes me, no one has made an improper advance. Lumpy and I are sitting in the lounge with Billy, who sets the monitors.

"You became one of us," says Billy to me, "when you punched Derek." He raises his glass in tribute, and I modestly accept this undeserved compliment.

After three days on the road, I lost my temper and decked Derek, the unbelievably annoying tour accountant. This scored major points with the crew, since he's not very popular, and they'd all like to take a shot at him. What's stopped everyone else is that it's just not smart to hit the guy who holds your per-diem money, and for them, hitting a nerd like Derek is like hitting a girl—not exactly a worthy opponent. I actually only bashed him with my duffel bag after I caught him trying to read what I had just written in my notebook, but the incident, in true crew fashion, has now been exaggerated and blown up into some kind of brawl with me the Sigourney Weaver type victor against a screeching alien. Given the nature of my daily duties and that I also managed to break off a bus door handle soon after the Derek incident prompted Louis to dub me "the Annihilator." Billy and Lumpy toast my slugging arm. I don't bother to tell them I never really used it; I'm enjoying my tough reputation too much for that.

We notice we're slowly being surrounded by girls. "She's a high-class whore," says Lumpy, about a groupie across the room who is wearing red shorts that fully display the bottom third of her astonishingly high and rounded butt. She waves at us. We don't wave back.

"How do you figure that?" says Billy.

"Because that's how she makes her money."

"No, I mean how do you figure the 'high-class' part."

Toots and I occasionally wondered what we could make teenaged male fans do in exchange for a backstage pass, but the closest we came to any sociological experiment along these lines was when I took one of Rachel Bolan's guitar picks down to the pit just before showtime.

"I have Rachel's pick here!" I announce, holding it up for visual inspection to the crowd behind the barricade. It's black with a white skull and crossbones, and a tiny replica of Rachel's signature is scrawled at the bottom. "What do I hear for it? What will you do for me?"

"ANYTHING!" begins the chorus of male voices. "I'll give you every fantasy!" "I'll fuck you eight times!" "I'll lick your whole body!" "I'll lick your feet!"

This last offer, from a young, fresh-faced guy, caught my attention. "Lick this," I say, picking up my Converse-sneakered foot. I expect him to reconsider or argue me down, but no, he instantly reaches over the barricade and grabs my upheld sneaker with both hands so fast that a security guard rushes over to prevent me from falling. The kid cheerfully, *lustily* even, licks the sludge-coated sole. He gives me a big smile. Shocked, I give him the pick. He's ecstatic. When I tell the crew, Smooth Dude in particular is disgusted.

"You're a sick fuck, you know that?" he says.

The dreaded twenty-seven-hour bus trip turns out to be more fun than I had imagined. "The secret," says Chris Reynolds, "is to drink as much as possible." We begin the drive with a stop at a liquor store. After loading our cooler and fridge with beer, Jagermeister, champagne, tequila, vodka, and several different mixers, we move on to a grocery store for such wholesome snacks between dinners as Cup-O-Soup and Fudgesicles. We pass the time by drinking, watching videos, listening to music, and bus surfing, a sport where each competitor stands on one leg as long as possible while the bus lurches and weaves through traffic.

After passing out in the middle of *Apocalypse Now*, I awaken to see we've pulled over to allow a very agitated Smooth Dude to board our bus. "He's trying to kill me!" he's shouting. This can only mean that Lumpy has decided he's had enough of Smooth Dude, and Tony, their bus driver, thought it best to get him out

SEX AND DRUGS AND ROCK AND ROLL

of Lumpy's sight for a few hours. After several more drinks, naps, arguments, jokes, and long stories, we pull into the hotel parking lot in Thunder Bay, Ontario, to check in at 4:30 in the morning.

"Are you guys with a hockey team?" asks a drunken guest in the lobby. Nearly everyone is wearing a Skid Row crew T-shirt, so we give him looks that convey that we're too tired, dirty, and hung over to answer stupid questions. "Why are you so mad?" he says.

During our last show on the tour, in Calgary, I realize with some sadness that this is probably the last time I'll make explosives. I used to be someone who was nervous around fireworks; I couldn't even light a match without flinching. Now look at me: I get a thrill out of the noise, the concussive effect, the burning, billowing white light. It doesn't scare me anymore. Maybe the Fourth of July will be different this year; I won't have the urge to hide under the bed.

Midway into the show, a note is passed to Sebastian from the security guards. He announces that a girl suffered an epileptic fit, and would her friend meet her in the first-aid room. A bit later on, Patrick asks me if I could go and check on the girl, see if she's all right.

When I open the door, I see her lying on a stretcher, surrounded by nurses applying cold towels. She's twitching and a bit bruised-looking, but immediately waves me over and tries to sit up. "Can I have a backstage pass?" she croaks. I should have known by then that it's the only possible thing she could have wanted to say to me.

Swag (roadie-speak for free stuff) is passed out at the end of a tour, and for me, collecting the T-shirts and saying goodbye felt like graduating from high school: beating back the knowledge that even though addresses and phone numbers are exchanged, the camaraderie and closeness will most likely end right here.

I pack my two Skid Row tour polo shirts along with a Skid Row baseball cap, several guitar picks, a set of drumsticks, and three crew T-shirts from Pantera. The Killer Dwarfs, our warm-up act for the last week, rather touchingly presented me with a T-shirt, a signed poster ("To the bomb girl!"), and a lovely bottle of red wine with a corkscrew thoughtfully duct-taped to the bottle. But there are parting gifts, and there are *parting gifts*.

One roadie brags about a video he copied from a fellow roadie who received it as an end-of-the-tour gift from a rock star known for his extraordinary sexual appetite. The video features this rock star having sex with various women, some famous, some not, but the salient feature is that none of the women was aware that this guy was secretly documenting these acts on film. When the roadie reveals the name of one very well known actress shown having anal sex with this guy, we're astounded.

"Why haven't you sold that tape?" someone asks when the barking dies down. "You could make a fortune!"

The roadie shrugs. "I'm not done with it. Besides, I like to show it to my wife and say, 'See, honey? *She* does it.'"

# 2

# White Collared

After so much traveling, I relish the thought of having a job in New York City. It will be the only job of the year where I'll be able to go home after work, see my husband and friends, and sleep in my own bed at night.

Being a self-employed late riser, I've been spared thus far the experience of rush-hour commuting by subway. Not anymore: Now I must get up like everyone else and claw and wedge my way into a packed subway car.

This means starting the day by standing less than twelve inches away from fellow commuters' freshly applied lipstick, bloodshot eyes, razor nicks, and coffee breath. I begin to notice that in addition to reading newspapers, people read more books on the subway at rush hour than they do at other times of the day. To my surprise, approximately one out of every five people reading a book in the morning is reading the Bible—most of them women.

Come to think of it, I could use a little strength and serenity myself. Is it an accident that, despite the close quarters, someone's hand just brushed against my butt?

My first day as a copywriter at the New York offices of one of the biggest advertising agencies in the world finds me sitting alone in my windowless office. My desk is completely bare except for a lamp, a telephone, and a tube of toothpaste. I'm supposed to be dreaming up ads incorporating this brand of toothpaste, so I open the box, unscrew the cap, and cautiously taste it. Fifteen minutes pass. I panic every time anyone passes my office, as I have no idea what a real copywriter would be doing under these circumstances. My nervousness isn't helped by the knowledge that Salman Rushdie started out as a copywriter, and look what happened to him.

I met my boss earlier, a large, congenial man of about forty named Tom. The air in his office felt about ten or fifteen degrees chillier than the rest of the well air-conditioned building, but when we shook hands, his fingers were toasty warm. This strange feat of metabolism occupied most of my inner thoughts during our brief chat, and he sent me off to a meeting with Joan, a small, intense woman who apprised me of the current market research regarding the toothpaste account.

"Here's where we are," she says with some exasperation. "People are embarrassed to admit they use this toothpaste! It seems frivolous." She flips a chart on her desk over. "Here's where we want to be: that it's the only toothpaste they and their friends would ever think of using." She hands me a two-page summation, known as a brief, of exactly what the client expects of the new ads.

Since she thinks I'm a real copywriter, I nod my head as if I'm really taking all this in about advancements in tube design, and whether caps that flip up sell better than caps that screw on, but I feel dangerously close to laughing. *Toothpaste!* She goes over the market research and quotes from toothpaste users listed in the brief while I nod and circle what I hope are the key points. Finally she pauses with a serious expression on her face. I lean forward.

"Every major brand of toothpaste is equally effective as far as fluoride protection goes," she says in a slightly lower voice. "It's all *exactly* the same."

"But what about the four out of five dentists . . ."

She holds up her hand to stop me from saying the dreaded competitor's name. "They've got the approval of the American Dental Association, but that also means the ADA has a say in the tone and content of their advertising. We don't want that."

"So these ads should push the fluoride protection first but then also emphasize fresher breath and whiter teeth."

"Exactly," she says, and hands me a tube of toothpaste. I thank her too profusely, not realizing at first that the toothpaste is probably for research purposes and not a gift. We shake hands. I wander around until I can find my office again.

As I sit mulling this over, my phone rings. Startled, I pick it up. "Lynn Snowden," I say tentatively.

"Hi! This is Tracy from the Washington office!" She mentions another account with the agency, a communications network, and says, "I was told I should speak to you about it."

"You were?"

"Tom just told me you would be handling this account." I get a knot in my stomach. Does this mean I'm supposed to have the toothpaste thing all sewn up by tomorrow morning? Isn't this an awful lot of work already? "I'm coming in tomorrow," she says, unfazed by my silence. "Let's get together before lunch. Where's your office?"

Since I have no idea how to get back to the reception area from here, I look for a landmark, and see a name on the wall opposite my door. "It's . . . right across the hall from . . . Raphael's office."

"Okay! See you then!"

I buzz my secretary. "Do you think I could get some office supplies and equipment?" I wonder why she's not replying until I look up to see her in the doorway. A wave of Rive Gauche perfume hits me a moment later. I eventually learn to track her in the agency by her scent. "You know, whatever the other copywriters have?"

She nods and disappears, leaving me grateful that I didn't have to be specific. Aside from watching reruns of *Bewitched*, I have no idea how, or with what tools, advertising campaigns are developed. I thought this would be an ideal white-collar job and a way to finally answer for myself the barroom questions "Why is advertising so stupid?" and "What ad wizard dreamed *that* up?"

I cling to the small hope that being able to write will come in handy, but judging from what's on television, it's hard to see how that could be true. When hired, I was told this agency recruits copywriters from different fields, so my saying that I have a journalistic background would not seem strange to anyone. The idea behind this sort of head-hunting is that someone who works outside the field of advertising might think in ways that could bring a completely fresh approach to a campaign.

Since I'm not getting a salary, I asked if I could have my own office and a secretary—I might as well make this as pleasant a corporate experience as possible. The company kindly cooperated, but the fact that I didn't start out in a lowly cubicle and work my way up gives the other copywriters and art directors the idea that I must be some big gun hired by the agency to shake things up.

So here I am, alone in my office, tasting toothpaste. If I admit my ignorance regarding advertising to anyone, it will become difficult to explain why I have my own office. My original plan was to remain as unobtrusive as possible and learn how to write an ad by watching others do it. I hadn't counted on being so cut off from the rest of the agency. I look in my purse for a piece of paper and make a note to stop in a bookstore on the way home. Maybe there's a how-to book on advertising copywriting out on the market.

An hour later I get a call from Val, Tom's multi-earringed secretary. She tells me I'm wanted in a meeting. I rush down the hall, still unclear as to the best route, feeling like a rodent looking for the wedge of cheese. I finally spot Val among the rows of secretaries, and she waves me into what turns out to be a group meeting of the ten or so art directors and copywriters working under Tom. When the door shuts, I see I'm the only woman in what feels like the freezer section of the supermarket. I cross my arms over my chest and make a mental note to always bring a suit jacket to work.

The real point of the meeting seems to center around trying to make Tom laugh. Alex plays at being the gruff overworked art director who throws his hands in the air every time another account is mentioned. Stan, a copywriter, throws out comments that alternately parody and faithfully imitate brownnosing; his art director partner, Keith, originally from Australia, has a wit so dry it seems to have evaporated altogether. It's a classroom filled with class clowns. In between the jokes, ideas are thrown out, and briefs are distributed.

To my immense relief, I learn exactly how ad campaigns are developed. It appears that the procedure is exactly what it is on *Bewitched.* I get an idea for an ad campaign—having a spouse who's a witch would help in this area—then I explain my idea aloud in a meeting. If my idea is approved, that is, if Tom nods and says, "Good one," a script is expected to follow. Artwork and storyboards come later for presentation to the client. Who says TV doesn't prepare you for real life?

Three days later, my office has a typewriter, a stopwatch (to time copy), a desk calendar, stationery, some legal pads, and In/Out baskets. The In basket has accumulated what seems to be an alarming number of briefs, the Out basket contains my notes on a script for a radio ad for the communications network. It seems as if we're receiving many more briefs than we are presenting ideas, and it's giving me the same sinking feeling I got in school when the volume of homework assignments exceeded what could possibly fit into the number of hours left between classes. All I have to show for the toothpaste account so far is a half-eaten tube, and I lamely wonder if I can somehow turn that sad fact into a brilliant ad.

I try to fashion a creative atmosphere in my dreary box of an office by spending $150 on a psychedelic poster of Jimi Hendrix, a vintage 1972 poster of a neon-orange smiley face, and an ad for the movie *Henry: Portrait of a Serial Killer*, along with a forty-eight-inch-long black light to zap the whole place with a weird glow. The smiley face and the *Serial Killer* poster provide what I hope is a yin and yang of the office worker, but the Hendrix poster has the not altogether desirable effect of drawing all the sixties folks in the agency to my doorway, where they stand and reminisce. The black light, however, has the advantage of making my whites look whiter. If only, I keep thinking, I was working on a detergent account.

I've been told by a vice-president here that an entry-level copywriter would receive a salary of $25,000 to $30,000 a year. I heard from other people in advertising that $50,000 to start would not be unusual. "Why are you working here?" says an art

Trying to look busy and brimming with ideas. And as usual, the legal pad I'm holding is completely blank. (*Jeremy Conway*)

director who watches me decorate my office. "Don't you know this place pays the least?" I can't tell if he's telling the truth or trying to psyche me out, since I've also heard that there's a rumor going around that I've been hired to replace someone who hasn't been fired yet. I raise my eyebrows and smile knowingly, as if I've got a special arrangement. I do; it's just not the one he thinks.

One bonus of my new, bizarre decor is that it signals that I am a "creative"—a copywriter or an art director—as opposed to an "account" person who crunches numbers and handles the business end of advertising. I'm told that because my office is on the border between the two factions of the agency, there were some creatives who were hesitant to come in and chat in case I was "one of *them*."

Creatives generally take great pains to express their individuality, whether it's in their clothes, their office decor, or their work, however misguided the effort may be. The account people revel in their ability to conform, to adapt, to please. Of course, the people they aim to please are not the creatives, but the clients. It sometimes works out that the account people are the ones to take your script and storyboards to the client, even though they may not completely understand the concept or, worse, leave out an important nuance that makes or breaks an idea. This arrangement keeps the clients massaged and happy and isolated from the volatile, unpredictable artistic temperaments of the creative people, but can also mean that briefs and consequent communications can be horribly garbled. I'm told that the prevailing philosophy behind this system is that creatives are too crazy and impetuous to be trusted in the same room with a client, as words may be exchanged that may cause the client to take the account somewhere else.

I linger behind after my third group meeting to show Tom my first piece of copy, a radio ad script, as I would rather see one person roll his eyes than a roomful. I've written it in the campy style of a 1950s sci-fi horror movie, and I sit waiting for a chuckle that never comes. "Never use the word 'it' when referring to a product or service," he finally says, circling at least five of them in red pen. "Work the name in as many times as you can. And all this shit," he says, circling the dialogue I wrote incorporating the necessary ad-speak, "should be said by an announcer. It never works otherwise." I meekly take the marked-up script back. "It's not bad," he says. "It'll be fine. Come back with the changes, and I'll put it through." I feel absolutely elated and suppress an urge to skip all the way back to my office, wherever it may be.

I soon discover that I have two things on my side with regard to successful copywriting. Since I've already seen millions of hours of television, it's fairly easy for me to mimic the style of dozens of commercials, and, two, my tendency toward rather extreme brand loyalty means I can write copy as if there really is a difference between brands. This doesn't mean that I'm likely to come up with a revolutionary new kind of ad; it means I'm all set to imitate someone else's revolutionary ad. I soon learn that there'll always be a spot for people like me in the ad industry, as clients, despite what they insist, don't really want anything new anyhow.

About five of us from the group tend to convene in Paul's office to brainstorm, as Paul, a copywriter, has the most toys. We take turns playing darts or shooting Nerf basketball while ideas and thoughts are also thrown out for consideration. We play with the Homer Simpson dolls (this requires fluency in the Homer Simpson voice) and Paul's treasured fart machine, usually employed when anyone bends over to retrieve the Nerf ball. Fake British and Pakistani accents are also incorporated into the conversation, mostly because Paul is very good at them and gets other people to play along.

As my radio ad is now in the loop for official approval from the client, I feel myself to be on a winning streak with ideas. I am, after all, an *idea person* now. "You know what's bad about toothpaste?" I say to the group. "The colors on the tube! They clash with every bathroom, they have nothing in common with any towel colors on the market, and it's the one thing that the consumer can't repackage the way they can with shampoos or liquid soaps. So why not market a white toothpaste in a plain silver tube? Or in a black tube? Or an elegant black-and-white tube?"

"Black toothpaste?" Alex says in his perfectly honed Homer Simpson voice.

"No, just the graphics. The toothpaste is whatever it is."

61

Four people shake their heads at me as if I'm an idiot. "People associate certain *colors* with certain *brands!*" The guys chuckle. "Jeez, Lynn." So much for a winning streak.

Back at my desk, I try to think about the ad and, at the same time, look as busy as possible for the benefit of passersby who may or may not be important. This effort brings on a longing for my days with Skid Row. As a roadie, no one really cared what you got up to during the workday as long as the work got done. In corporate life, getting the work done is not nearly as important as appearing to be busy at all times. Personal phone calls are camouflaged with businesslike noises the moment someone pops their head in. Aimless wandering around the hallways can appear to be a purposeful walk to a meeting, if you remember to bring a file of papers. A slightly late arrival to work can be concealed if you immediately make yourself visible, as if you've already been working and are simply taking a break or getting "more" coffee. And even though receptionists and secretaries pack up and leave at the dot of five, I hang around until the more respectable executive-class hour of six-thirty or seven, again making a final patrol of the premises so my late attendance is duly noted.

A brilliant strategy for a toothpaste account isn't going to come to me any faster because I'm spending more time in this eerily glowing room; in fact, I'd probably get more inspiration from walking down Fifth Avenue. These are my thoughts at two o'clock, as I'm fighting off the urge to lay my head down on my desk and take a nap. Should I shut the door? Or will people be fooled into thinking I'm reading if I lean on one elbow and shield my closed eyes with my hand? I yearn for my little bunk on the crew bus. What a great job that was, even if it was on the filthy side.

I'm irritated to be sleepy and cold at the same time. Outside, it's approaching a humid 95 degrees, but I'm wearing a crisp white long-sleeved shirt, a dark suit jacket, cuffed pin-striped trousers, and black leather lace-up shoes. I can feel my skin prickled into goose bumps where my knee socks end. The polar-level climate control is a never-admitted-to device in the white-collar world ensuring that everyone dresses in a businesslike manner no matter what blistering, asphalt-melting heat is endured en route to work. To wear shorts or a sundress in here would mean dying of frostbite before lunch. To go without nylon stockings under these fluorescent lights would mean walking around with legs the color and texture of dead mackerel. I sit on my hands and stare, glassy-eyed, at my desk.

Fortunately, Paul takes my mind off this by barging in and announcing that we've been partnered on the tea account. Our mission, as outlined in the brief, is to devise an ad that stresses the "freshness" of the tea. I go over to an account guy's office to get a box of the tea for inspirational purposes. While in his office, I see a can of the iced tea mix. "Oh I love this stuff," I say, picking it up. "I drank this all the time as a kid. In the summertime, I used to just eat the powder and chew ice cubes."

He gives me a deservedly peculiar look. "How much of that canister would you say is sugar?" he says.

"Yeah, I know, I know. It's probably seventy-five percent sugar, five percent lemon, and twenty percent tea."

"Try ninety-seven percent sugar, one percent lemon, and two percent tea."

"You're kidding," I say, shocked.

"No, I'm not."

"It's still good, though."

He gives me another funny look, but I'm wondering if the American public would go for a new taste sensation of eating this stuff dry. Probably not. Even astronauts added water to their Tang, although I used to eat that stuff dry as a kid, too.

Over the next few days, Paul and I come up with a couple of ideas, and meet in a conference room to explain them to three account guys. Paul and I hand out our scripts.

"Okay, we see a close-up of an orange being peeled," Paul says, reading aloud. "Then we see a champagne cork popping out of a bottle. The sound effects on all this are very exaggerated. Then an expensive chocolate truffle is unwrapped. Now we see the tea being unwrapped and pulled out of the box. The AVO," he says, meaning announcer voice-over, "says, 'Some things are sealed for freshness. Your tea should be too.'"

One of the account guys raises his hand. "You can't use another beverage in a beverage ad."

"The champagne?" I ask. "Why not? It's a great upscale image."

"Because we're trying to get everyone to drink tea, and nothing else," he says.

"Do you seriously think," I say, "people are going to go, 'Hey! Why don't I have a glass of champagne right now instead of a cup of tea'?"

"You're just not supposed to do that," he says with some condescension. "The concept is good, we just need to think of something else that's sealed up for freshness."

"How about a can of coffee?" says one of the other account guys. Paul and I exchange meaningful looks before we derisively say "Hel-lo!" to this guy.

"Hey!" he says, singling me out. "You don't know me well enough to talk that way to me!" We argue some more over the champagne, and eventually adjourn the meeting.

The champagne issue becomes moot when the spot gets cut down to fifteen seconds, which is enough time for the orange to be peeled. Three days after that, Paul and I are informed that the whole thing is bagged because the legal department says there's too much emphasis on freshness, something we can't legally claim to have over the other teas on the market. "But isn't that what we were told to emphasize?" I ask Paul. He shrugs.

Of course, this is nothing compared to the cookie-spot brief, a couple of pages that magically appear in my In basket one morning. In this case, the brief states that a series of magazine ads are to announce the "New Light Recipes" for the cookies, but "the following words can not be used in the ad copy: Light, Healthy, Reduced or Lean." This is because the FDA has issued guidelines regarding what can be labeled Light, Healthy, Reduced, or Lean, and this cookie doesn't measure up as it's just marginally less caloric than its regular recipe. I keep rereading where it says "New Light Recipes" and the part where it says not to use the word "Light" in the ad, until I give up and go to see Tom. Two other copywriters are already there with the same question. He's on the phone with the woman who wrote the brief, and Keith is sitting with a stopwatch, timing how long it would take for her to start crying. She cried once during a confrontation, so the group is betting Tom can make her weepy once again.

"Okay, so we can't call it 'New Light Recipes.' Then, we call it something else, like 'Smarter Recipes.' Can we get a batch of the new cookies over here?" Tom listens, then shakes his head no to us.

"Do they look the same?" whispers Stan, a copywriter.

"Do they look like the old cookie?" says Tom. He shakes his head no at Stan. "How about if we left them in the oven a little longer, could they get a golden brown color? What I'm saying is, can we do a convincing side-by-side shot with the two cookies?" He rolls his eyes and hangs up. "This is bullshit," he says.

"She never cried?" says Keith, a little surprised. He puts down the stopwatch. "Can we do a shot of a kid holding a cookie, but being lifted up off the ground by it like it's a helium balloon? We wouldn't use the word 'light.' It would all be by implication."

Tom sighs. "This is as close to a scam as you can get." No one wants to work on this because the ad is bound to look cheap no matter how it's done, as there's got to be a little clip-out coupon along with the recipes, and it will look like every other food ad in *Good Housekeeping* or *Family Circle*. I use the excuse that it's the art direction that's the real crux of the ad, and since I'm not partnered with an art director, there's nothing much I can do.

Those of us in Tom's office eventually end up in Paul's office where imitations of the president of the company are being perfected—the walk, the talk, the gestures. Being able to do the president convincingly is part of being an employee, and all of us try to fool one another with phony memos from the big boss announcing either raises, firings, or weird professions of love.

"There was a time," says Keith, "when we were on the same pee schedule," he says, referring to the president. "Every time I went into the men's room, there he was! At the urinal! And I couldn't walk out. It was really weird." He thinks a moment. "If he wanted to molest me, if it meant getting a raise or promotion, I would only be too happy to go along."

Being spared the experience of peeing next to the big boss is the only reason I'm happy to be the lone woman in our group. Whenever I use the cavernous women's room, I find it a strange yet totally accepted ritual of corporate office life to routinely urinate next to co-workers. We buy tampons, apply makeup, and carry on perfunctory conversation with each other all the while. It strikes me that I've never watched my best friend perform such intimate ablutions, but in the office, close proximity in the bathroom is part of the workday.

The agency also furnishes the restrooms with a very large bottle of mouthwash (another account), so gargling is another private activity done with public gusto in the restroom. I have to admit, though, that after trying this mouthwash one day, I buy it. For a brief moment I imagine an ad for this account where a company has it in their restrooms, and then the employees begin using it at home. Nah, that's stupid, I automatically think. No one would believe that would happen in real life.

I meet another female copywriter in the women's room, Ellen, who is working in another group. I tell her that I sometimes feel strange being the only woman. "I used to be partnered with a woman," she says, "the only other woman in my group. We'd do a presentation and someone would say, 'Are you girls doing your hair differently?' or they'd give us certain accounts and expect ads from us that could only appeal to women. Now I'm partnered with a man, who's real young, right out of school, but it makes a big difference. We're taken so much more seriously."

Briefs continue to accumulate in my In basket, but they no longer alarm me, as I've learned that you need to work only on the ones that Tom says he needs right now. A meeting is called for ideas for a computer company, and I don't have one until Tom asks me what my idea is.

"What about someone flipping the logo like a coin, and someone else catching it and flipping it to another person?"

"Good," he says. "Write it up." It didn't make the cut into the pile of ideas to be shown to the client, but at least I learned that an idea will come to you if you really need it to.

I'm finally invited along for lunch by some of the guys in my group; their initial hesitancy is due to the fact that lunch involves playing the Game. Players eat whatever lunch they bring or buy while sitting on the steps of a large office building on Park Avenue, and the Game involves selecting a passing member of the opposite sex with whom you would like to repopulate the planet after some terrible apocalypse. The Game is played in four-minute intervals, and the winner is the player who has made the most attractive selection, as judged by other members in the group. "This isn't really sexist," says one player to me, "because you're playing too, right?"

I occasionally win a round or two, as the guys sometimes concede that my male choice beats out any female they've chosen. I'm told I have an edge, as there exists the possibility of some athletic messenger going by on his bike. "Too bad we're not playing near a college campus," says Brad, a young art director, as he searches for suitable sex appeal among the crowds of businesswomen.

Back at the office, Paul and I are informed by Lewis, another creative head, that we're on the tea account again, but this time it's about making iced tea from the tea bags, not from their mix. The point of the ad, according to the brief, is to win back people (specifically southerners, who make the most homemade iced tea) who've been using a competitor's tea bag. The competitor's tea remains clear, while our tea tends to get cloudy. This ad will somehow make the case that cloudy is good and clear means "weak and watery."

"This is a problem," admits Lewis. "People really like clear things now. Pepsi is going with a clear beverage. People like to think that clear means no additives, that it's pure." Clear products are everywhere: Ivory liquid soap is available in Clear Ivory, Amoco is pushing clear gasoline, Gillette offers a clear stick deodorant, and the familiar Palmolive emerald green liquid is now absolutely clear. It's a bad time to be a cloudy beverage.

Paul and I sit down together to write. "Okay," I begin, "there's a backyard party in progress . . ."

"A pool party?" says Paul. He elaborates. "Where do we want

to be when we do the shoot? In a backyard . . . or in a backyard with a pool?"

"Oh, a pool. A really nice pool."

My pool party idea involves people surreptitiously pouring out their clear tea (Have I seen this before? I wonder as I formulate it out loud) and refilling their glasses with their neighbor's good (slightly cloudy) tea. It's a terrible idea, but it's an idea, nevertheless. We write up that one along with a few others, all of which are nixed by Lewis. He sends us away to think up "tag lines," or slogans for this tea.

Paul and I split up and agree to devise lists and work on ideas and then reconvene. I write at the top of a legal pad, "The classic tea." "The only tea you ever wanted to drink." "If it's gotta be tea, it's gotta be _____." I realize that everything I'm writing is unbelievably bad. I think of other lines, which are even worse, but at least I look like I've been working if I fill up the page. Finally, in desperation I write, "Just drink it." I wonder if Nike's "Just Do It" tag line came at the end of a long list of lame choices.

After about two weeks, when I see that good, creative ideas are routinely shot down by clients in favor of the tried and true, I begin to realize that the blame for the rotten, intelligence-insulting, hysterical, grating, or annoying ads on television lies not with the advertising agencies, but with the clients. "The product name comes up twenty-six times in thirty seconds," one art director tells me after a presentation. "And the client asked if it could be said more. I'm not kidding." After hearing about meetings where clients repeatedly voiced concerns over the faintest breath of a wisp of a controversy, and wanting viewers to be fairly bludgeoned with the obvious, I begin to wonder how we end up with any interesting, let alone original, commercials at all.

I begin to experiment with the tea at home. A thought is entertained as to whether we can urge people to "make it fresh every day," as we discover it turns cloudy after about twelve hours. There's also some experimenting as to whether the cloudy tea turns clear if more water is added, making the point that you can turn this good (cloudy) tea into the bad (clear) tea by adding a lot of (flavor-diluting) water. You need to add an awful lot of water to make it clear.

After several other failed ideas, Lewis reminds me rather ominously that "good advertising makes the viewer feel smart, not stupid." With this in mind, Paul and I write a script for a sassy southern woman confiding in the (smart) viewers about her silly and superficial girlfriend who's only concerned with appearances and so serves that "weak and watery iced tea." Surprisingly, this makes Lewis happy, and the idea begins its nine-month journey toward being shot as an animatic (a rough storyboard approximation of a commercial), subsequent test marketing and focus groups, and finally the real thing, if it makes it that far. It doesn't. It fails in the focus-group stage, and after attending one, I see why.

Tom picks Paul and me to drive out to New Jersey for an afternoon to monitor a focus group on a new series of breath mint commercials. We're being sent as insurance, to make sure that the account people watching the focus group come to the same conclusions about whether the commercials are successful or not.

This marketing survey is conducted at an industrial park in suburban New Jersey, where "ordinary, average consumers" are recruited through various means to come and see commercials and, for $25, give their honest reactions to them. But since no one wants to think of themselves as someone who *likes*, let alone watches, commercials, this arrangement, in my opinion, is flawed at the outset.

In this particular focus group, the members are taken in one by one to see the commercials so the opinions of others cannot influence their own. They are interviewed about their impressions by an employee of the marketing survey company while we, that is, the ad agency people, sit in a dim adjacent room and watch them through a large two-way mirror, and listen via microphones planted throughout the room. We pick through a fruit basket provided for us while we watch and listen, and even though they can't see or hear us, the close proximity causes us to whisper. Predictably, whenever the focus-group participants are left alone, they gravitate to what they believe to be a very large ordinary mirror, forcing those of us sitting behind it to witness rather intense personal grooming and primping at disturbingly close range.

One of the ads is a very funny spot featuring two cockney gangsters bickering about bad breath.

A male high school teacher: "Since I like Monty Python, I like anything with British accents. So I guess I liked it."

An incredibly sour-faced fat woman: "It was stupid."

A Mafia don wanna-be in pinstripes and pinky rings: "I didn't like it. Why? I don't like any ads."

"Can't we disqualify him?" Paul pleads with the scorekeeping account people. "He said he hates everything."

When they're asked what the point of the ad was, maybe a third of them are able to correctly guess that it's if you use breath mints you won't have bad breath. The fat woman, however, says, "Oh, that if you use these mints, you'll be one of the beautiful people," her face screwing up with contempt.

"What?!" Paul and I yell at the same time, as the guys in the ad look like ex-boxers, and are not attractive at all. In frustration, Paul throws a grape at the mirror, which makes a dull *thwack* and causes her to look in our direction, puzzled by the noise.

Mr. Pinky Ring on "What was the point of the ad?": "That I can't recall."

"Does anyone else think," I ask the room, "that this guy has testified in a court of law?"

"The reason he doesn't know," says Paul, "is because he was checking out his hair in the mirror the whole time."

When asked if he would watch this ad if it came on television, a Danny DeVito look alike said that "while it's funny, no, I wouldn't watch it. Why? Because I get up to go to the refrigerator or to the bathroom when commercials come on."

When asked what commercial they've seen on television that they've liked, none of them can remember a single one. "Oh, there's one that's really funny," says the Monty Python lover. "But I can't remember what it's for or what it's about."

Even though I had nothing to do with the creation of these breath mint ads, I find the experience extremely depressing.

"It's even worse when you wrote it," says Paul, "and some moron says, 'Who wrote this shit?'"

The account guys tell Tom the ad was a failure. Paul and I protest, saying it was the people who were failures. I read in *New York* magazine that advertising legend Ed McCabe has labeled the advertising of the nineties as "the dumb decade." I add focus groups to the list of reasons why ads on television are so lacking in any subtlety.

Back in my office, I pick up my tube of toothpaste yet again, and think of all the ads I've ever liked, and I try to imagine their format with this toothpaste. When I look up, I see yet another sixties person admiring my Hendrix poster. "You know, I used to hang out at the Filmore," he says. I nod with polite reserve to convey the fact that I'm not interested in hearing about Woodstock until I realize it's actually the president of the company. I met him weeks ago only briefly, and his every movement has been parodied so often in my presence I no longer recognize the real thing. My brain locks, preventing me from speaking and, worse, listening, as I'm too busy wondering what my initial facial expression was like. I snap out of it just in time to hear that good copywriters possess the gift for "condensing," he says, making a squeezing gesture with his hands. "You can't teach it. Either you have it or you don't." He then leaves. It occurs to me that a good suggestion to college graduates might be to decorate your office with sixties memorabilia, as baby boomers are now in power and it makes a handy little icebreaker. Too bad I was so busy having a panic attack that I couldn't really take advantage of it.

After tasting the toothpaste at least a dozen more times, I finally get the idea of "a toothpaste with looks and brains." That is, a fluoride toothpaste that also has whiteners and breath fresheners. I outline a snappy montage of everything that's beautiful but impractical, or ugly but useful. I show absurd efforts to merge the two, such as a Lamborghini with a bicycle strapped to the roof. We then see the toothpaste, the embodiment of finally having it both ways. I type up my script and take it into Tom's office.

He reads it. "You don't see that the spot's about toothpaste nearly fast enough, it only comes in at the end and we're looking at all this other stuff." He hands back the script. "You know, as innovative as the Nike ads are," he says, "they show the sneakers almost the whole time." I go back to my office and throw the toothpaste in the wastepaper basket. Eating it is making me queasy.

I learn that I've been chosen to go along to an afternoon casting for a spaghetti sauce commercial. The spot is called "The Happy Chef," and has to feature a gleeful chef tasting the sauce, which causes him to burst into a joyous boogie. After spending four hours watching actors moving and grooving in a chef's hat and tunic, often without any sense of rhythm, let alone style, I think I can say that actors are somehow beyond feeling anything that a normal person would call humiliation.

The audition is cruelly divided into two parts: the line readings and then the dancing. This means the actors have to file into an enormous mirror-lined loft, and put on the chef's hat and tunic over their T-shirts and shorts. With their bare legs hanging out, they resemble culinary flashers.

The suitably costumed actor then faces the casting committee, a boom box is turned on, and he's given the command to dance while he's recorded on videotape. This is so painful to watch that most of us choose to turn our heads slightly to watch the actor on the video monitor rather than to watch him live. The actors, on the other hand, manage to maintain a cheerful, I'll-do-anything-as-long-as-film-is-rolling attitude.

One of the actors introduces himself and makes the unnecessary trip across the room to shake our hands. "Did we work together before?" he asks me.

"No," I say.

"Are you sure? You look familiar."

"Have you ever done any movies?" I ask.

"Me?" he says. "Oh no. I specialize in *thirty seconds of magic*." He smiles obsequiously. I'm sure our entire conversation was engineered just so he could make that point.

He got the job, of course, despite my strenuous objections that we're hiring an insincere brownnoser with marginal talent. But since he's one of those actors who's in a million commercials, he instantly becomes the safe, cover-your-ass choice: If the commercial's bad, it can't be because we cast this guy. I start to see the spot on television almost immediately. While it's not exactly bad, it's not really very memorable. But after recalling all those actors desperately showing us their best moves, the irony is that we don't really see this chef dancing very much at all.

After a meeting in Tom's office, we're sent away to work on an ad that requires our group to think of several one-line gags concerning a father's disapproval of a boy who wants to date his daughter. The setup requires the wife to say a name and the father to give a negative reason. Apparently, the president feels the lines in the script "aren't funny enough," so we've been told to think up better ones. As usual, some of us gravitate to Paul's office to play darts while we think.

"Okay," says Stan. "The wife says, 'It's David Penner,' and the father says, 'The one with the Camaro without seat belts? I don't think so.' " Paul jots this down, and we all start to chime in, regressing more and more with each suggestion, going for the cheap laughs.

" 'The one with the van with "Do the Wild Thing" written on the side? I don't think so.' "

" 'The one with the leaky colostomy bag?' "

" 'The one who used to be Doreen Penner?' "

" 'The one you had an affair with while I was in Cleveland that time?' "

"How about if we change his name to Dick Beninya?"

"Or Gene Italia?"

"Or Phil McCrackin?"

We eventually type up our best, safest, least controversial lines and the script is tossed back.

An account guy eventually materializes at Paul's door, interrupting the Nerf basketball finals. "This is way too sexual."

"What is?" I ask, knowing that we culled out anything really overt.

" 'The one with the van with "Love Shack" written on the side?' " he reads.

"So? It used to be 'Do the Wild Thing.' "

"You can't say 'Love Shack,' " he says. Eventually, he returns to tell us that "even the word 'van' is too sexual."

"How are we going to be blamed for using sex to sell everything," I ask this guy, "if we can't even use the word 'van'?"

Keith mentions a reel he saw of an art director's work that featured a cereal commercial. "It was an animated spot," he says, chuckling. "A children's cereal. Absolutely brilliant. He stopped the tape and showed me, frame by frame, how one of the cartoon creatures lifts up his shirt, or tunic or something, and this giant erection pops out for a second! You'd never notice it normally, because it happens so fast and your eye is being diverted by something else." He laughs. This is the sort of retaliation art directors seek when faced with the intense frustration of difficult and highly conservative clients. I begin to suspect that this revenge scenario is the real basis for the fad of "subliminal advertising" in the sixties where the word "sex," among other things, was found to be airbrushed in print ads.

The popular myth that "sex sells" was to be shattered more completely, however, before I left the company. Since my radio ad for the communications network is approved and running in Maryland, I'm selected to write a radio ad for a computer online service concerning a back-to-school offer of a free modem. An account person named Tim hands me the brief, which is filled with so many mandatory disclaimers, offer specifications, reasons for purchasing, and explanations of services that must be included in the ad that I wonder whether there's time for any extraneous dialogue. Tim looks panicked when I point this out, and it turns out he's worried that extraneous dialogue could turn out to be controversial. "It's a very conservative company," he says. I tell him I'll call him when I have a script.

The script features a mother, father, and teenaged boy talking in between many necessary interruptions by an announcer. The boy is easily convincing his parents that they should take advantage of this offer, and it culminates with the boy remembering that "Hey, Cynthia Richards has _____," he says, naming the service, as if now he has an excuse to talk to a foxy babe. His father then admonishes him to "do your homework," to which the son knowingly replies, "I am."

Tim tells me that the client doesn't like the Cynthia line, as "it's unclear that she's a cute girl." I nod, since no one but me would know that a cheerleader by the name of Cynthia Richards stole my boyfriend in the seventh grade. "One more thing," he says. "They don't like the wife saying how she can find out the sports scores while the game's in progress. They want the husband to say that."

"But the husband says everything!" I protest. "Tell them that female sports fans definitely exist."

"They want her to say the line about how she can pay the bills at a touch of a button."

I reverse the wife's and husband's lines, and change the kid's line to "Hey, the head cheerleader has _____." Tim goes off with the new script and returns saying, "It's too sexual."

"The words *head cheerleader* are too sexual?"

"The client doesn't want anyone to think that they can get laid using this service. They were wondering if the cheerleader line could be changed to 'My friend John.'"

"In the first place," I point out, "if my line sounds sexual, your line sounds gay, and second, any father who hears that is going to say, 'Well, go over and play with it at John's house!' My point is that the cool kids use this service, and now this kid is in with the in crowd. Can you explain it to them again using that point? Or better yet, just let me talk to them?"

Tim looks frightened. "Oh no, I'll do it," he says, rushing off.

He calls back, saying that he's got the client on his other line, and if I don't like "My friend John," do I have an alternative to "head cheerleader"?

"Yes," I say. "Tell them it's 'All the Neo-Nazis at my school have it.'"

"I can't tell them that!"

"Why not? It's probably true, and it's not sexual at all. I think when you tell them that line, they'll see that the head cheer-leader line is really okay."

"Don't you have something else?"

I go find Tom, who takes my side. After making some phone calls, however, he's eventually informed that I'm just going to have to think up something else if I won't use the "My friend John" approach.

I give in. The kid says, "Since we're saving so much money, can I have a mountain bike?" which is followed by the admonition to do his homework and so forth.

"It's fine," says Tim, giving me the news while we sit in his office. "The client likes it." I try to smile. "This isn't really me," he says. "I've really got a lot of varied interests, and a terrific sense of humor," he says, rapidly blinking behind his Coke-bottle glasses. "I've only been here six months. I'm going to gradually show people my other, you know, crazier side. When it seems appropriate." I tell him not to wait much longer.

My last official day at work has me going to the taping of this particular commercial. The producer and I listened to audition tapes earlier in the week, and made our choices, and now at the recording studio I'm being introduced to these actors as "the writer." I've never been so embarrassed in my life.

"I'm really sorry about this," I say. "The lines are kind of lame, and you've all got to talk really fast to get this to fit in thirty seconds . . ." My voice trails off. The actors look uncertain as to how they should react. Two of them thank me for casting them.

Ten days later, I'm showering in the morning with an all-news radio station on in the bathroom. As I'm trying to get soap out of my hair, I hear the worst ad lines in the world, lines that I've written. I turn off the water and hear the kid asking for a mountain bike: my contribution to advertising's dumb decade.

# 3

# Those Who Can, Do. Those Who Can't, Teach. Those Who Can't Teach Are Substitute Teachers

I *learn that in order to qualify as a substitute teacher for the coming school year in Virginia Beach, Virginia, I have to attend a meeting scheduled in mid-August. "But I'm from out of town," I point out, thinking about the two plane tickets and two rental car agreements. I'm calling from the ad agency, making one of those long-distance personal calls so frowned upon at work.*

*The woman answering the phone at the Virginia Beach school system is unmoved by my situation.*

*"Okay, I'll make the trip," I tell her, circling the day on my desk calendar, "but you should know that you're not going to attract substitute teachers from other states with this system." I hang up the phone feeling foolish. Substitute teaching is not exactly a "have gun, will travel" kind of job.*

*I sit at my desk and imagine a class in front of me. It's not an unpleasant thought. When I was a kid, I used to love to be the teacher when my friends and I played "school." Teachers get to write on the board, they make important notations in the grade book, but the most appealing aspect for me was that good teachers*

*are loved. As a child, they seemed like benevolent gods.*
*What's it like to be a benevolent god these days?*

It takes a minute for my eyes to adjust, coming in from the bright glare of the Princess Anne High School parking lot to the comparative dimness of the school building. I can hear the familiar sound of dozens of lockers, handled roughly by students, rattle and crash. I was awakened this morning the way every substitute teacher hopes to be awakened, not by an alarm clock, but by a 6 A.M. phone call from a vice-principal telling me to get up and get in to work. Because of that phone call, I'll earn $48 today. I needed a college degree and a spotless police record to get this job, and after taxes, I'll take home about $44. It's only a few dollars a day more than what I will earn as a factory worker, where education and lack of jail time are not a priority for employment.

When I drove into the school driveway at 7:20 A.M., I was stunned by the traffic, the slow parade of cars pulling into the large student parking lot. This is supposed to be an average, suburban middle-class high school, filled with kids from my old hometown of Virginia Beach, Virginia. The passing years have put a wider mix into the student body, both racially and in socioeconomic terms, but unlike my school days, it seems as if everyone who is of driving age has a car already. I also don't remember students having nicer cars than the teachers, but this too seems to be the case.

If no one beyond tenth grade is riding the bus anymore, the hallways, at least, smell exactly the same as they did when I was in school, a universally recognizable mélange of chalk dust, disinfectant, and floor wax.

At the principal's office, I sign in and the secretary hands me

**81**

the lesson plan that was dictated by the absent teacher over the phone. A student is standing next to me pleading with her to be allowed "to call my grandmother! The wind blew my car door shut and locked my keys inside. All my books are in there. And the engine's running!" After handing the student the phone, the secretary produces an I.D. card for me to clip to my clothing. It says "Staff" in bright red letters, and features a drawing of a rapier-wielding fop, a rendering of the school team insignia of the Cavaliers. This ridiculous-looking badge apparently prevents me from being accidentally ejected from the school as unauthorized personnel. "Remember to turn in any absentee attendance cards before nine o'clock," she says, as more students come in with other crises. She hands me a Xeroxed piece of paper. "Today's announcements," she says, and gives me a map of the school along with a class schedule, hurriedly circling my room number.

My first class is called "Office Systems," but judging from the electric typewriters on every desk, it looks to me to be more like plain old Typing. The bell rings, and I shush everyone before reading the announcements. In the middle of a notice that band practice is canceled, I see that several students are giving me and each other funny looks. Suddenly the public address system crackles to life with the Pledge of Allegiance. Egad! I leap to my feet and wildly look around for the flag, finally spotting it over my shoulder. I pledge in the loudest voice possible, with a perfectly straight, highly patriotic face, exactly the way I remember other teachers doing it.

That over with, I sit back down and resume the announcements. Three students straggle in, and it hits me. Of course—the funny looks were because teachers always take roll first. I look at the brief, handwritten lesson plan the secretary handed me: "Home room attendance cards are in top right desk drawer," it says at the top of the page. I dig them out and call the names, stacking the absentee ones to the side, as these must be the things that have to get to the office by nine o'clock.

I notice in calling out the names that there aren't any boys in the class, and I ask the students why this is. One African-American girl wearily raises a hand: "Because they know they can pay us to type stuff for them." A few others assure me that it's coincidental, and that boys are in all the other classes.

Aside from the brief excitement of a fire drill, where I have to follow, rather than lead, the students to safety, the day is little more than glorified babysitting. I say glorified because I've got that impressive college degree that a real babysitter wouldn't be expected to have. Unfortunately, I daren't read a book or attempt any work myself beyond a few scribbled notes, since students instantly begin to chatter the moment I look down. I realize that their occasional eye contact with me is only to see if Im watching them. Anyone who's seen the film *The Blackboard Jungle* could probably guess that maintaining discipline is the largest part of a teaching job; actual teaching is worked in and around what can feel like lion taming. As a substitute, I'm wondering when the actual teaching part starts.

At certain times of the day, I'm required to go next door where there are computers on the desks. This is for classes called Word Processing. They're learning WordPerfect software, and my enthusiasm for seeing something not only useful but fairly cutting edge taught in an ordinary high school is entirely wasted on the students. They feel that computers are made for games, not this boring crap. While they work, I pace around, shushing people, looking over their shoulders, feeling not unlike a prison warden.

A hand goes up. A student has a question about the software! I'm even more pleased to discover that I know the answer. Hey look, I'm *teaching*. The moment passes quickly.

The truth is that I'm much more bored than they are. As a student, I thought the clock moved abnormally slowly during certain classes. As a teacher I wondered if it stopped altogether.

I spot potential trouble when a six-foot-tall student walks into the word processing class with heavy stubble and two earrings. He doesn't let me down. While the rest of the class works, he amuses himself by either talking out loud to himself or calling across the class to Jenny, a pretty blond.

"Shhh," I tell him from my desk, knowing how ineffectual and prissy I sound. He ignores me and continues his chatting. "Hey, you're disturbing the class," I say, my voice sounding a bit shrill. Jenny is now giggling at everything he says, and the rest of the class is getting restless with the knowledge that order is breaking down.

I get up and slowly walk over to his desk, trying to look as menacing as possible, but smiling out of nervousness. "Hey," I say, putting one hand on his computer monitor, wishing I could remember his name. "I mean it. Shut up."

A cloud passes over his face. His eyes narrow. "I'm asking her something about homework," he says loudly, which is blatantly untrue.

"Ask her later."

"It's later *now*," he says arrogantly. *Now what*, I wonder helplessly. Some laughable threat about sending him to the principal's office? What if he won't go? It's not like I can call security and have him removed.

"How many of you plan to go on to college?" I ask the class, still standing over his desk. He looks confused as to why I'm no longer speaking to him, but has shut up. Hands are raised. "Good. How many are trying for scholarship money?" As I ramble on about the value of an education, he looks bored and begins to type again. A teacher I briefly spoke to passed on the tip that troublemakers and chatterboxes are usually inhibited by close physical proximity; you just have to teach the class standing over them. Providing, of course, that you have the good fortune of having only one per class. I eventually wander back to my desk, and the room is mercifully quiet until the bell rings.

Recovering in the faculty lounge, I remark to one teacher that some of the students seem much older now than when I was in school.

"Some of them are," she says.

At the end of the day, I walk back to the office to put returned homework assignments in the teacher's mailbox, and I think about how the day could have been worse. I could have been teaching math.

I nod at Mr. Sykes, who is sitting in his office. In any other line of work, I would feel free to call him Ralph, but school may be the last bastion of formality in the workplace: Everyone is referred to using a courtesy title. I began each class by pointing out my first and last names on the chalkboard, but the students scrupulously avoided calling me Lynn, choosing instead to dub me either Miss or Mrs. Snowden, the latter making me think that my mother is in the room. When I told them it's really Ms. Snowden, they thought it was "weird" that I kept my name in marriage. Teenagers can be surprisingly traditional.

"Mrs. Riley won't be here tomorrow," says Mr. Sykes, knowing that I'll be pleased. I am, briefly. "She teaches advanced math."

"Oh great," I say weakly. "See you then." I walk out into the parking lot to find my car. I feel like it's been several months since I parked it. Zombie-like, I drive home and instantly fall into a deep, three-hour sleep, waking up in time to watch the local news.

The top story concerns "a gang incident" at one of the high schools I had visited in the previous few days. The news report mentions the assistant principal I had introduced myself to as a new, eager-to-be-called substitute teacher. She tried to break up a gang fight and ended up in the hospital with a broken nose. My hopes of steady employment leap with the thought of all the chickenhearted teachers who will suddenly call in sick.

The next morning, I get to school early to familiarize myself with whatever advanced math could entail. I walk into Mrs. Riley's empty classroom, and any feeling of confidence is rapidly replaced by the old familiar armpit-igniting math anxiety as soon as I see the posters she has up featuring graphs and numbers. I read the lesson plan she left for me, which is to have the students (mostly seniors) "read Chapter 4 and do the problems. Whatever they don't finish in class," her note says, "they have for homework." I open up the *Math Analysis* textbook and examine the problems they'll be doing.

Solve each inequality over $R$ and graph
each nonempty solution set.
$$6(4x + 1) \geq 12x + 6$$
or
$$n \geq 2n + 3$$

Who am I kidding? I got here early to *familiarize* myself with this as if it would all come flooding back? Even with after-school tutoring, I was lucky to get C's in Algebra II. Whatever I knew about Algebra II has faded to the point where I can't tell if this is even algebra. I take several deep breaths, and try again. The numbers and symbols swim meaninglessly in front of my eyes like so many minnows. I stare at the page for half an hour until the students trickle in, hoping for a miracle of comprehension that never comes. Unwilling to endure the boredom of simply babysitting, but unable to actually teach the material, I resort to Plan B.

I manage to call the roll, pledge allegiance, and read the announcements in the correct order. "Before we get started on what Mrs. Riley left for you to do" (a groan rises up from the class) "I'd like to teach you some math you'll probably use every day of your adult life. It's about how to figure the tip in a restaurant." Thirty-five pairs of eyes blink at me in the silence. This is Plan B, or what I like to think of as practical math, something I happen to be good at, and it wasn't taught in school. "Now, what do you consider to be a good tip?"

"Ten percent," says one kid. Others murmur their assent. When I tell them it's 15 percent to 20 percent, the students look shocked. I briefly wonder if this is due to their own cheapness or because 10 percent is what their parents are tipping. (I learn in my next job it's the latter.) I draw an American Express charge slip on the board and explain about life in restaurants beyond Sizzler and Chuck E. Cheese. We go over the amount written in for the tax and the blank lines for the captain and the tip, and how you must total the bill yourself, and take the customer copy. Even though the math is pretty elementary, it's obvious that no one has told these seventeen-year-olds anything about the facts of life concerning money. After twenty minutes on tips (including the European concept of *service compris*) and credit versus charge cards, I tell them to open their books and get going on their assignment.

I sit down at the desk, a little shaky from adrenaline and nerves. Ten minutes pass and a nerdy-looking student with a shock of black hair approaches my desk with his book. He says the one thing I've been dreading.

"Can you explain problem four?"

I look around the room, trying to remain calm. "Who's done

problem four?" Fortunately, five hands go up, and two of them, I notice, belong to recently emigrated Vietnamese students who can barely speak English. "You," I say, pointing to a non-Vietnamese, as there might be a need for a lot of explaining, "go up to the board, and tell us, step by step, how you arrived at your answer. I think a lot of people are having trouble with that problem." Yeah, like me.

I nod wisely at his solution, hoping it's correct. As no one objects, I have to assume it is. It amuses me that the students, cynical as they are, would be completely shocked to discover that I have no comprehension whatsoever regarding the scribbled numbers on the board. They believe, quite sensibly, that I have to know the subject in order to get hired. This is also the same silly assumption I made when I was filling out my application form.

There is a section on the form for substitute teachers that says "Subjects you wish to teach." *English*, I wrote down with confidence. Art, history, and social studies came next and then I hesitated. I loved biology, but am I really qualified to teach it? I asked my husband, and he responded to the question with raised eyebrows, indicating that I'm being perhaps too ambitious. I added gym, home ec, and health.

When I handed in my application, I was told that if I cross all that out and write in "Will teach anything" I'll get called a lot more often. Forty-four dollars a day is, after all, $44 a day. For that amount of money, we can't be expected to be experts in everything, and we don't need to be. Our job is to make sure the students don't burn the school down while the real teacher is sick.

At least the advanced math classes are fairly easy to manage, since they're generally very bright students, but I did have to break up a card game. "Come on guys," I say, standing over them. "Let's do some math."

"We are," says one with glasses and braces, his voice cracking. "We're playing blackjack."

"And we finished all the problems anyway," says the other, showing me his paper. I tell them to study something else "in case the principal walks in, because it'll make me look bad if you're playing cards, okay?" They seem to appreciate this bit of honesty, and put away the cards.

I notice I have a remedial math class coming up, which is ninth-graders who are, judging from the textbook and worksheet, still trying to master the basics of addition, subtraction, multiplication, and division. Obviously, my little chat about restaurant tips is out of the question, as they haven't quite made it to figuring percentages yet, but at least, I console myself, I'll have no problem with the material.

I'm getting used to the rude responses students have when they see they've got "a sub." This sobriquet is delivered in tones of voice ranging from slight disappointment to bitter resentment, the latter emerging if they made the supreme effort of doing their homework assignment or studying for the test that is now postponed. Unprepared students take the news of their teacher's illness joyously, but all students see my presence as the signal that liberties can be taken. This means that before I can call roll, I must spend about two minutes dealing with the onslaught of requests for hall passes "to go to my locker, I forgot my book," "I need to go to the bathroom," "Can I get a drink of water?" before getting down to business.

The remedial math class turns this usual two-minute, White House press conference type of badgering into ten minutes of an angry mob swarming around my desk like villagers in a Frankenstein movie, all demanding hall passes. "SIDDOWN!" I finally screech. "NOBODY'S GOING ANYWHERE! SIT! DOWN! ALL OF YOU!"

After a few minutes of handing out worksheets and desperately trying to keep order, it becomes obvious just how many of the kids in here are, in the private language of teachers, "LDs," meaning students with a learning disorder. Some are literally unable to sit still, a few are continually drumming on desks, humming tunelessly, rocking in their chairs. Some are kids who should be taking Ritalin or put in special classes, but who have been misdiagnosed or have, according to one teacher, parents who refuse to "face facts." Mixed in with these unfortunates are kids who could care less about learning anything. Trying to get absolutely everyone to be quiet seems impossible, so I settle for a dull, continuous buzz, only objecting when it escalates into a roar.

I ask one chubby boy who will not stop drumming to open his textbook. I ask three times, to no avail. "Get out your book!" I say again, standing over him. It's become a question of honor, since I know he'll never do any work, but I at least want him to do something related to math, even if it's only getting the book out.

He ignores me and continues to drum, causing a noticeable rise in the noise level of the room, as I'm temporarily distracted. "If you don't stop that drumming right now," I say, gripping a pencil with palpable frustration, "I'm going to *stick this pencil right in your eye!*" This sentiment flew out quite involuntarily, and I'm momentarily appalled by my hideous threat, but it actually does the trick. The kid stops drumming and searches for his book in his knapsack. Still white-knuckling the pencil, I tell him, "Good! Open it and keep it open! The rest of you had better be working! I'm coming around to check on your progress!"

I compliment one heavily made-up girl who actually finished her worksheet. "I took this class last year. I flunked," she says, smirking. "The teacher hated me. So I told her right where to go. So she flunked me." She says this proudly, as if she's somehow gotten the last laugh.

By the time the bell rings, I feel like a boxer in a ring who's just received the long-awaited signal to retreat to a corner. If only someone would squeeze a sponge over my head, I think, as I make my way down to the faculty lounge for a free period.

As a teenager, I always thought this mysterious sanctum was where teachers went to smoke, curse, badmouth their problem students, and swig out of flasks. Much to my disappointment, this is not the case at Princess Anne High School. There's not even so much as an ashtray out, let alone anyone smoking or exhibiting any other antisocial behavior. Teachers spend most of their time there Xeroxing materials or repairing the Xerox machine, which inevitably involves getting smudged with some greasy black ink that's very difficult to remove. There's a bulletin board with various announcements and items for sale, along with quite a few Xeroxed cartoons that are classroom related. Aside from using the adjacent men's or women's room, teachers use the telephone (chiefly to make doctor's appointments, I notice), eat a snack brought from home (no one seems to patronize the vending machines full of chips and candy), and grade papers.

The lounge could also be subtitled The Land of Floral Print Dresses. All of the women are in calf-length skirts of cotton or rayon—simple, matronly garments that could be made quite easily from a Butterick pattern. The men wear short-sleeve shirts and a tie, and plain trousers. My business wardrobe that served me so well as a copywriter now looks a bit too flashy and upmarket. I know that their decidedly unhip "teacher look" is partly due to choice but mostly due to economics: If I earned $44 a day for any length of time, I'd be running up a few items on a sewing machine myself. As it is, I weed through my clothes and see—for the first time—that all of my skirts are too short, and some of my shirts are a little too transparent. Dressing for success in high school is like dressing to visit someone in prison.

As much as I would like to sit and complain about some of the wiseass kids, I worry that it will reflect poorly on my competence as a disciplinarian. I realize that all the substitutes in my youth who threatened to report troublemakers to our regular teacher were probably bluffing. I know I was when I turned to one kid and demanded his name, presumably for reporting purposes.

"Eddie Vedder," he says with a smirk, not realizing that the aged substitute facing him actually owns an album by Pearl Jam, and recognizes this as the name of the lead singer. The rest of the class is holding its collective breath, as they wonder if I'm buying it. I think back to fifth grade when Bob Warwick had that substitute refer to him as "Mick Jagger" for the whole day. It really is true that kids think they invent everything.

"Oh—Mr. Vedder," I sneer back, "why don't you sing 'Jeremy' for us?" This lets the class know that old people watch MTV too, and may pick up a few facts about the repertoires of popular musicians. The kid laughs, red-faced at being caught so easily.

This is when I vow to pay closer attention when calling roll. Being able to address a troublemaker by name carries a lot more power than asking him what it is as he's glowering over you. I'm the type who can't remember five names from a cocktail party, so the thought of learning 150 names in a day was so daunting I didn't even try at first. But looking up after each name is called and placing a face with it helped me remember more names than I thought possible. If only I could do that at a cocktail party—of course, not drinking probably helps too.

I find it refreshing to come from the business world where people lie so expertly, and watch these teenagers bungle the truth in the most amateurish, transparent way. Lies such as "He started it!" "I already finished my report, it's at home," "That book was out at the library," and "It wasn't me talking!" seem really pathetic, small-time stuff compared to the deft, professionally delivered lies one encounters in adult life. Faced with these novices, I feel like a mind reader.

While talking to one class, I lose my train of thought entirely when a girl props up her notebook to reveal a picture of Sebastian Bach taped to the back of it. My old boss! I flash back for a moment to my days as a pyrotechnician and drift back to the present to see that the students are waiting for me to complete my sentence. I stammer around, eventually finishing up, and while they're working, I approach the student and ask to see her notebook. She looks stricken, but hands it over. I flip it over to Sebastian's face and give her a stern look. She thinks she's in trouble.

"That's not a very good picture of him," I finally say.

"Yeah," she says, visibly relieved. I hand it back to her. She giggles with relief. Playing head games with students is a fun way to break the boredom.

Seventeen-year-olds haven't yet seen the need to disguise any of their feelings for the sake of politeness, so when they're bored, they really let you know it: blatant yawning, and heads sinking down on folded arms. Still, seeing two or three students adopt this posture makes me wonder how many aren't bored at all but high, hung over, or tired from after-school jobs. I look over the rest of the class wondering how many are sexually or physically abused at home, how many of the girls have eating disorders.

When I ask students what they want to do when they finish school, it's always the brightest students who seem unsure of

their ambitions or desires, and the least prepared, least participatory ones who have the loftiest career goals. "Engineer,"
says one boy in a Def Leppard T-shirt who habitually sleeps
through remedial math. "Lawyer," mumbles one pregnant girl
who never does her homework. I ask if anyone wants to be a
teacher. No one does. "I can't wait to get out of school," says
one blond surfer. "Why would I want to come back? Look at
you, you're stuck in here same as us."

Seeing me gazing out the window in the faculty lounge, a
teacher in her thirties who is working on the couch holds up a
sheaf of homework assignments. "At least you don't have to do
all this," she says, spotting me as a substitute. We begin to chat,
and she says she usually works twelve-hour days, with all the
paperwork. "And I just pass out at around nine-thirty at night. I
have exactly one hour to myself, if I'm lucky. After my kids are in
bed, I sit and watch my soap opera that I've taped. It's tough if
you have to be up by six A.M. to get everyone, including myself,
off to school." I mention the low pay, which causes another
woman, who may be in her forties, to look up from her paperwork.

"I'm married to a lawyer, and my oldest daughter is thinking
about becoming a teacher," she says with a pained expression. "I
know this sounds terrible, but I don't want that for her! She'll
never be able to support herself in the style to which she's
become accustomed. She has to be self-sufficient. You can't depend on the fact that some man is going to support you forever
and ever."

It occurs to me that this is why all the teachers I meet seem so
idealistic. They have to be, or they'd quit. No one does this for
the money.

Since substitutes are usually marking time until a full-time
teaching job opens up, they ask me where I hope to teach. We

chat about the area for a while, and they encourage me not to lose faith in myself. "I've seen a lot of good teachers leave because they just get burned out," says the older one. "It's not what they thought it would be. I'm sure you can see that already."

Teachers eat in their own lunchroom, which is just down the hall from the cafeteria. Despite the brightly decorated bulletin boards, it's a dreary windowless room with a microwave, a refrigerator, and still more vending machines. Almost everyone brings their own lunch. The alternative is to purchase one from the school cafeteria.

I'm told that as a teacher, it's my privilege to cut in on a line of students waiting to be served, as we only have a half hour to eat. So do the students, I think to myself, but a teacher assures me that the students will think it far stranger if I actually wait in line. "Would it seem unusual if I sat down with a table of students?"

She smiles as if to say *You're new, aren't you.* "Yes," she says "It would seem very unusual! Students don't really like it when we do that. You bring back your lunch and eat it here."

I walk into the noisy cafeteria. "Excuse me, I hate to do this," I say to a girl at the head of the line. "I'm a teacher," I say, gesturing to my I.D. badge.

"Well, I'm pregnant!" she says.

"Oh," I say, noticing that she is. "Well, I'll just cut in behind you, then." Not much has changed in school lunches since I was a student, despite the cheery signs announcing that "Nutrition starts here." Besides the rotating specials of the day and an abundance of sugary desserts, two items are always available: greasy french fries and a ghastly invention called chicken burgers. The pregnant girl in front of me gets two orders of fries and an ice cream sandwich. I opt for an anemic-looking salad and make a mental note to bring my lunch from now on.

Back in the teacher's lunchroom, I sit down in the middle of a conversation. "I have one girl spelled D-E-N-I-C-E on the roll," says one teacher, "but she'd sometimes hand in papers with her name as D-E-N-I-S-E. 'So which is it,' I asked her. She says, '*I don't know.*' " He doesn't laugh; this is not a funny story. "So I told her I thought the spelling in the roll was probably what was on her birth certificate."

An older female teacher nods. "I have one Michele—spelled with one 'el.' Her momma just didn't know how to spell Michelle, is what it is."

Fortunately for me, enough teachers are sick or called away on personal business over the next three weeks to ensure me steady employment at Princess Anne High. I become familiar enough to some students for them to greet me in a singsong "Hi Miz Snowden!" as we pass each other in the hallway, something I find deeply pleasurable. If they can remember my name, maybe I'm having some sort of positive effect. The other bonus is that I get to teach some classes over longer periods of time. Unfortunately, one of these subjects is advanced math.

"Are you going to teach us about tipping again?" asks one of the students. I had other math problems for them, such as how to balance a checkbook and how to figure out what you're really earning after taxes. There are enough real-life problems of money for me to assure that they never realize that I can't help them with their math homework.

After substituting for a science teacher, I see him the next day and mention a five-dollar item that he might consider buying for the aquariums in his classroom.

"Are you kidding?" he says. "I make twenty thousand a year. I'm not buying anything." His remark reminds me of the time my friends and I saw our history teacher selling ties in a department store in the mall. We thought it was tremendously funny. It never occurred to us that he was doing it because he needed the money.

While teaching, one of my biggest fears is that I'll accidentally swear in front of the students. Knowing I can't swear makes me feel as if the forbidden words are perpetually ready to fly out of my mouth. The dreaded event happens when I'm teaching social studies, and am required to show a video. (The days of film strips, I'm happy to report, are well behind us.) Since I'm usually not up and dealing with large groups of people so early in the morning unless I'm at an airport, I'm hardly in the mood at 8 A.M. to discover that the volume control isn't working, leaving us with picture but no sound. The classroom chatter escalates into an insect roar while I fiddle with every knob and control panel. I finally send someone out to "find someone who can fix this."

A khaki-clad handyman appears, complete with steel-rim glasses and a crew cut. He's clearly appalled at the noise level, but raises his voice to tell me he'll wheel over another TV and VCR. When he turns to go, he loudly slushes the room and points his finger at the entire classroom in a threatening way while wearing the fiercest expression imaginable. The room now silent, he points at me, as if he's handing over the magical control of his finger. This strikes me as such a pompous, dime-store-magician gesture that I accidentally burst out laughing. The class, unfortunately, follows suit, and the handyman storms out.

"Shush!" I plead with the class. "You're going to get me fired!"

"You started it!" one student says.

"Okay, but when that guy comes back, I want this room to look like a stuffed exhibit! No laughing, no talking, no moving! Got that? Otherwise I'm in deep trouble." When the handyman returns, everyone is perfectly behaved. I pop in the tape. The volume works. The handyman leaves. I check my watch and see that we have just enough time to see the video in its entirety before the bell rings. As the opening credits roll, the fire alarm goes off, signaling yet another drill, the second in a week.

*"Fuck!"* I explode. I couldn't stop myself. Mortified, I apologize. They file out, smirking and giggling. I try to look dignified.

The students in my later classes have heard about this little scandal from the students in my morning class blabbing during lunch. "Heard you got mad when the VCR didn't work," says one kid.

I say nothing. By this time I've learned that the best part about being a teacher is that you don't have to answer a student if you don't want to. Privately I'm wondering if saying the F-word is grounds for dismissal. As a student, I can remember a teacher swearing exactly once: After most of us failed a test, our seventh-grade science teacher told us to "knock off the bullshit!" It had a galvanizing effect on the class; no one breathed for at least a minute, as we were sure the world was coming to an end. Even though my word was technically worse, the effect it had was far from galvanizing.

It's easy to say that kids are different today, but, I can't help thinking, look at the teachers! I got hired, and here I am swearing, telling kids that their parents probably don't tip enough, and laughing at the handyman. I recall the time I made two African-American kids who were shouting "faggot" at each other discuss with the class why homophobia is as bad as racism. I wonder now if their parents would agree with my prompting the conclusion that it *is* as bad. When covering imperialism and the balance of power, I tried to get kids to relate to it more by asking if the girls felt they owed something to guys who bought them dinner. Would parents approve of this—or any—discussion of sexual mores? I remind myself to cool it, since Virginia Beach is, after all, televangelist Pat Robertson's home base. If I got a steady teaching job here, I'd probably get fired in a month, F-word or no F-word.

After two weeks, I settle into the routine of being a teacher. This means completely cutting out all social drinking, as I can't imagine anything worse than teaching with a hangover, no matter how slight. Nights where I stayed up past 10 P.M. are fast becoming a distant memory.

I am getting better at maintaining discipline, for even though I've always been able to handle rude cab drivers, indifferent clerks, and the occasional stubborn co-worker, these social skills don't help in the world of teenagers. You can tell an adult to "please be quiet," and they'll do it even though you're wearing a pleasant expression. Teenagers know you're serious when you stop smiling, so it's necessary to develop an almost sociopathic ability to switch moods from a fierce reprimand to one of pleasant encouragement when you move on again with the classwork as if nothing untoward has happened.

Even so, my proficiency as task mistress has its limits. A huge kid with pristine sneakers and a hooded sweatshirt refuses to slide his desk toward the middle of the room to see a video. His inaction is preventing several students from moving their desks within the sightlines of the television, so I ask him again to "please move."

"I moved!" he says, sullenly.

"Yeah, about a quarter of an inch," I say, irritated that he's taking up so much time. The video on Christopher Columbus is almost forty minutes in length, leaving me not much time to review the vocabulary, which includes words like *Eurocentric*. Frustrated, I grab the side of his desk. "Don't be a jerk," I say, as I bodily drag him three feet over in one short yank. When my eyes meet his just before I let go of the desk, my heart skips a beat. His face is a mask of hatred; I have no doubt he'd like to kill me on the spot. Afraid that he's about to lunge at me, I turn and walk away, chattering about the video. By the time I get up the nerve to manage a casual glance in his direction, I see with some relief that he's not pointing a gun, but has instead settled for giving me a series of dirty looks. I pretend not to notice, but the encounter leaves me shaken.

One other essential teaching skill that doesn't come naturally is timing. Experienced teachers know how to vamp, ending their lectures just when the bell rings, whereas I finish up too soon, and stupidly tell kids to work on their homework. This means they pack up everything five minutes before class is over and begin to talk. While I'm trying to quiet the noisy ones, others are sneaking over to the door, where they stand like cows waiting to get into a barn to be milked. "Hey, everyone sit down!" I cry helplessly, right when the bell rings.

"You can't let them do that," one teacher advises me. "Never let them even stand up! They'll really take advantage, especially of a substitute."

This is the month for the big fund-raising candy drive, so not only are students selling chocolate bars and gum to one another, there's a stand set up in the school's front foyer. This means the kids are eating the stuff all day, when they're not chowing down on chicken burgers and greasy fries. It astonishes me to hear that most teachers allow students to chew gum in class, but no one lets them wear their baseball caps. Since I can't abide the smacking and cud-chewing that accompany gum and candy consumption, I'd much prefer the students wear their hats, a comparatively quiet, healthy activity. I decide to make a deal. "Here's my rule," I tell my students. "You can wear your hats in my class" (a cheer goes up) "but if I catch *anyone* chewing gum or eating candy of any kind, *all* the hats come off." This actually works, as they police one another, and besides, I like the way kids look in baseball caps. My policy gets me dubbed "the cool substitute."

The oceanography teacher will be absent for a week, and tells me that the students are to check out any book from the library that has to do with the ocean or water, and to write a book report on it. This is clearly busywork, so after an entire class returns with the thinnest books imaginable, such as *My Friend the Dolphin* and other tomes appropriate for the second-grade level, I decide to make this a more meaningful project and write a "suggested books" list up on the board.

One girl in a cheerleader uniform raises her hand. "You read all them books," she says, in the southern manner of speaking, where questions are phrased as statements and statements sound like questions. She has the expression of someone who knows they've caught you in a lie. I've only listed ten titles, including Hemingway's *The Old Man and the Sea*, Conrad's *Heart of Darkness*, Thoreau's *Walden*, and Melville's *Moby-Dick*. I'm trying to think of some short stories, or shorter novels, since I'm teaching five classes.

"Yes," I tell her.

"Like, *all of them?*" She looks around the room in search of other incredulous faces.

"Don't anyone read *Walden*," cautions one thin blond kid.

"Why not?" I ask.

" 'Cause it *sucks*," he says. "I had to read it for English."

Despite my assurances that these books are far more interesting and entertaining than A *Child's Book of Shells*, very few students return from the library with anything I've suggested. I can't say I blame them for trying to take the easiest route, and I lack the desire or the real authority to make them do otherwise. I console myself with the thought that at least a few kids are reading something challenging.

One afternoon class is preempted by a school assembly concerning class rings, to be led by a representative of Josten's, the jewelry company. Shortly after we file into the auditorium, a smarmy and overly enthusiastic salesman in a suit and tie introduces himself by pumping the air with his fist while proclaiming, "We are the same company that makes *the rings for the Super Bowl!*" He pauses to drink in the cheers. "This is a *once in a lifetime* purchase, Juniors!" He then spins an unlikely story that even the ultra-sappy disk jockey Casey Casem would reject as too sentimental: He gave his class ring to his high school sweetheart, whom he eventually married (after college, of course!), and now she wears that *very high school ring every day on her charm bracelet!* The relentless hard sell complete with slide show goes on for forty-five minutes but never mentions the actual cost of the ring, which I later learn is about $200, and can go much higher. The salesman urges students to arrange to receive their rings at the Ring Dance, a formal event that is held two months before the prom. Ah, the ring and the Ring Dance. Yet another expensive high school ritual whose real function, as far as the students are concerned, is that of a bargaining tool for sex.

At some time during this assembly I turn into the pompous handyman, as I'm now shushing people like a pro, pacing the aisles, incorporating the pointing-a-finger-like-it's-a-warning and the snapping of fingers in a quick, gunshot style. I have no doubt that my friends would find my behavior hysterically funny.

As a kid, I used to wonder if the teachers who habitually

pointed at the board using their middle finger were really as oblivious to what they were doing as they appeared, since there's no way a kid can look at a teacher who seems to be flipping the bird without having to stifle a giggle. As a teacher, I can now say that yes, they knew exactly what they were doing. I contemplate doing it myself a few times, but I know I'd never be able to keep a straight face. This ability must come only after years of frustration and practice.

On my last day, I'm assigned to "Front Foyer Duty" after school, the regular post of the teacher I'm subbing for. Because of the scheduling of the school buses, students must wait for anywhere from five to forty minutes for their bus. In the meantime, they must be corralled in front of the school and monitored, lest they fight, smoke cigarettes, or do whatever high school kids these days might do. My partner in this duty is a young, timid teacher who asks me if I'm subbing for "Jim."

"Uh, Mr. Nixon," I say, since I have no idea of anyone's first name. I know he's a burly, no-nonsense guy, the ideal choice for keeping order. Since the woman asking me this has the physical presence of a Chihuahua, the tough-guy vacancy created by Jim's absence will have to be filled entirely by me. She brings up "the gang incident" at the other high school—something that happened during the wait for buses—and talks about all the troublemaking students "here from the Bronx!" There does indeed seem to be a strange pipeline from the Bronx to Virginia Beach, as if parents in New York who feel their kids have committed one too many felonies send them down here to stay with friends.

Since several students have now disappeared from our sightlines, she urges me to go out for a quick patrol. I walk outside, my "Staff" badge flapping impotently in the breeze, and I say a silent prayer: Oh please, please, don't let me deal with anything unpleasant. No crack smoking. No guns. No broken noses, especially mine. Please.

Fortunately, it's only three kids smoking cigarettes at the side of the building. One of them, a girl who looks like Bernadette Peters, is having trouble lighting her cigarette. "Okay," I say loudly. "Put that out!" The look of shock and surprise on her face causes her almost to drop her cigarette. The two boys just stare.

"Who are you?" one boy asks.

"I'll ask the questions around here!" This is actually a line I heard a New York City cop use. "You know the rules: Get in front of the building."

"We're allowed to stand here," says the girl.

I shake my head, my hands on my hips. "Look, you know the rules. Get over there." I don't sound like Clint Eastwood at all, and so I stalk back into the building without waiting to see if they're going to obey. As I walk to the door, I can hear the faint, off-key strains of the school's marching band trying to play Queen's "Bohemian Rhapsody." The other teacher seems relieved to see I'm okay. I feel stupid.

Teaching is exhausting. It involves talking all day, and even on their best behavior, students require the expenditure of an incredible amount of energy, leaving me with precious little by three o'clock. Even so, I've enjoyed being able to say "I'm a teacher" for the last month. I feel a strong sense of pride, and find it interesting to see how many people automatically treat me with respect and admiration. "You must be really smart," says one woman waiting in line with me at a bank. "What do you teach?"

"Advanced math."

"WOW!" she says. At this moment, I know just how the

Scarecrow in *The Wizard of Oz* felt when he got his diploma. Despite the dismal pay and the troublemaking students, teaching is fulfilling, important, and deeply satisfying. As much fun as it was being a roadie, if I had to choose one job to do for the rest of my life, it would be that of a teacher.

At the airport, waiting for my plane home, I add up what I earned, and I see it doesn't even cover the cost of my rental car. If I stay in town, and am lucky enough to have Mr. Sykes call me every school day of the year, I can expect to earn approximately $8,600 by June. I would not be covered by a medical plan.

Back in New York City, it takes a while for me to stop acting like a teacher. I snap "No singing!" at a man droning to himself on the subway. I become impatient with people slowly filing out of the elevator in a building lobby and suddenly clap my hands loudly, "Let's go! Come on, let's go!" My husband stares at me. I realize too late that I'm not in high school anymore.

# 4

# Fear, Loathing, and Working for Tips in Las Vegas: The Horror, the Horror

**I**f you're going to be working in Vegas as a cocktail waitress," says Jerry, "you've got to master 'the lean.' "

Jerry is addressing me from across the table at a dinner party at a friend's house. He worked in Vegas for years in hotel management before moving to New York. He's waggling his eyebrows at me.

"The lean?" I ask politely, my heart sinking.

"Here's what you do," he says, shifting his chair back to demonstrate. He stands up as if he's holding a tray. "You get yourself a push-up bra, and then when you serve a drink to a customer," Jerry bends over at the waist, offering an imaginary drink. He's jutting his chest out farther than even his chin. "You lean way in like this. See? That's how you get big tips."

I look over to see what my husband's facial expression is like: nothing more than polite interest. My own facial expression might be faint panic covered by slight amusement.

"Great," I say, "I'll keep that in mind." It's going to have to be a hell of a push-up bra, I think to myself.

"The lean," Jerry says again, sitting down.

*The next morning, I'm walking around the apartment in heels, a short skirt, and my most ambitious push-up bra. I'm holding a dinner plate as if it's a drink tray. I practice Jerry's lean on an imaginary customer and almost pitch forward into his imaginary lap, soaking us both with imaginary liquor.*

*"Damn," I murmur, steadying myself on the chair. My center of gravity is way off in this position with these shoes. Maybe the push-up bra is throwing me off with the extra ballast. I try again. It's no use. I decide to forget the lean in favor of fretting about standing in these high heels for eight hours. I plop down on the sofa and try to remember which brand of shoes is the "looks like a pump, feels like a sneaker" variety.*

*I call up a set decorator for the movies and ask her if she remembers. She's a great source of information.*

*"No, but you should buy your pumps out there," she says. "Vegas is filled with showgirls and waitresses who've got to wear heels all the time. They've got that shoe stuff down to a science. You can select color, width, heel height, everything."*

*"Great idea!" I tell her. "Thanks."*

*"Aren't you worried about the outfit?" she says. "Some of those Vegas waitress getups look really humiliating."*

*"Well," I say, thinking of all the tip money I'm going to earn, "I think if I get the right kind of shoes I can deal with anything."*

*Little did I know.*

The week before I left for Las Vegas, the *New York Times* reported that Nevada leads the country in alcoholic beverage consumption, with the average citizen sucking down a whopping 44.8 gallons per year as compared to the rest of the country, which consumes a mere 26.3 gallons per person per year. The reason for these skewed figures is obvious: The country is doing all of its serious drinking in Las Vegas.

And it's not just drinking: Two weeks after I arrive the front page of the *Las Vegas Sun* reads, "Screaming Man Dies On Strip," about a guy who was running around in his underwear on the main drag at 6:45 A.M., flagging down cars and screaming "Praise the Lord." He died suddenly when the police arrived and attempted to subdue him. Two days later it is reported that the dead man was "a 33-year-old COMDEX conventioneer who went crazy on cocaine." The *Las Vegas Sun* thoughtfully published a postmortem photo of what presumably once was a happy-go-lucky computer geek from San Diego, but who is now a bruised, bloated, dead whale on a slab, photographed with his eyes shut and his mouth open. Like all the other cocktail waitresses reading the paper that morning, I couldn't quite say whether I'd waited on him or not. He looked like an awful lot of other customers.

One of the hard lessons Las Vegas taught me was that it's not necessarily true that in a town with that much alcohol consumption there'd always be openings for cocktail waitresses. Everyone wants such a presumably glamorous and lucrative job, from the girls who work as Keno runners in the hopes of hearing of an opening to women like me who stupidly figure they can start at the top with no experience. The forms I had to fill out and have notarized to get a job educating the youth of Virginia were nothing, a cakewalk, a casual inquiry, compared to the monumental paperwork—tests, reference checks, and identity verification—required just to serve drinks to crazed tourists in Nevada. You see, cocktail waitressing in Vegas isn't an interim job the way it is in New York or Los Angeles, where serving drinks is a brief embarrassing stop on the way to stardom, or at least to an occupation that allows one to sit down. In Vegas, cocktail waitressing is an actual career in itself, and, thanks to the Culinary Workers

Union, to which almost all casino cocktail waitresses belong, it can be a very, very long one. It's easy to spot the many thirty-year veterans of the business. The face-lifted battle-axes marching around on stilettos and slinging Bloody Marys are women who were no doubt considered "babes" during the Kennedy administration. They still sport the same French twist hairdo, false eyelashes, and long pale nails that they had when they first put on the uniform fresh out of high school.

I thought being a cocktail waitress would be one of the easiest jobs in this book. While in college, I had a summer job waitressing in an Italian restaurant, and it occurred to me back then that just serving cocktails would be a lot simpler—there's not as much to carry, you don't have to remember how certain dishes are prepared, and you don't have to recite any daily specials. Also, people come and go in a bar and tip all the time; in a restaurant, you're stuck with the same duds for a couple of hours.

The following summer, I had an opportunity to work as a cocktail waitress in an Atlantic City casino, but my parents—who both worked in casinos at the time—disapproved of the sexy outfit I'd have to wear and told me I'd "get pinched" a lot. For three months I listened to them tell stories of waitresses handing one drink to a gambler and receiving a $500 chip as a tip while I—smart college girl too good to wear a sexy outfit—earned $150 a week as a typist in Caesars' purchasing office. I've never forgiven them for it. Until now.

I thought this would be my chance to get some of that easy money. I chose this job because it would provide the union experience, and it's the antithesis of a teaching position: high wages for unskilled labor. The sexy outfit and the casino setting provide elements of glamour and vice; cocktail waitressing has long been a career option for the uneducated, reasonably attractive woman.

When I arrive in town, I am blissfully ignorant of the fact that this would be the worst job in the book. I'd been told by the Culinary Workers Union that just knowing my own Social Security number wouldn't be good enough for the folks in Vegas, and neither would pay stubs with my number printed on it, so I've come prepared with a Social Security card. I lost the original one while still a teenager, but even though my number has served as bank identification, a driver's license number, and my student I.D. number in college, no one has ever asked to see my actual Social Security card before. This was an omen of the scrutiny to come.

I had been to my doctor for a tuberculosis test as part of the requirements to become a teacher. My seven-week-old doctor's note announcing the negative results wasn't a recent enough determination in Las Vegas, so my first order of business here is another TB test. This involves driving down to the Clark County Health District offices, taking a number, and paying $10. After telling a clerk that no, I am not pregnant, I join a long line of people waiting to be injected subcutaneously on the forearm. After my shot, I'm told to return if there is a reaction to the injection, and I'm sent to another line for a required photograph. I emerge, three bone-crushingly boring hours later, with a temporary health card (which indicates that I'm not pregnant with a large NO, something every potential employer will see) and a paper explaining that I have thirty days to come back and see a health film before I'm issued my permanent card.

I'll need another three hours in order to secure my next new piece of identification, so I rush downtown to the Las Vegas Metropolitan Police offices to apply for what is known as my sheriff's card. Taking another number, I sit next to a well-dressed couple who look fresh from job interviews, and begin to fill out my form. There is a section for "Distinguishing marks or tattoos," and while I do have a fairly unique C-shaped scar on my hip, I write "None," in a tiny act of rebellion against this incessant prying. As I flip my form over, my ears prick up as I hear the well-dressed couple talking about guns.

"I'm going to drop off the .38 in Arizona and pick up the .32," the man is saying.

"Yeah," she says. "That'd probably be a good idea."

"Excuse me," he says, tapping my shoulder. I turn, startled. "Does every job in this town require a card?" He gestures to the huge crowd in the room. "Like, even fast-food workers?"

"I don't know," I say politely, wondering if he's carrying his .38 right now. "I think it's just for casino employees."

This is the second conversation about guns I've heard in two days. While waiting for my luggage in the Las Vegas airport, I listened to two men talk about getting federal permits so they could carry their guns across state lines. "I'll just say I'm in the jewelry business or somethin'," one of them said.

"I don't know if you can lie on a federal permit," says his friend. "Just find out what it needs to say and write that." While I know there are plenty of guns in New York City, I never hear anyone talking about them; in Vegas, guns seem to be a topic of idle chitchat.

Getting a sheriff's card involves presenting plenty of identification to a clerk who then checks you out via a computer for outstanding warrants, traffic tickets, unpaid child support payments, the works. "People get carted away in handcuffs in that place all the time," Sandy Turner, a dispatcher at the union office, warned me. "They go in there trying to get a sheriff's card to get work and end up in jail for unpaid parking tickets or something."

Since my record is clean, I'm sent to the next room to line up for mug shots. "Don't smile," the technician tells me, as we do a front and profile view. I feel exactly as if I'm being arrested, a feeling only heightened by getting fingerprinted directly after the little photo session. "Relax your hands," I'm told, as a woman presses my inked fingertips and thumbs, then all four fingers down to the palm, onto two sheets of paper. After I wash up, I proceed to another window to pick up my laminated photo I.D. In this photo, taken after my mug shots, I am requested to smile. "This is the one you carry at work," the technician tells me. "So, you know, look happy." The card specifies NON-GAMING beneath my picture, and has a number on the back that I'm to call if I spot any of my co-workers engaged in illegal activity.

The next morning, I sign up and pay $20 for the four-hour class on "Techniques of Alcohol Management," in order to get my TAM card, another requirement. This is where you learn how to spot phony I.D.s when minors come in, and how to tell if someone is too drunk to be served, since you, the cocktail server or bartender, can be held responsible if the drunk manages to kill someone on his way home. "Keep a diary," says the woman teaching the class, "and note anything unusual on your shift. It comes in handy if you're required to testify in court later." But in Las Vegas, I wondered, exactly what would be considered unusual? And in a town where each person presumably glugs down approximately three and a half quarts of liquor a week, isn't being drunk only a matter of degree?

After passing a written test, I fill out another form which asks whether I own or rent my home and if I'm married, single, or divorced. "It's just for statistical purposes," explains our instructor. I get photographed again, and receive another laminated card to add to my collection, which is now complete, and I'm finally eligible to look for employment.

"A job in the show room is a possibility," says the food and beverage manager at Bally's, whose eyes keep flicking down to my breasts and up to my face, "if you're a real hustler. If you're aggressive, it's a good job." He's talking about serving drinks in a room where there is no drink minimum and where drinks are not served while the show is in progress. A waitress at the union office told me that she reads a book during the show to pass the time. Sounds like the perfect job for the independently wealthy student.

Now his eyes are roaming around over my entire body, as I perch—back straight, legs crossed—on the edge of a chair. I stared quite a bit at my own reflection in the morning, as I put on what Sandy told me would be "a good interview outfit": my trusty push-up bra under a leopard-print turtleneck, a black miniskirt, sheer black hose, black pumps, and an awful lot of makeup. I feel like a delinquent hooker, but I've managed to make it through the first cut in the interview process and am now facing the big boss, who's smiling like a shark. Knowing that it would look suspicious if I listed my address as Caesars Palace, which is where I'm staying, I write in Sandy Turner's address and phone number. We chat about how eager I am to be part of the "Bally's team," and as he drones on, I look up and notice a surveillance camera pointing at me from the corner of his office. "I'll call you," he says meaningfully, shaking my hand on the way out.

When I tell Sandy about him, she laughs and says, "That's nothing! There was one food and beverage manager who'd make the girls get into a string bikini and then he'd take Polaroids!

We complained and complained and nothing happened, but then the son of a bitch was caught loading bottles of liquor he'd taken from the hotel into the trunk of his car and was fired on the spot."

The good news about the food and beverage manager at the Dunes is that he's a really nice guy; the bad news is that he tells me that the Dunes is in the process of being sold to Steve Wynn and will close down in a matter of months, so he doubts he'll be doing much hiring. Noting my drink-serving ambitions, he warns me that the pay as a cocktail waitress may be lower than I'm expecting. "Fifty to a hundred a night is good these days, now that Las Vegas has been marketed as a Disneyland. We're attracting a lot of midwestern families who're used to tipping Mary Lou in the diner fifty cents and she's happy. It used to be, ten years ago, that money was just thrown at the girls, they'd be carrying three hundred, four hundred a night. Not anymore." I reluctantly loosen my grip on my long-held fantasy of being tipped a $500 chip for bringing one drink. "And the jobs that are lucrative," he says, meaning the blackjack tables and the baccarat pit stations, "are held by women who were hired in 1970, and we can't get rid of them." He chuckles. "That's why this place is closing down. Steve Wynn doesn't want to inherit sixty-year-old cocktail waitresses."

Since Steve Wynn is so anxious for young blood that he's tearing down casinos to get it, I decide to apply at one of his properties, specifically the Mirage, home to Siegfried and Roy and a giant flame-throwing fake volcano. Like other casinos, the Mirage's personnel office has a large sign forbidding people to leave with an application form. Unlike Bally's and the Dunes, the Mirage's application form has a section on the front for "Hair color____ Eye color____ Height____ Weight____." The word *discriminatory* comes to mind as I hand my completed form over to the clerk, who makes a Xerox of my cards and staples the sheets together. "Can I see the food and beverage manager?" I ask.

"No," he says. "We don't have any openings." He hands me a card with a phone number on it. "You might call this number. It has a recorded announcement of job openings, and if there's anything else you're interested in, you should come back." Disappointed, I jealously eye all the cocktail waitresses working in the casino on my way out, and glumly tip the valet parker.

Just as it's telling that the Mirage is concerned about physical appearance, every casino reveals its own priorities on the employment application. While every application eventually asks if you've ever been convicted of a felony, the Dunes positions this information on the front page, with a box for the details of your criminal record. While in the Dunes' personnel office, I was standing behind a gum-chewing twenty-five-year-old, whose hair was pinned sloppily up on top of her head. She handed in her application to the woman behind the counter, who looked it over and asked, "Were you employed anywhere during these two years?"

"Naw," she says. "I had two kids." There's a minute or two of silence as she flips the application over and scans the rest.

"Well," sighs the woman behind the counter. "The man you need to see isn't here right now, so we'll call you. Thank you." When I go up to the counter, I can see her application lying on the desk. While my form is being perused, I see that the previous applicant was applying for a job as a "busser—snack bar," but she had checked "yes" to a felony conviction, and wrote in "Grand Theft Auto—1990." Yikes. The woman behind the counter looks up, smiles brightly, and asks me a few questions before Xeroxing my cards. She then tells me where to find the boss's office, the man she just said wasn't in.

Sitting around the union offices later, I relate this story to Bobbi Dugan, a feisty blond dispatcher who worked at the Golden Nugget for twenty-five years as a cocktail waitress. "I know exactly the girl you're talking about!" she says of the car thief, as she's sent her around town a lot recently trying to get her hired. "She's a wild one! And yeah, if you're a felon, forget it! The El Cortez and the Horseshoe used to hire felons all the time, but all the hotels now, if they see *felon*, they won't hire. When the mob ran this town, if you were a felon, all they cared about was if you were a good employee, the rest didn't matter. When the corporations moved in," she says making a face and lowering her voice, "everyone became a number."

A few more days pass with no calls for employment, not even, I notice, for the show-room job I was looking forward to turning down at Bally's. I complain to Sandy that I've given out more personal information in the past five days than I have in my whole life, and am starting to feel a little paranoid. I've become so used to looking for video cameras everywhere I go that I didn't realize at first that the bellman who showed me to my room at Caesars Palace was joking when he pointed to the mirror above the bed and said, "When you see a little red light go on there? Smile, 'cause you're on candid camera!" Sandy, who is never without a cigarette dangling from her lips, nods. "In Las Vegas," she says through a plume of smoke, "Big Brother is definitely watching you." Big Brother also requires a drug test.

Some casinos give you a list of three places to go for a urine test, but at Bally's they use the DNA test where they cut sixty strands of hair from the back of your head. "Which is a big clump," says Bobbi, scandalized, clutching reflexively at her own mane of candy floss hair. The woman who initially interviewed me there turned and parted her hair. "I had it done two months ago," she says. "Can you tell?"

"No," I lied. Caesars takes thirty hairs from each of three sites, rather than one clump. "You can't even tell," says Phil Cooper, a vice-president at Caesars, who thinks I'm silly for being upset about it. "I have to have it done again soon. It's no big deal."

Even a cameraman I meet from a local news station tells me he had to take a urine test to get his job. "I drove out here from West Virginia and while I don't do drugs, it could have come back a false positive and I would have been S.O.L." I tell Sandy to find me a job in a casino that does urine tests, not the hair-cutting thing. Bobbi is sympathetic. "I still can't believe you didn't get hired yet wearing that outfit," she says. "You look as cute as can be."

Later that afternoon, union big cheese Johnny LaVoie emerges from his office to announce that I've got a job at the Tropicana ("They owe me a favor," he says) and that I should go down there to get "processed"—more forms and photographs. A guy in his office tells me to make sure I buy the book *How to Become a Casino Cocktail Waitress* by Sally Fowler, and memorize the section on "How to Order Your Drinks" so I'll know the system with the bartenders. I roll my eyes and give him a withering look, as I consider myself someone who not only knows her way around alcoholic beverages, but has certainly held tougher jobs than this.

"If I can make explosives," I tell him, "I think I can handle ordering drinks."

Forty-eight hours later, I realize it's much easier to make explosives. And I thought *teaching* was exhausting? It's been twelve hours since I got off work, and I can barely contemplate moving from a prone position. This is what happens when you have to work an eight-hour shift in high heels, rushing around with a heavy tray full of drinks. And since I was working in the lounge off the casino, I had to run up and down a short staircase to and from the bar. I stare resentfully at the measly $56 in tips lying on my dresser. *Christ!* Even prostitutes get to lie down on the job sometimes; we can't even sit unless we're on our one-hour meal break. I keep catching sight of my uniform, which is the very small, only slightly crumpled mass of color on the floor. The thing is so stiff with artificial fibers it can almost stand on its own.

"What size do you wear?" the German lady in the uniform room asked me last evening.

"An eight? I don't know, maybe a six?" She handed me a size four of a tiny garment cut low in the front and low in the back, with an extremely short flared skirt. The fabric is a tropical print of screaming magenta, blue, and turquoise. When I inhaled sharply and carefully zipped it up in the ladies' changing room cum bathroom (wondering where the inevitable surveillance cameras are hidden), I checked myself out in the big mirror as I positioned my headband in accordance with casino regulations. As to the entire effect, the word *garish* doesn't begin to describe it, and my job interview outfit suddenly seemed dignified in comparison.

For a lousy $56 in tips I had to endure hour upon hour of the loudest lounge band in the world singing "Celebrate good times, come on!" which meant creepy fat guys would interrupt their clapping just long enough to beckon me over and put their arm around my waist. This intimacy is performed under the pretense of pulling me close so I can hear their drink order. Meanwhile, I'm trying to crouch, and lower myself down by bending my knees. I don't want to risk falling into his lap by performing the Vegas lean. I also had to cope with another snippy waitress—"Honey, I had to bus your table over there!"—who happened to be a transsexual, a fact that did not go unnoticed by a table of

On the edge of the desert in fabulous Las Vegas. I'm dressed in what's laughingly known here as work clothes. (*Jeremy Conway*)

men at the tag end of a bachelor party. At 3 A.M., one of the
married members of this party decided to put his head up my
skirt while I was taking their drink orders.

I wheel around furiously, and hear one of his friends say,
"He's just makin' sure she's a real woman!" That I didn't just
wrap my tray around this guy's head is something of a miracle;
what stopped me was the Tropicana motto: "The Friendliest
Employees in Las Vegas!" And I was worried about ass-pinch-
ing?

"If you do that again, sir," I tell him through gritted teeth,
*"I'll break your glasses."*

A man ordering on behalf of his table says he wants "Four
Screaming Orgasms." I write this down. "Repeat the order back
to me," he says, giggling. His date looks uncomfortable.

"That's okay, I got it."

"No," he says harshly, his humor now gone. "I want you to
repeat it back to me. Say it! I want you to give me *Four Screaming Orgasms.*" I repeat it. When I bring the drinks—disgusting
concoctions involving vodka, amaretto, and Kahlua that only
someone who likes to say the words *Screaming Orgasm* to a
stranger would enjoy—I announce, "That'll be eighteen dollars,
please." He tips one dollar. Gee, a whole dollar *and* plenty of
abuse.

A man introduces me by name to his family at the table, and
makes a big show of ordering everyone's drinks and telling little
jokes. I bring the drinks and tell him, "That'll be fifteen fifty."
He hands me $16 and rather grandly insists that I keep the
change. This is apparently the guy who tips Mary Lou fifty cents
at the diner back home. The scary part is that the IRS is assuming I'm getting tipped fifty cents for *each drink* I serve, not each
round.

I feel something desperate emerge once it clicks in that I'm now forced to depend upon tips to make more than my $5.35-an-hour salary. This is accompanied by an almost blinding fury when people withhold what are actually my wages. I want to grab them by their lapels—if their jacket has such a thing, it's probably a nylon windbreaker—and scream, "Why do you think I'm dressed like this? Because I *like* it? Do you think I'm hanging out here fetching drinks for everyone because it's *good for my health?* Goddamn it, I brought you your two drinks, I laughed at your stupid lame jokes, *now you owe me a dollar!*"

The worst part of all this is that I have to do it all over again tonight. This is now my job. I look up at my exhausted reflection. Now I can't remember exactly why I envied those smiling waitresses at the Mirage.

I open my manual and again bone up on the incredibly complicated section on ordering drinks, and study the Tropicana's long list of drink prices. The drink-ordering system is designed to make the bartender's job easier, and I remember Bobbi's last-minute advice for me to suck up to the bartender as much as possible. "The bartender can screw you up real bad, you're dead if you can't make up to this guy. You have to order the drinks, do all the work," she says, "and then you have to toke him!" *Toke* is the old, insider Vegas word for tip, as in short for token, and Bobbi reminds me that a 10 percent toke to the bartender, no matter what, is expected. "*And* he makes twice as much as you just by walking in the door!" Thanks to the union, waitresses earn more than the usual $1.00 an hour salary they're paid elsewhere in the country, but bartenders here earn even more: about $90 a shift.

When we approach the all-powerful bartender (almost always male) with a drink order, we must rearrange the drinks in our head so when we call them out, the bartender can hold two drink guns, one for liquor and one for mixers, over a row of ice-filled glasses. He's then set to pour our orders by moving his thumb over the buttons in a clockwise direction. All "well" (using house-brand liquor) drinks are ordered first before moving on to the "call" brands, as he's then obliged to drop the liquor gun to reach for specific bottles, but still holding on to the mixer gun. Beer and wine are ordered last, when both guns are dropped, along with any blender drinks. If you forget a drink, the bartender may send you to the back of the line behind the other waitresses, rather than pick up the guns again for you.

It gets more complicated. This system was instituted in the days when bourbon was the most popular drink, so all the bourbon drinks are ordered first, but, the manual points out, *without* using the word "bourbon." Calling out "Water! Soda! Ginger!" to the bartender means you want a bourbon and water, a bourbon and soda, and a bourbon and ginger ale. (Yelling out "Plain water," "Plain soda," "Plain Coke" means you get it without the bourbon.) Scotch drinks are ordered next, then brandy (Brandy is next? Who drinks brandy?), rum, vodka, gin, and tequila. You also have to remember how much everything costs, which means mentally rearranging the drinks again by price.

When you work in the lounge, you have to buy the drinks from the bartender, and you're reimbursed by the customers, who should consider it something of a miracle when they receive what they ordered, since everything has been shuffled around at least twice. I practice adding up random drink orders: two well drinks at $2.75, one Dewar's . . . I glance at my list to see that it's a premium brand, which is $3.75, Bombay gin is only $3.50 . . . add 25¢ per drink if the band is playing . . . is it possible I taught math only a month ago?

This system of purchasing drinks from the bartender and selling them to the customers makes their inevitable, conspiratorial question "Can't you just give me this drink for free?" incredibly irritating. They think they're trying to cheat the casino, but they're trying to cheat me. Lounge waitresses receive $100 at the start of our shift and must return $100 at the end of it, so any screwups or free drinks come out of our pockets. Looking at my $56, I can't escape the nagging feeling that I gave some guy a $10 bill thinking it was a $1 during a hectic period.

I flip the list over to review again all the drinks with names like Hairy Navel and Alabama Slammer, and how much they cost. I'm beginning to think I know how cocktail waitresses got the reputation for being stupid—just for taking the job in the first place.

On my second night, I'm assigned to the coffee shop, and I see that getting out of the lounge and being put in here is the difference between hell and a kind of living death. Patrolling a coffee shop and trying to sell drinks to disgruntled people who can't afford to eat in the casino's nicer restaurants is a losing proposition. This is the traditional spot where you "learn" to be a cocktail waitress, as there's about one drink order an hour. Tips are scarce. Some people think they'll tip at the end of the meal, without realizing that the waitresses don't share any of their tip money with me, and people who have been comped for free drinks also rarely tip. They have the mindset that the casino, which I apparently represent, owes them.

"I'll have a Bloody Mary," says a man who's dining with his wife and another couple, who've introduced themselves as Canadians. I write up a check, pay for the drink at the coffee shop register, and rush off to the casino service bar to stand in line behind the other waitresses, get the drink, and trot back to the coffee shop in a record four minutes.

"That'll be two seventy-five, please," I say, setting it down.

"So," he says, digging in his pockets, "how do they handle tips here? Are they automatically factored in the cost of the drink?" He hands over a $10 bill.

"Oh no, sir! Tips are definitely *not* included in the bill." I make change, which he, incredibly, pockets, thus stiffing me.

"Oh. I wondered," he says, rather smugly, ending our exchange. His tablemates look uneasy in a way that suggests this is a favorite routine of his. I feel foolish standing there in my tropical monkey suit with my huge fake gold nameplate blaring "Lynn" in such a presumably friendly, at-your-service way. The amount of humiliation and anger one feels at such a moment is completely out of proportion to the money one would have earned in a tip. At the end of the night, I have $15. I'd probably do better standing outside panhandling.

I tell Larry, the food and beverage manager, about the Canadian. He nods. "Canadians are the worst tippers."

"Notoriously cheap," says Sandy the next day, when I report my experiences. "The worst in the world, I think."

"The Japanese are supposed to be bad tippers, but there are some who tip very well," says a room service guy. "But there aren't any Canadians you can say that about."

Thanks to Johnny LaVoie's influence—or as we say here in Vegas, "juice"—Larry is obliged to put me on the casino floor. He introduces me to my fellow waitresses and the bartenders at the service bar. Since it is unheard of for a brand-new waitress with zero experience to land a spot on the floor during prime time, the entire group instantly assumes I must be screwing somebody fairly important, somebody beyond even Larry. I decide to ignore this response, but it isn't easy. The group is about as friendly as a school of barracuda.

Maria, a short waitress approaching fifty, eyes me suspiciously. She has the beginnings of a dowager's hump—an easy diagnosis, due to the cutout back of her waitress uniform. This hump seems to serve as ballast for her large, jacked-up breasts and prodigious cleavage. "You got dancer's legs," she says accusingly.

"Really?" I say. "I'm not a dancer." She looks at me as if she knows I'm lying.

"Where did you work before?" another hard-looking blond asks.

"Uh, one night in the coffee shop and before that, the lounge."

"Huh!" she says. "I had to work in the coffee shop for nine months before I was put here." Larry had warned me that I might find these women "pretty bitter and hard. The job does that." Later I tell him that I'd be pretty bitter if I had to work in the coffee shop for nine months.

"Only nine months, she said?" chuckles Larry. "It's usually a year."

Despite this less-than-genial atmosphere, I find the work on the casino floor infinitely preferable to lounge work, since gamblers are more interested in gambling than in cruising the waitresses. The tips are generally better, but it's not the gravy train I'd previously imagined. While some people are prone to tipping generously because the drink is free, others feel that a free drink means *free*—so they don't tip at all. And standing in line at the service bar mentally rearranging my drink orders subjects me to language from fellow waitresses that even Skid Row's roadies would object to.

"There are some stupid motherfuckers out there tonight," says the hard-looking blond, who happens to be working on her fortieth birthday. "She's pumpin' quarters into a hundred-dollar machine! When I tell her, she thinks I mean the machine *costs* a hundred dollars. I thought I was gonna wet my pants—"

"—that's what happens when you turn forty!" cracks another waitress.

"Hey, no more fortieth jokes!"

"Isn't the bartender cute?" says Laura, one of the few younger waitresses. She's speaking to me, but it's obviously for the bartender's benefit. She sighs as if lovestruck. "Too bad he's married." He makes a joke with her about how she forgot to wear underwear last night, and had to go back home for it. "I just forgot!" she says. She flips her skirt up to reveal blue panties. "I've got them on tonight."

"Hey, how cold was it last night?" says Maria to the bartender. She turns around to give me a fishy stare, as if I'm standing too close to her in line.

"Really cold, maybe forty degrees," he says.

"Oh, no wonder my pussy was so cold," she says. This is said with such serious macho swagger that I want to burst out laughing—*Say, Maria, you are one tough little hombre!*—but I keep my response down to a contemptuous smirk.

As she walks past with her drinks, I resist the temptation to add, "Maybe your pussy's cold because no one's been near it in years." You have to be Jack Nicholson to say this right, and besides, I've heard the stories of how waitresses get back at colleagues they don't like by "accidentally tripping" and sending a tray of drinks cascading down some unfortunate's front. I heard about this tradition from waitresses at the union office. "Make it a whole tray of spicy Marys," says a brash twenty-five-year-old originally from Bangkok. "Then when they reach down in front of you to get some napkins—right in the face. Pepper in the eyes, and stain her uniform." She smiles coldly. "You say, 'Oh I'm sorry.'" She demonstrates by fixing me with a stare I'd hate to meet in a women's prison. "But then they know not to fuck with you, and they respect you after that."

"Oh God, oh God," says a waitress rushing in, "we are being audited!"

"Honey, it's happening to everyone," says Laura.

"Audited! Audited!" she says.

"I declare everything," says the forty-year-old. "Everything."

While the drinks are free to gamblers, we still must "ring them up" on the register near the bar using our identifying number, so the casino can declare how much it spends on liquor, and the IRS can keep counting our drinks and our alleged fifty-cent tips.

After a couple of weeks of this, I come to the depressing conclusion that it really is true that women generally do not tip well. They're also the ones who order fairly complicated or unusual drinks ("Cranberry, peach schnapps, and vodka with a slice of orange peel," says a brunette in her twenties), and I've learned that the more exciting the order, the better the chances that absolutely no tip is involved. "Let's see," says one pudgy middle-aged woman at a slot machine, clicking her long red nails against the machine as she speaks. "Kahlua and cream in coffee with whipped cream on top and Sweet and Low on the side." I dutifully bring it, even though it's closer to dessert than a drink. "I know," she says with a giggle, when I set it down. She reaches for the drink greedily, neglecting my tip. "I'm a glutton!"

I hear one woman hissing at her husband, "A quarter is fine! She makes plenty of money," meaning me. "I mean, *look at her.*" Another man asks me, "How much do I give you for you to come home with me?" I smile nervously, but before I can decide to tell security, he says, "Just kidding," and hands me fifty cents. I begin to wonder if the sexy outfit doesn't actually cut down on tips, since women feel threatened by it, and men tell themselves we're only waitresses after all, and with an outfit like that, flirting is part of the deal. We're supposed to humor their oh-so-tantalizing attempts at seduction if we want a tip for bringing them a drink.

I begin to appreciate bikers, who tip well, at least a dollar a drink, and who always order simply, either a Jack Daniels and Coke or a Budweiser. Best of all, they're quiet and treat waitresses with respect, probably because they've dated a few.

"Doctors are atrocious!" a waitress tells me. "I have a plastic surgeon who tips maybe one dollar for fifty drinks a night. Lawyers are bad too. I'll take a working person any day." She tells me a joke that waitresses like to share with non-tippers. "What's the difference between a [insert appropriate description of the non-tipper here: doctor, Canadian, cowboy, whatever] and a canoe?" Answer: "Canoes tip."

I expect nothing from couples in their twenties or thirties who have a furtive look about them. This happens when they're down to their last $20, and their inclination to tip is long gone. The woman seems to be the one holding the cash at this point, as the man can no longer be trusted with it. One couple with that look about them pretends to play a slot machine by dropping a quarter when they see me. "A margarita," says the guy, "and a Long Island iced tea for her." When I return, they take the drinks and immediately order another round. "By the time you get back here we'll be ready," he says nervously, handing me a dollar bill as a tip. I know they're almost broke, and that in the lounge these drinks would cost $11.75. I admire the fact they're still tipping, and I notice he's got the hands of a slot player. His fingers are covered with a shiny gray film, as if he's been rubbing them with pencil lead, the telltale sign of handling so many coins. I pretend I don't know what they're doing and bring them another round. I figure the casino owes them that much and, anyway, people like this will always be back with more money to lose.

Las Vegas is a cash town. I never see a brand-new bill of any denomination; money is as soft as old suede and as faded as worn denim, all of it tainted with the residual sweat and grime of the thousands of people who've passed it back and forth. Money just never seems to make it to the bank here. Bobbi tells me stories about the good old days of cocktail waitressing back in the sixties and seventies, when girls bought brand-new cars with shopping bags of cash. But the days of waitresses never using credit cards, and paying cash for everything so they can hide from the IRS, are over.

"There are waitresses who haven't filed an income tax return in ten years!" says Bobbi. "I always tell them, 'Honey, I'll bring you fresh fruit in prison, because that's where you're going.' One waitress is losing her house, her car, and she's going to jail. It's different now. There's IRS in the cage," she says, referring to the casino bank. "Everywhere. *They've got you.*" And if the IRS doesn't get you, there's always a gambling addiction. "I know cocktail waitresses who've been working thirty years," she says. "And don't have a dime. They're players."

Most casinos forbid employees to gamble at their place of work, unless it's making a bet on a sporting event. Most, but not all. "I worked at the California, downtown," says Susan, a waitress I chat with on my break, "and they'd let you gamble on your break or after work! There were women with two kids gambling. A lot of people gamble away their wages." She contemplates this for a moment, and adds, "We have a high divorce rate here." She's on her second marriage herself at the age of thirty, but not because of gambling. "Everyone works different shifts," she says, as if that should be obvious to me. "When one gets home, the other's going to work. I didn't see my ex-husband for five years."

I eventually get moved from the slot machines to the blackjack tables, which turns out to be far more lucrative, as a dollar a drink, rather than a quarter or fifty cents, seems to be the average tip, and with the dealer and pit boss looking on, there's more pressure on the player to do the right thing. "Always serve to the left," says Karen, a waitress designated by Larry to give me a few pointers, "and pick your moment when you ask someone if they'd like a drink, you know, wait if they're being dealt a hand."

One card player stops me after I serve him and says, "Show me your left hand."

I carefully transfer my tray of drinks to my other arm and hold up my hand, thinking he wants to see if my forearm is bigger from carrying trays of drinks all night, something I'm beginning to suspect is happening. "Oh, you're married," he says. "The pretty ones always are."

"I would have told you," I say, irritated that I shifted the tray just for that, "if you'd just asked."

Ask any casino worker in Atlantic City about strange occurrences on the casino floor, and they'll always tell you about some guy "urinating right under the table," or women "peeing into their clothes," because they can't bear to tear themselves away from a slot machine or the cards. "I can't tell you how many blackjack chairs get ruined in a year, from people takin' a leak into them," a Showboat employee once told me. But ask a casino worker in Vegas the same question and they'll tell you about the time some guy died. For some reason, Vegas gamblers seem far less inclined to urinate in public than Atlantic City gamblers, but they drop dead at what seems to be an alarming rate.

"We had a guy die at the bar of a heart attack," Susan tells me. Other things happen too: "There was a guy jacking off behind the Whirlwind of Cash one time, and one guy in the poker area likes to finish up other people's drinks." But death is the

Big One in a casino, the thing that people really remember.

A dealer tells me, "People die at the tables. We had one old guy at the Flamingo playing twenty-one who keeled over backwards, stiff as a board. His arms raised and everything. He wasn't dead, he was on some kind of medication and just took too much. He was so stiff, they couldn't fold him into a wheelchair, so they got a hand truck and wheeled him out! He looked just like one of those mannequins."

"One night at the Golden Nugget," says Bobbi, "a guy dropped dead right in front of us! A heart attack! And you know what? People kept on playing, they didn't miss a play. They walked around him, stepped over him. The paramedics came, and people never missed a card!"

While I don't see anyone die, despite my fervent wishes, I do notice that the figures quoted by the food and beverage manager at the Dunes regarding what I will earn turn out to be completely accurate: $50 to $100 is about average, and on a really good night, $150. I look forward to cashing out at the end of my shift, since there's an undeniable thrill from watching all of my coins get poured into the change-counting machine on the casino floor. A magic number appears as the total, something like $38.10, which feels, despite the sweat and blood of the past eight hours, like found money, and yet also leaves you wondering who had the balls to tip a dime. For utterly childish reasons, I never change in all of my singles for bills of a higher denomination: This is so I can have a few minutes of pleasure sitting in my car in the employee parking lot at 3 A.M., giggling at the effort of trying to stuff all my cash into my wallet. The hypnotic effect of cash in your hand means you'll work for a lot less of it: $150 in singles seems like a lot of money, but a check for $150 looks pretty paltry.

While the tips at the blackjack tables are larger, you also have to constantly bus ashtrays, a job I recommend to anyone who wants to quit smoking. There's very little in the world that's more disgusting than having to carry stacks of ashtrays, dump them out, and wipe them clean with a bar rag. My manual contains the disturbing news that "ashtrays are one of the worst health menaces to cocktail waitresses. . . . Your fingernails may be weakened from the ashes and there are girls who are afflicted with infections and rashes on the fingers, hands, and faces. And these same hands go from ashtray to drink." Good point. I also begin to notice how my chest will actually ache during the day. Between the smoke and my near constant diet of steak dinners for $1.99 and steak-and-egg breakfasts for 99¢, this chest tightening is from either my two-pack-a-day secondary smoke habit or my arteries clogging.

Since my co-workers aren't exactly thrilled about my mysterious ability to leap ahead of other workers with more experience, my days are fairly free of social events or companionship. I relax and vent my work-related anger and frustration at the video arcade at Caesar's Palace, the place where parents drop their kids while they gamble. Here I spend hours and untold numbers of quarters at the Terminator 2 game holding a machine gun, pretending I'm Arnold Schwarzenegger and deftly mowing down my enemies. I get so good at this that I enter my initials onto the list of top ten players: me and nine teenaged boys. It's hard to get a game going with anyone, though. A woman who plays with that much grim determination and skill probably looks pretty scary to kids who are used to seeing adults behaving this way only at a craps table.

On my last week, Larry suddenly tells me he can't put me on any shifts, explaining that "there are about ten waitresses on the wait list with more seniority than you." Johnny suspects that the waitresses have threatened Larry with a grievance to the union, unaware, of course, that the union is behind me working in the first place. To resolve matters, Johnny tells me to quit, and sends me over to work at the Stardust for my last four days, as they need more waitresses because the big rodeo is in town. This is the annual National Finals Rodeo—the three-day event that is the cowboy equivalent of the World Series, and all the serious rodeo partying goes on at the Stardust.

I never got around to being drug-tested at the Tropicana, but during orientation at the Stardust, we're told that the food and beverage manager will hire on the best waitresses among us after the rodeo, and then we'll have to submit to the DNA hair drug test. "They say sixty strands, but it's more," murmurs one waitress, as we stand in line to get our forms processed and our I.D. cards checked.

"I'll tell you how to beat the drug test," whispers Tyler, a waitress in her early twenties with short curly hair. "Nexxus makes this shampoo called Aloe-Rid. This girlfriend of mine got hired by Caesars?" Tyler ends almost every sentence on an up note, as if it's a question. "She graduated from college about a week earlier and had every drug known to man at a party, and then found out she had to get drug-tested? She heard about Aloe-Rid, and we were pouring it into her hair every day! It really strips and dries your hair out, but we did a deep conditioner right before the drug test—and she passed."

"God, why do they take hair?" complains a beautiful African-American waitress wearing glasses. "Why don't they take pubic hair?" The line erupts in laughter. "Here, take all you want, knock yourself out! But seriously, why not?" she says. "DNA is DNA, right?"

We talk about previous places of employment. I mention my

Tropicana nemesis, Maria. "I knew her from Vegas World!" says Cindy, an older waitress. "Man, is she a bitch! She hates every-one, don't feel bad."

After one night of working the tables at the Stardust Rodeo Party it becomes apparent that couples tend to sit at tables to listen to the band, whereas single people stand. In cowboy cul-ture, women hold the money, and they're not terribly interested in tipping, preferring instead to count out exact change. I end up making a scant $36 in tips, although one waitress working near me says she only made $20. The second night, I tell the manager I'd really like to be one of the "Shooter Girls," the ones walking around the party with a bottle of Crown Royal in a hol-ster and a bandolier full of shot glasses. I figure I have a better chance selling shots to single cowboys than fighting to get to the bar to bring drinks to non-tipping couples. This strategy works, and I end up with $120 at the end of the night, along with the distinct, disgusting impression that I've been dipped by the heels into a bottle of Crown Royal. My cuticles constantly burn from sloshing the stuff over them.

"Guess you didn't recognize me without my orange hair," says one cowboy to a woman, as he offers to buy her a shot. He introduces himself as a rodeo clown. She mentions the name of another rodeo clown. "That guy?" he scoffs. "He's a scumball. Now me, I'm a *class* act." Little did I know that I would end up sitting next to the class act on an airplane.

After working until 4 A.M. on my last night in town, I barely had time to rinse off the whiskey before catching a 7 A.M. flight to New York. Through some bizarre twist of fate, I find myself seated next to the above-mentioned Mr. Orange Hair, who, in-credibly, carries a leather briefcase. His occupational title— "Rodeo Clown"—is branded into it, along with what seems to be his personal motto: "Wherever you go, there you are."

"I plan to sleep the whole flight," I warn him, as he recognizes me as "the Shooter Girl!" and insists on shaking my hand.

"Me too! Is it okay if I lay my head on your shoulder?" After I growl a response about how I'm in no mood after the day at work I just had, he smirks. "Oh, go on," he says. "Your job isn't so bad." This is coming from somebody who distracts angry bulls for a living, so I decide not to argue—even though I know his job isn't any harder than being a cocktail waitress.

# 5

# There's No Such Thing as Bad Publicity, Only Bad Publicists

So what job are you up to now?" My friend Nicole is asking me this over drinks in a bar. This place in SoHo is her hangout, and she's busy looking over my shoulder to see if she knows anyone here. I know it's only a matter of time before she spots someone.

"Well, next week I'm going to Los Angeles to be a publicist," I say. "I just finished being a cocktail waitress, which was really . . ."

"When are you going to be a stripper?" she says. Now she's waving at someone behind me.

"Nicole, I keep telling you: Not for a while, okay?" She asks me this every time we see each other, and it's beginning to wear on me. The thought of being a stripper is unsettling enough for me to contemplate without the prurient interests of other people to contend with.

The person she was waving to, a fresh-faced man in his twenties, is now kissing Nicole on both cheeks. Where are we, Paris?

*"This is Lynn," says Nicole. "She's going to be a stripper." I roll my eyes.*

*"Hello!" says the man, who takes my proffered hand and uses it to pull me into kissing range. I resist this maneuver, and our minor struggle nearly pulls me off the bar stool. This kissing business between strangers has gotten way out of control.*

*"In New Orleans, right?" says Nicole.*

*"When?" says the man, excitedly. He takes a step back to check out my body. I want to slug him.*

*"Later this year," I say. "I'm actually a writer. I'm going to Los Angeles soon to work as a publicist. That should be really exciting."*

*"Nicole, you look so good!" he says, checking her out as well.*

*"I think I'll be able to go to the Golden Globes awards," I say to Nicole. She smiles, sipping her drink.*

*"Hey, why don't we plan a trip to New Orleans!" says the man, squeezing Nicole around the waist. "When your friend is stripping!"*

*"Yeah!" she says. "We could get a whole bunch of people! You'll have to tell me," Nicole says, waving her cocktail straw for emphasis, "exactly when you're going and the name of the club where you're stripping."*

*"Yeah, sure," I say, "I'll tell you as soon as I know." I actually know already, but nothing, not money, the promise of eternal life, or threats of torture, could make me tell these two. Or anyone else I know, for that matter.*

In a handbook for publicists, rule number one would be: Badmouth whomever you like, as long as it isn't a client. I learn this right away, shortly after I introduce myself to Tom Esty, a man who is now one of my colleagues at the Beverly Hills publicity firm of Baker Winokur Ryder. I see a copy of Richard Simmons's latest book on a table in his office. I pick it up with a chuckle. "Richard Simmons," I say to Tom, who is Simmons's publicist. The frizzy-haired, campy former fatty known for his aerobic workout tapes called *Sweatin' to the Oldies* has now written a self-help book. "He's so scary," I say with a laugh.

Tom's face, normally pleasant, changes to a mask of stern disapproval bordering on outrage. "Scary?" he says, although it's not a question. "I don't think he's scary at all. I think he's *absolutely brilliant.*" He says this with nothing less than total conviction. "He's got worldwide recognition! He's *changed* millions of people's lives! Did you see Arsenio last night? Richard Simmons was on, and he was *brilliant.*"

As a journalist, I'd often wondered if the publicists who raved about their clients like proud grandparents ever admitted to family, friends, or co-workers that perhaps one client or another is hard to be so unrelentingly positive about. The answer is no. Celebrities are often accused of believing their own hype, but publicists are the ones swallowing it whole even as they're manufacturing it.

Tom is still brooding about my disrespectful comment about the brilliant Mr. Simmons when Cindy Guagenti, a tall blond with a lispy childish voice, walks in carrying *Daily Variety.* Cindy represents Brad Pitt, among other actors. "I was thinking," she says, plopping down in a chair, "of writing Barbra Streisand saying 'If you're ever thinking of changing publicists . . .' Like when the one she has dies, because he's been with her thirty-three years. There's an article in here," she says, waving the paper, "that says he's resigned! But forget it," she says morosely, "everyone's calling her now."

"I hate every magazine in the country," says Tom.

"Yeah," she says, still glum. "I called up an editor and talked to her about a client of mine and she says, 'I'm done with April and May's booked up.' So that's that! And I know they say, 'Oh those publicists, they think they know everything!' when we're gone. They're *soooo* two-faced."

*We're* two-faced? is the comment on the tip of my tongue until I remember that I'm a publicist now. We sit in silence and I try to see Cindy's point. I think it is this: Writers are seemingly nice and positive to the celebrity but then turn around and print that the movie he's in is a dog. Cindy says two-faced; we journalists prefer the term *objective*. Journalists and editors lack the professional ability to love someone unconditionally the way a publicist can, and therefore we can never be trusted.

As a member of the camp that can't be trusted, it takes me a few days to shake the feeling that I'm working for the enemy. Publicists are the people that journalists and celebrities only *pretend* to like. I decided to be a publicist to find out what it would be like to be someone so loathed and dreaded. Would I even be conscious of it? I imagine I'd have to be like a television producer I know who is disliked by everyone she works with, but she manages to believe they all love her dearly.

Before I worked at BWR, I viewed publicists as people who interfere when I'm trying to interview a celebrity. Instead of letting me talk to the star directly about where and when we should meet, the publicist prolongs this rather simple bit of business into a two-day blizzard of phone messages. Inevitably, the publicist asks to be present during the interview, which feels a bit like having your parents out with you on a date. There they sit, a parasite growing fat on the fame of their celebrity host. If you manage to shoo them away, the publicist won't stay banished for long, and will call during the interview—or just show up—"to see how things are going." Perhaps it is fun to annoy people in this way. It certainly wouldn't be work.

I pull into my parking space at BWR's offices every morning at 9:30 A.M., and enter the modest building on a quiet street in Beverly Hills—but then, every street in Beverly Hills is quiet. Within a few days of this peaceful, insulated existence, I begin to feel resentful of any attempt to upset the new, positive status quo. My initial attitude toward this job—antagonistic journalist in the midst of sycophants—has imperceptibly given way to a publicist's warm, cozy, yet morally righteous demeanor: *Can't we all just get along?* Unlike the journalist I used to be, and may become again, I only want to draw attention to my clients in the most *positive* way. I realize now that I was deluded in thinking that publicists ever do anything stars don't want them to do. I soon learn that an accepted practice is for the star to whisper to the publicist, "Come and get me in half an hour," and then complain to the journalist how annoying it is to be interrupted by his or her overprotective flak-catcher.

As time goes by I began to feel defensive and protective every time a journalist calls the office, and I am soon rebuffing these damned vultures with pleasure. After all, celebrities love us publicists! And we love them! They love us so much *they insist we come along* when they're being interviewed by a two-faced journalist! Did I realize as a journalist how universally loathed and dreaded I was?

My first task at this firm is to drum up interest in the pilot for a magazine-format show that Malcolm-Jamal Warner is co-producing, something called *All-Ax-S*—which is pronounced "All Access." Malcolm, you'll recall, played Theo on *The Cosby Show,* and even though his involvement with this project is fairly minimal, his co-producers see the benefit of pushing his name forward to get interest in the press. My job is to persuade local news stations to send camera crews out to various locations in Atlanta, Phoenix, and Los Angeles, where segments of the pilot will be filmed. My tools to accomplish this are a dictionary-sized reference book filled with phone numbers of television stations, a legal pad, a pen, and a telephone.

Three days and dozens of calls later, I feel like Jack Lemmon's character in *Glengarry Glen Ross*, sweaty-palmed and desperate to make a sale, running my hands through my hair in the effort to summon the enthusiasm and confidence for yet another cold call. I've nothing to show save a few local affiliates who tentatively agreed to send out a crew if "nothing else is happening." I see the media as Cindy does, a mass of two-faced opportunists, hungry for scandal, so quick to dismiss a perfectly nice actor and his new project as "Not interesting enough," or "Not for us," and "Sorry, I don't think so." *Entertainment Tonight*, our big hope, is enthusiastic, but says they don't have a crew available on the day we're shooting in Los Angeles. I call CNN to try to entice them to send out a crew to cover the filming of the Atlantic segment on the rap group Kris Kross, but the answer is a polite no thanks. I feel as if I'm letting little Theo down.

This exercise in frustration also illustrates perfectly how the fax has replaced simply listening. When I call a news director, I deliver a mini-pitch about the show, which is actually a pitch to receive the fax. The fax is my brief, easy-to-read, media-friendly press release. After sending the fax, I make a follow-up call to see if they're interested. In the old days, this entire process could probably have been handled with one phone call. And of course, in the old days, when there were a handful of television stations, a job like this could have been accomplished in an hour. I end up with a stack of cover sheets and faxes to stick in the file for this account, but no firm commitments. I hand the file over to Angela Cabel, the office manager, who is also trying to drum up publicity. "I think BET is interested," she says, meaning Black Entertainment Television, a cable channel.

"Really?" I say, relieved. "That's great!" Malcolm and his partners will be pleased.

Since I'm the new person here, I'm given work that just about anyone could do, but no one particularly wants to. This includes requesting two tickets to a taping of an HBO comedy special for a client of ours, Victor Love. In sharp contrast to my last project, this is deftly accomplished in a single call. I feel suddenly powerful.

I then tackle the job of calling critics and press people who have not RSVPed to our screening invitation to *Watch It!*, a film starring Peter Gallagher. I leave thirty-five messages on voice mail. Twenty people eventually call back, and even though they all received an invitation in the mail and have heard my highly detailed message, I still have to repeat again the name and basic plot of the movie, who's in it, and when and where the screening is being held.

Redundant explanations are part and parcel of the job. Even the follow-up calls I made for Malcolm's show often involved me reviewing and explaining the fax, which has clearly gone unread, despite the demand that it be sent in the first place. It occurs to me that this is exactly how functional illiterates get by without detection. Very few people seem to be actually reading faxes or memos, and with the advent of voice mail, no one has to read phone messages either.

"People used to *pretend* they read all that stuff, even when they hadn't," says one assistant, who hears me complaining about this. "Now they say they *haven't* read it even if they have." She crumples up a fax of a gossip column from a New York newspaper and tosses it into a wastepaper basket. "It's real hostile, don't you think?"

Admiring my *All Ax-S* press release, Cheryl Lynch, another publicist in the firm, asks me if I could rewrite some of the celebrity biographies in her files. She asks me to start with Sherrie Rose's biography. I look at her résumé and 8 × 10 glossy and see that Sherrie is a pretty, curvaceous actress who's made quite the career in B movies. Cheryl needs this written quickly, as she's about to send it out to garner publicity for *Double Threat*, Sherrie's newest picture, with Sally Kirkland as a co-star. Picturing the physical assets of the two stars, the real meaning of the title of the film becomes all too obvious.

I show the finished draft to Cheryl. "I like the way you say she worked with Roger Corman," she says, reading aloud from my copy, " 'the man responsible for launching the career of Academy Award–winning director Jonathan Demme.' "

I smile modestly. "I thought that if someone just glanced at the page, the words 'Academy Award–winning' would spring out." Cheryl invites me to a party for Sherrie at Ava's, a small nightclub in the Beverly Center.

"I'm with Baker Winokur Ryder," I say at the door, which is rather unglamorously located in the parking deck of a shopping mall. The velvet rope is magically opened, and I squeeze past the crush and spot Cheryl. She introduces me to Sherrie as the writer of her bio. "Really?" Sherrie squeals, resplendent in a low-cut gown. "I loved it! Thank you so much!" She hugs me, attracting the envious stares of every man in the room.

I discover it's much easier to become a publicist than it is to stop driving like a New Yorker. After two weeks in Los Angeles, my motoring spirit is finally broken and I stop trying to get anywhere in a big hurry. Traffic in Los Angeles has become so bad that people have accepted the inevitable and are now working out of their cars: faxing and phoning, applying makeup, typing on laptops. Using the car as a work space has robbed them of the incentive to rush to the office, so the space is slowed even more. On the freeway, vehicles drift from lane to lane and slow to a near standstill, only to leap back to life when the fax is un-jammed or the phone call is completed. As an antidote to this poke-along driving, I rant and rave along with Howard Stern on my twenty-minute crawl down Santa Monica Boulevard from the fashionable Chateau Marmont hotel, my new place of residence. Working in such a status-conscious business, I figured I had to live someplace cool if I was going to be driving a completely unimpressive rented Chevrolet Cavalier. Avis, unfortunately, is not in the business of renting out Porsches, Jaguars, BMWs, or anything else worth stealing or car-jacking.

I've taken the step of altering my appearance slightly for this job. My new hairdo as a publicist includes a dark rinse to eliminate all my blond highlights to emulate more effectively the Sherry Lansing serious-brunette power look. In deference to the more relaxed business dress code on the West Coast, I pair black jeans with my suit jackets at the office. I notice that the casual look is completely sacrificed at night in Hollywood for the hooker-on-the-town effect, when restaurants and gatherings are clogged with women of all ages wearing leather micro-minis, bustiers, lace outfits, and high spike heels.

Since ample time is needed to make this dramatic transition from day to night, Cheryl and I leave work early to prepare for the Youth in Film Awards ceremony. Cheryl's client, Brian Austin Green, an actor from the enormously popular television show *Beverly Hills, 90210*, is a presenter. Since I'm to be his publicist during the Golden Globes ceremony next week, Cheryl wants tonight to serve as a dry run for me. Like everyone else in Hollywood, publicists find most awards ceremonies to be three hours of boredom, and are eager to pass along this duty of attending with a client if they can.

Suitably attired for the event, we drive out to the Valley in Cheryl's champagne-colored Nissan Pathfinder. As her assistant for the night, my first task is to look up various numbers in her Filofax and dial the carphone for her.

"Hello, this is Cheryl Lynch," she begins, after I hand off the phone, "I represent a number of celebrity clients." She gets down to what she needs immediately; in this case, it's "tickets to see the Black Crowes at the Troubadour." The tickets are for someone who hasn't actually signed with her yet; it's a gesture that she hopes will coax him along. "Now I'll pay for them," she says, which is an unusual offer from a publicist, "I just need the tickets. Def American can't help me, and the Troubadour says a hundred tickets will go on sale tomorrow morning."

She pauses to listen as we sail down an exit ramp. She frowns. "Thanks anyway," she says, passing me the phone. She flips on the overhead light so she can touch up her nail polish now that we're likely to stop at traffic lights. These Black Crowes tickets are important, so she racks her brain to think of someone she can call for help. "I represent some people for free," she explains, lest I think this is all about getting a commission, "because I believe in them. And I know once they get a deal, they'll take me along."

In addition to a starting salary of anywhere from $25,000 to $30,000 a year, a publicist takes 15 percent of the retainer paid by a client they bring in themselves, and 5 percent of the retainer on a client brought in with other people in the agency. A client must pay the agency a minimum retainer of $1,750 a month but, depending on the services involved, it can go to $2,500 a month and beyond.

Cheryl instructs me to look up another number, and this time she gets the tickets. As we glide into the parking lot, she says, "You carry my Filofax." Cheryl drove in her stocking feet so as not to ruin the back of her elegant high heel on the floor mat. The valet parker opens her door, she puts on her shoes, and, after much dithering, she leaves the cellular phone in the car, since it won't fit in her tiny evening bag.

We fight our way backstage to find Brian. My job is to organize the film crews who want to interview him after the show; Cheryl will be the media watchdog. This means she'll stand within hearing distance of Brian during the interview in case any difficult or personal questions come up, in which case she can intervene. "Be on the lookout for *Hard Copy*. They're doing some sort of story about a fight Shannen Doherty was in," she says, naming Brian's tempestuous co-star on the show, "and they may want to ask Brian about it." I'm confused as to whether this means I welcome *Hard Copy* with open arms or put my hand over their camera lens, but since I never see them, the question is moot.

Cheryl scoots in beside Brian to check herself out in a mirror. She fluffs her long, curly hair, which is the color of a perfect apricot. "Look at me," she says. "I've got bimbo hair."

"People in this town pay a lot of money to have hair like yours," I tell her.

"Yeah! Bimbos! It takes me an hour and a half to blow dry it straight, but I can't do that all the time, so I end up with *this*," she says, holding out her big, soft, strawberry-blond curls. She fixes her lipstick, I dust off Brian's lapels, we both wish him luck and then head out to find our table.

The "Youth in Film" descriptive led me to expect—or perhaps hope—to see teenaged movie stars, but a large number of winners are very young children on television shows. An early award recipient was like a little Elvis Presley, complete with pompadour and a humble southern manner, saying, "I'd like to first thank the Lord Jesus Christ." This sets off a wave of copy-cat piety, prompting such speeches as "I'd like to first thank God, my family, especially my mother," followed by a surprisingly long litany of appreciation for such brief careers. After about an hour of this, I hear one mother at the next table say to her ten-year-old actress daughter, "If you thank God, I'll kill you."

A man with the BBC finds our table and crouches between us. He flirts for some minutes before getting around to asking for an exclusive interview with Brian. "No," we tell him. He politely flirts for an additional thirty seconds before retreating, a gesture I think is pretty classy under the circumstances. He promises to find us after the show.

"I can't believe Brian's not wearing any of the Armani," Cheryl mutters. "I got a deal with Armani, and after all that, he doesn't wear it."

Two extremely dull hours and a rubber chicken dinner later, the ceremony is over, and we rush backstage to the press area. I tell the fawning man with the BBC that his crew can "set up right over there. Brian will be over as soon as he's finished." I trot across the room where Brian is giving an interview to Britain's ITV. With Cheryl in place as the watchdog, she instructs me to be the "buffer," the person who stands and makes sure the fans don't crowd in around Brian or take any photos while the crews are filming, since flashes are distracting on video. I take my position and realize that I'm also blocking the entrance to the ladies' room. "We'll be done in two minutes," I tell the waiting crowd of women, not all of whom are fans of Brian, but are desperate nonetheless. "No photographs," I remind a pack of squealing girls. I see one girl raise a camera to her face. I point with authority. This is just like being a teacher again. "Hey," I bark. "No pictures until the interview is over, okay?" She quickly lowers her camera.

"You're good at that," says Cheryl as we pull Brian away from the autograph seekers and rush him over to the BBC. "You could be a bouncer." We go through this drill with three more crews before finally escorting Brian out to his car.

While we wait for our own car to be brought around, I tell Cheryl how I can't get over how much the guy from the BBC sucked up to us. He acted like it was a bigger deal to meet us than it was to meet Brian.

Cheryl nods with satisfaction. Apparently the BBC guy knew who was more important. "To be a publicist," she says, "means that you're also somewhat of a star in your own right." I had heard this before in the agency from other publicists, and dismissed it as wishful thinking, but it occurs to me now that it's true. Not because publicists are actually stars, but because they must be treated as if they were stars if people wish to get anywhere near their clients. This big difference becomes a very subtle one in Hollywood, where perception is reality.

Some nights later, I see a woman who identifies herself as a publicist with a big firm being denied admission to Tatou, a nightclub. The polite, not to mention dignified, thing to do once the velvet rope has not opened immediately is to leave, but this woman can't quite grasp the fact that she's being turned away.

"Do you know who I am?" she screeches at the bouncers. "I call you people all the time! And I'm going to call everyone and tell them never to come here!" The Tatou employees have clearly heard this many times, and remain unmoved. The woman turns to her friends in the crowd and explains in a loud voice, "You see, I'm worried that if one of my star clients comes here," she says, dropping several directors' names, men who I think would be scarcely interested in going to Tatou in the first place, "they'll be treated this same way, which means that I get a phone call at three A.M. because they're mad that they didn't get in!"

But, one is tempted to point out, your star client won't get turned away because *he's famous*. Publicists believe themselves to be on equal footing with their clients: Wouldn't a big star want the very best, someone they consider a peer, to represent them? At the very least, publicists think of themselves as a kind of vice-celebrity, just a heartbeat away from stardom.

"You know Dwight Yoakam?" says Paul Baker, one of the three partners in the firm, on one of his rounds through the office. "He's my neighbor. In fact," he says, glowing with pride, "we're both having pools put in at the same time! So mine was three weeks late because he's a big star and they did his first." Paul adds this modestly, but the real point is that the difference between Dwight Yoakum, a multi-platinum-selling country superstar, and Paul Baker, publicist, is a mere three-week wait. We're practically peers!

One of Paul's clients is the *L.A. Law* actor Corbin Bernsen, a guy I used to know in 1981 as the Winston cigarette model when we were represented by the same modeling agency. As long as we're chatting, I tell Paul that Corbin was a very successful full-time model back then, something he seems to be sweeping under the carpet now.

"Female models who become actresses are always 'model turned actress,' " I say to Paul. It's always bugged me that Andie MacDowell, Kim Basinger, and Geena Davis are still referred to as ex-models, but actors who were full-time models, such as Matthew Modine and Corbin Bernsen, escape this stigma. "How did he avoid that?"

"Do you want to meet him?" Paul says brightly.

"No. I mean, I've met him. I was just wondering . . ."

"Listen," says Paul, eager to wrap things up now that he's being paged, "next time he comes in, I'll tell him you're here."

A week later, Paul ushers a confused Corbin Bernsen over to my desk and happily introduces us. The moment is incredibly awkward, as we haven't seen each other in ten years, and I was really only friends with his wife, a woman he's since divorced. "Sure, I remember you," Corbin says. "So! You're doing this now!" He gestures to my legal pad and my telephone directory as evidence of my new career. It's clear that he thinks I just quit modeling last week. "Congratulations!" he says, in a heartfelt way. I'm at a complete loss for words, and since I've forbidden Paul to discuss my book with anyone, he can't really add much either. "Nice seeing you again," Corbin says as Paul ushers him out. I try not to feel embarrassed. It's not something a real publicist would feel.

On my way over to the fax machine, I walk past an open office. There's a cartoon on the wall: A man is beseeching a UFO, "Take me! Take me!" The UFO's pilot replies, "No, you're ugly." An apt metaphor for Hollywood.

While standing in line to use the fax, I can see a big open box of fan mail for Michael J. Fox. "He's Nancy's client," says Angela, meaning Nancy Ryder, one of the partners. Angela's ahead of me in line. "I don't know why we're getting this stuff," she says. I can see letters in the box from places as far away as Japan and Thailand. "I think we send it all to someone else who handles his mail."

So besides an agent, a manager, and a publicist, the larger stars have security experts, bodyguards, and perhaps a personal mail handler. This explains why certain stars get involved in so many terrible movies: It's expensive to be a celebrity. I'm told that even reclusive stars who shun these trappings of stardom hire publicists. I smell hypocrisy: "Oh, so they pretend they hate attention," I say to Angela, "but they hire someone to make sure their name is in the news every month?"

She shakes her head no. "Some people use us to shield them from publicity. We field requests, answer questions, take all the calls they don't want to be bothered with."

I walk into Cindy's office as she's returning a call from a journalist who wants to interview Brad Pitt. "Tell him," she says into the phone, "in your dreams." She pauses. "That's the message. *In your dreams.* He'll know what it means." She hangs up with a giggle. I smile with her: mean old nasty journalist! I privately wonder if the delectable Mr. Pitt ever comes into the office, and if he did, if Cindy would introduce me. I doubt it: The really important clients are quickly ensconced in an office with the door shut, and, if possible, locked.

Publicists guard their clients closely, even, or perhaps especially, from their co-workers. The big dilemma comes when one publicist is very friendly with, say, the producer of an important late-night talk show that another publicist in the same firm wants to get his client booked on. Ordinary folks might think that, being co-workers, one might approach the colleague about putting in a good word, perhaps getting an introduction to the producer. But in the world of publicity, this is tricky stuff indeed. There is a danger that the celebrity might think he'd be better off with someone with *real contacts,* so the publicist would rather approach the producer cold and take the rejection than risk asking for help. The failure to get the booking can always be blamed on the dim wattage of the star.

I'm invited to dinner with a few publicists. We're all from different firms, and over dinner we talk shop. This means we gossip about stars. The real business stuff is too dangerous to discuss, for fear of someone swiping a client.

"So I was in this frozen yogurt parlor last night," says one publicist, a twentysomething woman with curly brown hair. "And there was Jerry Seinfeld! With a date. *And* they were making out!"

"Making out! Beyond kissing?"

"Are you sure it was him?"

"What frozen yogurt parlor?"

"Oh," she says, savoring our attention. "He's *so much* better-looking in person, so handsome! *She* was very Laura Ashley, bobbed blond hair, very attractive, and the two of them were laughing *a lot*. In between kissing. He had her *in hysterics!*"

We nod, smiling. That Jerry's a funny guy. Who wouldn't be in hysterics?

The gossip goes on in this vein, titillating but undeniably positive. How fabulous Cher looked trying on clothes in a boutique. Keanu Reeves certainly looked hunky when someone spotted him in a pool hall. If a scandal is mentioned, a moue indicating regret, distaste, or exasperation is more appropriate than an actual remark. Rule number two in the nonexistent handbook for publicists would be: If you can't say something nice, don't say anything at all.

At the office the next morning, I see that my name is misspelled in a memo. "What about that rule," I joke to Cindy, "about how it doesn't matter what they say about you as long as they spell your name right?"

"Oh, I don't think that's true," she says with a straight face. "It matters what they say. A lot of people really care about that." Okay, so there we have rule number three.

Cheryl comes in to tell me that we're going to spend the day "media-training" the Team Suzuki motocross riders. This is a group of ten or so testosterone-crazed jocks in their teens or early twenties who are sponsored by Suzuki, and who tour the country competing in motocross events. Motocross is a sport where competitors race specially made motorcycles around a stadium that is piled high with giant dirt cliffs. Spectators must enjoy eating and inhaling dirt and sand, listening to what sounds like twenty chain saws going at once, and watching guys soar from precipice to precipice, rising and falling like a flock of birds. These events attract much the same dirt-happy crowds as tractor pulls and mud wrestling. Nevertheless, Suzuki wants their competitors to say the right thing in front of the cameras if they're being interviewed pre- or post-race.

We drive out to Orange County to a firm that specializes in media training. "Bring up the name Team Suzuki in the first sentence of the interview," instructs the consultant. We're sitting with the team in a video room. "Remember your message points: Team Suzuki is first, then how motocross is a family sport, then mention how people who purchase a Suzuki are eligible for a lesson at the Tony D School."

One of the motocross riders murmurs, "Is the sport safe? Sure! Tony D's in a wheelchair!"

The biggest problem during the mock interviews is to break the team of the habit of describing everything as "good." We're fighting a long sports tradition of using one adjective to describe everything: "My bike's doin' good," "The track looks good today," "I think our chances are real good." We urge the use of more meaningful adjectives and try to get these guys to be more like themselves on camera instead of straight-faced stiffs by reminding them of possible endorsement deals and maybe even acting jobs.

Team Suzuki's biggest star is Jeff "Chicken" Metiasavich,

who is presently chewing tobacco and spitting into a paper cup while listening to all of our advice. "And Chicken," I tell him, "lose the tobacco when you're on camera, okay?" He rolls his eyes in exasperation. He opens his mouth by way of editorial comment.

"Remember to turn a negative into a positive," Cheryl adds. "When faced with a negative question, 'You had a lousy season last year,' don't get defensive or agree with them, say something positive incorporating the word Suzuki instead: 'Maybe, but I'm happy to be on Team Suzuki, and I'm looking forward to an outstanding year.'"

"Remember," warns the consultant, "the media is *not nice*." Cheryl and I nod in agreement.

To keep the team's spirits up amid all our nitpicking, Cheryl tells them that she's arranged for a "special surprise" later.

"Does it involve pussy?" asks a team member named Factory.

"Uh, no," says Cheryl, smiling brightly. "But it's still fun!"

When the surprise turns out to be two limousines to take them to dinner, Denny, another team member, registers excitement, "And there's girls in them, right?"

"No," says Cheryl. "It's a *limo!* You get to ride in a limo! Isn't that great?"

"No girls?" says Factory.

We threaten to beat them with bats if they fail to show up at Saturday's taping of MTV's *Inside Sports*. Brian Austin Green and the show's host, the Burger King spokesman Dan Cortese, are going to learn motocross with Team Suzuki. "See, I'm always thinking," says Cheryl about the two-client combination of Brian and Team Suzuki.

We get to the stadium on Saturday with the personalized motocross outfits for Dan and Brian: head-to-toe neon Spandex affairs with giant boots and face-obscuring helmets; the only way to tell them apart is to look at the name on their backs. The Team Suzuki guys are suited up and roaring around one track, being filmed while they soar twenty and thirty feet into the air, while Dan and Brian putter around the other, much less dramatic track, which somehow reminds me of miniature golf.

"Why don't we just get Factory and Chicken to put on their outfits," I suggest, "and do some really outrageous stunts as if they're Brian and Dan?" I'm not a journalist anymore, I don't have to worry about ethics.

It was a thought all of us had much too late. At this moment, Dan and Brian are seen putting on their helmets and taking their first real spin for the cameras around the baby track. At the first hill, one of them flies off the bike, pinwheeling his arms before disappearing behind a ridge. We climb down the bleachers and run closer to see a very still, helmeted figure lying flat on his back, and all I can think is *Please God, don't let it be Brian.* Aaron Spelling will kill us. He'll be written out of the show. We've ended his career.

It turns out it's Dan who's lying on his back, which is an immense relief. Brian has leapt off his bike and is crouching over Dan along with the entire MTV film crew. Since no one is shouting for an ambulance, we assume he's okay, and remain at a respectful distance. A few of the Team Suzuki guys have ridden over and are standing on the track looking down at the prone Cortese. They're smirking and shaking their heads.

Denny and Chicken have roared away from the accident scene and are heading our way. I flag them down. "What happened? Is Dan okay?"

"He busted his ass," says Denny with rather studied indifference.

"What does that mean medically? Is anything broken?"

"Bruised ribs," shrugs Chicken. "We were laughing. We

thought it was funny. People think what we do is easy, and it isn't."

"Yeah," says Denny, "you gotta learn to tuck and roll first thing. We get back on the bike after we bust our asses, no one gives us any sympathy."

Dan left shortly afterward. He looked hugely embarrassed, hobbling around like an old man. He walked off by himself to sit down and ease off his boots. Brian, on the other hand, stuck with it and did really well on the bike for the cameras. The segment aired, and was cut together so it looked as if Dan's fall wasn't a segment-ending catastrophe but a manly roll in the dirt. Well, that's show biz.

Back at work, I'm enjoying the fact that on this job, I get to sit down whenever I want to and wear comfortable clothes, things I never fully appreciated before working as a cocktail waitress. I also don't have to work hard every single minute. On a leisurely walk to the water fountain, I hear that the daughter of a TV producer will be strongly urged not to patronize the Gate, a Los Angeles nightclub that happens to be a BWR client.

"Why not?" I say, popping into a discussion already under way.

"Because," says a guy whose name I can never remember, "her father has already slapped the Roxbury with a lawsuit regarding her being underage—she's nineteen—and getting into the club."

"But how can he sue them if they're not serving her liquor? Why can't he just take it up with his daughter and not threaten to sue every nightclub in Los Angeles?"

"Look," he says, exasperated. "He's such a player here you don't want him trying to close you down! *No matter what the reason!*" Whoops. I said the wrong thing. Yes, far better to keep her as far away from our client as possible. Forget *the law*.

I pop in to Felice's office to ask about tickets to the Golden Globes. Felice is planning to be there, as she represents Jason Alexander of the NBC sitcom *Seinfeld*. "You have to call the Hollywood Foreign Press Association," she says. Seeing my blank look, she adds, "They're the ones who vote on who gets the awards."

"You're kidding," I say. "Foreign journalists decide?"

"It's all these . . . octogenarians," she says. "Not unlike the Academy."

I call HFPA's offices and, during my lunch break, pick up my credentials. I'm handed a large envelope with a parking pass, a meal ticket, and my huge identification badge: two six-inch lengths of very wide brown ribbon proclaiming "P.R." (as in Public Relations) that are attached to a white name tag—"Lynn Snowden, Baker/Winokur/Ryder." There's also an instruction sheet regarding dress (formal or dark suit) and places where I, a publicist, am allowed to go during the event. Reading between the lines, I see this means that while I will not be seated at a table with my client, I am free to hang out at the bar in the back of the room.

On Saturday afternoon, I remove these valuable pieces of paper from my room safe at the hotel. I feel as if I'm going to the *Beverly Hills, 90210* prom. In lieu of a corsage, I pin on, with trembling fingers, my huge brown-ribboned I.D. badge just so. I'm incredibly nervous. Formally dressed in a black pantsuit, I stride out to my car at the ridiculously early hour of 4 P.M., and drive out to the Beverly Hilton Hotel. Like the Academy Awards, the Golden Globes is timed so it can be broadcast live during prime time on the East Coast.

Felice had coached me as to my responsibilities for the evening, and the first order of business is to wait out front with the other publicists and keep an eye open for Brian in the flood of limousines. I see Felice in what appears to be a roped-in area for publicists. "They've got us in a pen!" she says, as I join her.

"Well, we've always got them in pens," says another publicist behind us, referring to the press, "so I guess this is their revenge."

"I know both of my clients will arrive at the same time," says Felice fretfully, adjusting her glasses. "You're lucky you just have the one. Oh look, there's Brian!" I dash out of the pen and meet him at the curb, nearly knocking heads with a woman who's the publicist for *Beverly Hills, 90210.* I introduce myself, and she abandons Brian to my trembling care. The paparazzi and the fans, both in their respective pens, are screaming at us, so I have to lean in close to hear what he's saying.

He's introducing me to another arrival, a young movie actor I'll call Ricky who has a past history of drug abuse. We shake hands, and I herd Brian over to the fan pen first.

I stand a polite distance away while the point-and-shoot cameras flash nonstop and the yowling fans hand over their autograph books. After three minutes of this I step forward to announce, "That's all! Sorry! Thank you!" Being the bad guy is part of being a publicist.

I usher him over to the paparazzi, who shout, "Over here!" "Brian!" "Brian!" "This way!" When the flashes seem to reach a crescendo I move in to interrupt it, as it wouldn't do for him to still be standing there when the flashes have died down. "Okay guys, thanks very much!" I shout at the photographers. "Brian, we have to go in now." We're lucky so far, I think to myself, trying to relax. Thank God Al Pacino didn't pull up at exactly the same moment.

The lobby has an inside pen of paparazzi, and attention must be paid here as well. Brian dutifully stands on the red X taped to the floor for proper exposure and focus as the flashes commence. I glance over at the wall of television cameras and the mayhem of the shrieking media and the bright lights. A woman is gesturing to me to bring Brian over for an on-the-spot interview. I lead him over.

While Brian gives an interview, I keep an ear cocked to what he's saying, and glance down the line at the other crews. They indicate their interest with an excited nod or a polite "no thank you" shake of the head. When Brian finishes, I gently guide him down to the nodding and waving crew from E! Entertainment Television, a cable channel. As he begins to speak, I look to the next group, *Good Morning America*, to see if they're interested. I catch the eye of Mark McEwen, the roly-poly weatherman cum celebrity reporter. He responds to my questioning look with a hugely exaggerated, condescending smirk, rolling his eyes and shaking his head as if the answer is *no, we're not interested in him at all, not even if he's the only celebrity here.* This unnecessarily negative reaction infuriates me. Thank God my client didn't see it! How unprofessional! And you're *a weatherman masquerading as a journalist!* is what I hope my facial expression conveys to him as I protectively lead Brian past to the MTV crew. When Brian is finished, the MTV host waves over Ricky, who's been hovering in the background.

This bit over with, we creep down another press gauntlet, where reporters shout out questions. "Hey Brian," says one, "who's your date?" I turn so she can see my P.R. badge. "Oh," she says. We eventually get to the end, where an autographed poster for the 1993 Golden Globes is positioned against an easel. A smiling young woman hands Brian a felt-tip marker. He signs the poster and hands the pen to Ricky. The press animal caged safely behind us, we head through the open doors into the ballroom.

"Oh, man," laughs Brian, adjusting his suit. I'm pleased to see it's the Armani tuxedo. "Let's get a drink!" We flag down a roving waiter. Ricky seems to be suffering some sort of crisis.

"My fuckin' manager isn't here, man!" he says angrily. "I should be on E! Where the fuck is he!" He glances around the room. "He's a short guy with big teeth." He turns to the waiter. "Double rum and Coke."

"A Heineken," says Brian, as the two light up cigarettes. The character Brian plays on *Beverly Hills, 90210* is so nauseatingly wholesome that I have to admit I'm a little shocked. *Beer? Cigarettes?* "You know, *my* people were waiting at the curb," Brian adds with a touch of pride. I remain silent, as if it's all in a day's work, but I'm glowing with pleasure.

"Can you take me back out there?" Ricky says to me, his eyes desperate. "I came here so I could be on E! and my fucking manager doesn't even care!"

The waiter appears with our drinks. "Sixteen fifty," he says. Brian and Ricky look dumbfounded.

"Isn't this a free bar?" says Ricky.

"I didn't bring any money," says Brian, taking out his wallet for proof. It's one of those bike wallets with a green cannabis leaf stenciled on it. "Put that away!" I hiss at him. God! Can't have people seeing *that!* I fork over the cash.

"Please?" says Ricky. "Will you take me back out?"

I look at Brian. "Will you be all right here? Is it okay with you if I go outside for a minute?" He nods, and I take Ricky's hand to fight against the incoming tide of stars. We unfortunately get to the television crews just as Clint Eastwood, Tom Skerritt, and Lauren Bacall make their entrances. The crews are going wild, desperate for them to stop and chat. Ricky, meanwhile, skulks nearby while I make the inquiries on his behalf, but it's no use.

Unlike Ricky, I ended up on E! Entertainment Television without even trying. I'm looking down the press gauntlet while my client, Brian, to my right, gives an interview.

Ricky looks stricken. He drains his drink on the way back inside, and orders a triple rum and Coke.

"What do you think, I'm made of money?" I ask him.

"Stay away from me, man," he says to Brian. "I'm poison."

"No you're not," I tell him. "It was bad timing. Everyone walked in at once."

Brian tries to cheer him up, but Ricky won't have it.

"It's really important that I show everyone that I'm, like, clean and sober right now!" Ricky says through gritted teeth while I pay for his drink. He shakes his head. "If my manager was here, I would have been on E! I'm leaving! I needed to be on E!"

"The people who will hire you," I tell him as he gulps his drink, "are not at home watching E!, they're right here in this room watching you throw a tantrum! So stop it already, and start smiling! Take it easy and go around and introduce yourself! Show people you're okay."

He takes a deep breath.

"She's right, man," says Brian.

"Okay," he mumbles, and rushes off. Jason Priestley, another *90210* star, sees Brian and walks over to us.

"This is my publicist," says Brian, introducing us.

"Oh yeah," says Jason, all smiles. "At Baker! I remember meeting you there."

"I don't think so," I say, "I'd remember." I tentatively pull out my camera. Brian asks on my behalf if he can take our picture.

"I'd be delighted," Jason says, putting his arm around my waist, "because she's such a babe." Jason's a bit on the short side, so I try to scrunch down without slouching. "In fact," he continues, "I suggest you take her out after the show."

"She's my *publicist*," says Brian, lining up the shot.

"Nothing wrong with mixing business with pleasure," says Jason, squeezing me tighter as the flash goes off. Jason takes one of Brian and myself, which makes my prom night experience complete. We notice Ricky waving us over. He's chatting with rock star Jon Bon Jovi and looking very pleased.

Skid Row toured with Bon Jovi, I think to myself as we walk over to shake hands. What a perfect conversational opener! I get as far as saying "We have a mutual friend," before remembering that the two bands are no longer on speaking terms owing to a bitter financial dispute. Mentioning Sebastian's name would not be the best move in the world.

"Really?" says Jon with a smile. "Who?"

My smile is frozen. Fortunately, I see a way out. "Chris Reynolds," I say, naming Skid Row's production manager. Chris called me last week to tell me he'll be touring with Bon Jovi.

"You know Chris?" Jon says. "How about that! Where did you two meet?" Before I can answer, two women rush up and interrupt. "Nice meeting you!" I call out, walking away, "I'll see you later."

I duck into the women's room to see Sean Young trying to decide exactly where to place her AIDS awareness ribbon. I'd always wondered where stars got these things, and now I know: They're at every place setting in the ballroom. She moves it around across her chest before deciding to pin it to the back of one of her opera gloves, just above the elbow. She smiles brightly at me and Susan Sarandon, who's putting on lipstick.

I walk back out to see Craig T. Nelson, of TV's *Coach*, in a very natty vintage tuxedo. "Wow," says a woman from a photo agency. "Who'd of thought a big guy like him would dress so stylishly?" Later, when Craig passes by the bar, an actor says, "God! He wears the same thing every year."

The show is about to start, so everyone is urged to take their seats. This leaves me as one of the only people left hanging around the bar area except for the self-consciously eccentric young movie actor Crispin Glover, who is rather mysteriously pacing about the premises wearing a tuxedo and what look like black gardening gloves. I overhear him talking to someone. "Well," he says heartily. "I've got to go! I've got to circulate!" What's strange is that he literally means circulate, not meet other people.

After the first commercial break, there's a virtual stampede up the aisles, and the bar remains crowded until the end of the show. A group at the bar has also noticed Crispin's gloves. "Is he wearing them because his last name is *Glover*?" says a pretty brunette, sotto voce.

"Maybe his hands are injured," says a long-haired actor tugging uncomfortably at his collar. Crispin, only a few feet away, overhears this, and rather pointedly removes a glove and whops his other gloved hand with it. His hands are fine. "Oh no, he heard us," says the brunette. "We've made him self-conscious."

"So what? He wears big gloves to a formal event, and we're supposed to pretend it's not happening?"

The awards are given out, one after another. *Beverly Hills, 90210* loses, and I barely notice; from the hubbub of the bar, the ceremony seems to be incidental. In fact, I'm wondering how they manage to broadcast over the din we're creating. I can see the stars going up onstage—Lauren Bacall, Gregory Peck, Gene Hackman, Clint Eastwood—I just can't hear them. The roar of the bar goes on, no one pays a bit of notice or has any interest in what anyone might be saying. Robin Williams accepts an award for *Aladdin*, and I strain to hear his presumably funny acceptance speech. I turn around to shush the incredibly loud guy holding court behind me until I see it's Jack Nicholson. I withhold my shush. I move as far forward into the auditorium as I dare with my brown-ribboned pariah status.

I see Ricky leaning against a wall and walk over to him. He seems much calmer. "I'm not as big as I used to be," he explains glumly. "And that's, like, *everything*."

"No," I tell him. "You're not *dead*, and that's, like, everything."

Even over the racket, I can tell that the mention of Robert Altman's film *The Player* as a nominee stirs thunderous applause. Hollywood seems to view the film as being "About *us!*" rather than about everything that's horrendously, stupidly wrong with movie-making. The star of *The Player*, Tim Robbins, rushes up to the bar to grab a couple of drinks to take back to his table. Suddenly, he's mobbed by well-wishers, and the scene is eerily reminiscent of much of the movie. Tim looks distracted and a bit desperate to get away as people are falling over themselves trying to kiss his ass. "I loved *The Player*, didn't you?" says another publicist loudly, as she breaks into applause as Tim hurries past.

Al Pacino wins for *Scent of a Woman*. Suddenly, all chatter in the bar ceases as Al mounts the stage. For the first and only time during the entire ceremony, the room is so quiet you could hear a drink being spilled. Even the Beverly Hills cops leaning against the wall step forward respectfully to hear what Big Al has to say, and a bartender dumping a bucket of ice into a tray is glared at for being noisy. Sir Anthony Hopkins didn't even get respect from this crowd. "Pacino's a *real* actor," whispers the toadying publicist.

"I bet it'd *really turn you on* to do his publicity," says an Australian wire service reporter to me, a strange note of excited disgust in his voice.

The evening winds down and I perform my last official act: I tell a man with a walkie-talkie that Brian needs his limo now, and I escort him outside. "Thanks a lot," says Brian. "One more thing. Can I borrow some money? I'll pay you back, I swear. Just remind me."

Sure, I love lending money to TV stars who make thousands of dollars per episode. I hand him a $20 bill, which prompts me to remember that I lent $20 to Sebastian Bach so he could buy a bottle of tequila in a place that didn't take credit cards.

Sebastian still hasn't paid me back, and neither has Brian. Being a publicist may mean being a star in your own right, but you'd better carry a lot of cash.

# 6

## Women's Work

The phone rings at my desk. It's my friend Anne.

"I think I found a family for you," she says.

This is terrific news, since I've had no luck in finding mothers willing to let me replace them temporarily for my next job as housewife. Anne fills me in on the pertinent details: three boys, nice parents, large house in Darien, Connecticut.

"The husband knows that my sleeping with him isn't part of the deal, right?" I ask. "He knows and the wife knows and everyone else knows that I stay in the guest room, right?"

"Oh yeah, I explained all that," she says. "This Saturday might be a good day for you to meet with them."

"Look, unless there's something egregiously wrong with them that you're not telling me about, I'll take them sight unseen. They sound perfect! Is it okay with them if I start in two weeks?"

"Yes, but it might be a good idea to meet them first so you can get all the ground rules straight about what you want to do. You know, get to know them, put everyone at ease."

I take the train up to Darien on Saturday and return the same

*day. I leave home brimming with charm, anxious to reassure every-*
*one; I return a beaten woman on the brink of a nervous breakdown.*
*I curl up in a fetal position on my bed and jot down some notes.*

1. *The house is freezing. I guess the good news is that if I'm slav-*
   *ing over a hot stove all day, I won't notice.*
2. *Today was laundry day, and every available surface in the living*
   *room was stacked with clothes! I'm told this is only a week's*
   *worth.*
3. *I got there in the middle of a family meeting. The wife asked me*
   *to join them in reading aloud from a book on unconditional*
   *love. The wife got teary-eyed and emotional; I wanted to run out*
   *of the room and hide in a closet.*
4. *An argument broke out over television viewing being restricted.*
   *This resulted in the youngest child having a tantrum and leav-*
   *ing the room in tears.*
5. *I was accosted by a cat, which prompted the news that there are*
   *six pets in residence, not counting the mother-in-law, who*
   *seems to be deaf.*
6. *I'm completely stressed out, and I was there only ninety min-*
   *utes. Maybe I should ease into this job by first becoming an*
   *air-traffic controller.*

I had wondered what the job of housewife would be like
if love and duty were completely divorced from the equation.
The answer: unpaid labor. Lots and lots of unpaid labor. In other
words, no one would do this if love—or money—weren't involved. I was actually hoping that this job might entail a lot of
lying on a recliner, watching soap operas, and eating bonbons
until the kids came home from school. I'm starting to suspect
that it's only writers who can lie down and watch TV on the job.

Temporarily replacing a housewife who has kids is not at all the same thing as working as an au pair. Despite the obvious similarities in their routine, only the au pair is acknowledged as a member of the work force. Unlike the housewife, she earns a salary, has time off, and is perhaps eligible for unemployment benefits. The popular misconception that the women's movement decrees that no woman is fulfilled unless she works outside the home has stigmatized the woman who chooses—and can afford—to stay home. Of course we're periodically reminded to recognize the important job mothers perform in staying home and taking care of the kids—"the hand that rocks the cradle is the hand that rules the world"—but it's obvious that we as a society don't really believe that. A woman today who does not work outside the home is, more often than not, quietly viewed as . . . a slacker.

This is particularly galling when most paying jobs involve far less work. A woman once told me she returned to her job only six weeks after the birth of her child because (a) she and her husband needed her paycheck, and (b) she needed the rest.

My interest in being a housewife is simply to tackle the physical aspect of the job, to compare it to other workplaces on a task-by-task basis. I replaced someone we as a society believe "has it good"—a middle-class woman who has been married to the father of her children for over twenty years. In other words, a slacker who probably sits on the couch eating bonbons until the kids come home from school.

As far as how being a housewife compares to the other jobs I've held, there's one major difference: There's no quitting time. As rotten as it was working as a cocktail waitress, I found it immensely consoling to remind myself that my shift would eventually end. I could abandon my post, stagger home, relax, and brace myself for the next day. As a housewife, I'm already home.

Quitting time is when I'm in bed with my eyes shut, a status that is by no means permanent and is likely to change without warning.

I'm taking care of three boys, whom I'll call Tom, Kyle, and Bill, ages seventeen, thirteen, and nine, respectively. Bob, my temporary husband, is a pleasant gray-haired, lanky man in his forties who works as a computer systems consultant to various firms. His mother, Eleanor, an outspoken Sherman tank of powdered flesh, is in temporary residence while her apartment is being renovated.

The mother I'm replacing, Sally, is viewing my two-week visit as a total vacation from housework, and an opportunity to see friends and take dance classes. I will rarely run into her during the day, and when I do, she is updating and adding to the long lists of chores, errands, and carpool schedules, carefully outlining exactly what she would be doing if I weren't here.

Rounding out the household are two Labrador retrievers, who are supposedly confined to the yard and the kitchen; four cats, whose whereabouts I'm never quite sure of until one of them hisses at a dog; and two aquariums. I like the aquariums. I know where they are and they're very quiet.

The house I now call home is a sprawling two-story affair built next to a pond and a stream. There are four and a half bedrooms and three and a half bathrooms. The furnishings are eclectic and careworn, the detritus of three generations—it is Sally's family home. The garage contains a washer and dryer, an additional refrigerator, and a large deep freeze. Gardening supplies, camping equipment, and the cats take up the rest of the space; the cars live outside.

Like most homes, the heart of the house is the kitchen, a place where the linoleum is rubbed raw in front of the sink, where workspace is cramped because of a bowl of fruit here, a toaster oven there, the microwave, mixing bowls, other labor-saving devices, and an ever-shifting slag heap of newspapers and school notices. A dog bed is in the corner, recycling bins are shunted near the television on a counter, a table for four occupies center stage.

When I first arrived, coming from a one-bedroom apartment, I was impressed by the size of the house. By the time I left I could only think about how long it takes to vacuum it.

This wooded, residential area is filled with so many twisting roads, new highway extensions, and poorly marked streets that it's like wandering in an enchanted forest: impossible without getting lost, even if you carry a map or remember to strew bread crumbs. This becomes a major problem for me, for, like most suburban housewives, driving is about 50 percent of the job: The younger two boys play on six different sports teams between them. Carpooling is a way of life.

The average week in this house requires the washing of at least nine loads of laundry and the purchasing and hauling home of a staggering thirteen gallons of milk and orange juice. Dinner involves cooking for a minimum of six, but usually seven, two of whom are fussy eaters. After two days of what I had hoped would qualify as domestic bliss, I find myself staring wistfully at a bottle of champagne in a liquor shop window. It's only nine in the morning. I hum "Mother's Little Helper," the Rolling Stones' anthem to housewives on Valium. It seems to me that being a housewife is not so different from the hard physical labor of working as a roadie. Unfortunately, recreational drug use among housewives isn't quite the accepted tradition it is among roadies.

On the third day, my alarm clock rings at 7 A.M. I'm sleeping in Tom's bedroom, as Eleanor has the guest room, and Tom is bunking in with Kyle. When I open my eyes, I look out the window, which has been decorated with the names of various bands in colored paint. Skid Row is scrawled in red. A year ago I'd scarcely heard of them; now they seem to be following me everywhere.

I can hear crows cawing in the yard. I reluctantly sit up and grab a sweatshirt and sweatpants. Clothes in this job must meet three requirements: They must be warm, comfortable, and something I don't mind getting dog slobber on.

Eleanor and Tom are already up reading the paper in the kitchen and drinking coffee. "Kyle!" I holler. "Let's go!" Kyle, the middle child, attends a private school, and must be driven there every morning. "Kyle!" I yell up the stairs, gulping down coffee, which is a thin brownish-gray liquid: decaf with 1 percent milk. "Come on! Hurry up!" He emerges, dressed in a shirt and tie, carrying his books and lacrosse equipment. He grabs a corn muffin from the kitchen while I trot out to start the car. I crank up the heat and pop open the trunk so he can stow his gear. He climbs in the front seat. Of the three boys, Kyle's the most outgoing. A cheerful kid, the beginnings of a mischievous smile are usually playing at the corners of his mouth.

"Turn left here," he says at the end of the driveway.

"That part I remember," I tell him. Kyle must prompt my every turn as we make our way to school, and I blame my inability to remember the route on caffeine withdrawal. We pick up three of his classmates along the way. They're all girls.

"So guess what?" says one girl from the back seat. "Guess who Eric asked out yesterday!"

"Susan?" say the other two in chorus.

"Uh-huh! And they're supposed to be broken up!"

Kyle sits quietly in the front seat. He finds these discussions tiresome and occasionally embarrassing. "Why do they talk

**171**

about stuff like that?" he asks me before we pick them up. "They've got their noses in everyone else's business except their own."

Discussion has now turned to practical jokes played on shopkeepers during a recent school outing, modern versions of do-you-have-Prince-Albert-in-a-can. I turn on the all-news radio station and am surprised to hear of certain current events. I haven't read a newspaper in days.

The school is a beautiful brick building at the top of a hill. I wave back to the other mothers pulling up. "Have a good day!" I tell the kids as I join the cavalcade of cars pulling out of the school drive.

During my forty-minute absence, Eleanor has thoughtfully cleaned the coffee pot, which unfortunately means she's dumped out all the remaining coffee. Even though it's decaffeinated, I miss the ritual of drinking something. As usual, I say nothing to her about it, and gnaw instead on a bagel while I hurry Bill out to the end of the driveway to wait for his bus. If he misses it, I have to run him to school too. Fortunately, Tom has his own car.

Since there's no more coffee to dump out, Eleanor has moved on to her ritual of turning all of the televisions in the house to different channels, and leaving them blaring. She wears a hearing aid, although I'm told that sometimes she doesn't. I can't see that there's a whole lot of difference in her behavior either way.

I run upstairs to fetch the boys' hamper from their bathroom, and contemplate why it's so difficult for them to put clothes *in* it instead of just around it. I stuff balled-up socks and T-shirts into the rattan hamper; knee pads, shoulder pads, and lacrosse balls that are strewn around the bathroom get tossed into the no-woman's-land that is the boys' bedrooms.

That hamper and the one in the master bathroom are lugged down to the garage. The clothes are sorted, and the first wash commences. I set up the ironing board in its usual spot in the kitchen, so I can hang Bob's soon-to-be-ironed shirts from the chinning bar in the doorway to the dining room. My list decrees that several individually wrapped chicken breasts are to be removed from the large freezer to defrost for dinner. I wrapped these and several pork chops only yesterday after grocery shopping for the week. I'd never actually filled up a shopping cart before; just unloading the car and putting everything away took an hour. I take care of the defrosting and sequester the dogs out in the yard.

Eleanor suddenly appears, and announces she's going to work in the kitchen as well, as she's restapling seat covers to the dining room chair panels. "I'm a conservative Republican!" she shouts at me, while turning on Rush Limbaugh's TV show.

"And I'm a femi-Nazi," I say for my own amusement. Eleanor can't hear me.

Sally already warned me that Eleanor believes that Republicans are all Christians and Democrats are everything else, which means they're destined for hell. My idea of hell, I decide, is doing laundry and ironing with Rush Limbaugh's voice bellowing out at 110 decibels. My jaw remains clenched the entire time he's on the air.

When I go back into the garage to check on the laundry, the dogs rush in from the back door, and mill about while I bend over the washer. They watch my movements closely, as they're eager to return to the warm, food-filled kitchen. I keep them at bay most of the morning, but one of them, Celeste, sees her chance to get back in the house when I'm struggling to carry a plastic laundry basket full of freshly dried clothes and open the door at the same time. Darting between my legs, she bolts in, knocking me off my balance and pitching me and the laundry down in a heap in the doorway. The other dog, Fred, takes the opportunity to vault over me, muddy paws and all, into the kitchen. I hear Eleanor's shouted greetings to the dogs.

"Goddamn it!" I shout. "Celeste! Fred! Get back here!" I race after them before they can track mud into the living room. Grabbing both dogs by their collars, I tug them back to the garage, kicking the laundry and the basket out of the way. I shove them out and shut the door.

I check my watch. It's 10:30 already. I pick up the laundry, brush off any dirt clods, and carry it into the living room to fold it on the couch. There's no way I'm rewashing anything, I'm behind on my list as it is. The television is blaring in here, too. "Ladies and gentlemen! *Welcome to Fam-i-ly Feud!*" I nervously check to see if Eleanor can see me. She can't. I turn down the volume a tad. I fold about 400 boxer shorts. I can't be bothered to figure out whose are whose, so I decide to leave them all stacked on the couch and let everyone get their own.

According to my list, today is also the day to clean the bathrooms. I take a pair of rubber gloves, a bucket, and several cleansers from a closet off the kitchen and ascend the stairs yet again. The boys are responsible for cleaning their own bathroom, which inevitably means that Mom has to do it. I tackle this fresh horror first, thinking about all the grimy locker rooms I showered in throughout North America. Working slowly and methodically, I finish up with the toilet and then the floor. I can hear snatches of three different television programs rumbling through the tiles and up the stairs: *The Home Show, The Young and the Restless,* and *Maury Povich.*

Thinking about television programs prompts a few nostalgic thoughts on my minor involvement with *Beverly Hills, 90210.*

Did I really go to the Golden Globes this year? My life used to be so glamorous. I flush the now-clean toilet.

"Lynn!" It's Eleanor. She's undoubtedly jammed the stapler—again. I go downstairs. "I think it's broken!" she says.

I open it. "It's just out of staples again. See?" I show her how to reload it—again. "You just drop them in here, and close this."

"I think it's broken."

"Look, it's fine. See?" I staple a piece of card. "See? Just out of staples." As long as I'm downstairs, I check the laundry. More folding. I resume activities upstairs and clean the master bathroom. It's not that this job is so difficult, it's just tiring, boring, and filled with interruptions that are also tiring and boring.

Taking a quick break for lunch, I make myself a sandwich. Eleanor tells me about her recent experiences, which includes being hospitalized for breathing difficulties. I heard from the family gossip line that these breathing difficulties were greatly exacerbated by the rather extreme amounts of cat hair, dust, and debris in her apartment. This situation came about because of her bizarre ability to break any appliance (not just staple guns), including all makes of vacuum cleaners, electric brooms, and Dustbusters. Her three children took her hospitalization as an opportunity to have the place gutted, cleaned, painted, and completely renovated with all new—and at least initially—working appliances. A cleaning woman will come in once a week to try to maintain this new status quo. Is Eleanor happy about this? Not a bit.

"Can you believe what they did?" she says with indignation. "They had to get the doctors to keep me in the hospital or I would have never agreed to this. *Never!*"

She tells me about the pills for her condition. "I didn't like the side effects," she says, "so I've stopped taking them."

I pause in mid-chew. "Does your doctor know about this?"

"I'm not going to take them anymore!" she says angrily. I make a mental note to tell Bob this. Or should I? Eleanor is an adult and should be able to decide what she wants to do. No, she's not. I decide to tell Bob.

The kids have noted her weird, almost telekinetic ability to destroy all things mechanical. "She messes up the TVs," said Bill, who worries she'll blow out all four of them at once and he'll miss his beloved X-Men cartoon on Saturday. It's not an unreasonable fear.

"She's not very mechanically minded," is how Bob puts it, suffering from the usual blinkered denial of a family member. As an outsider observing Eleanor, I see her more as a Weekly World News headline: Woman destroys appliances by touching them!

Like millions of women with an in-law in residence, I come to the conclusion that I'd take two extra kids over a mother-in-law any day. For one thing, you can tell kids to go to their room or to turn off the television. Disciplining your elders is pretty much out of the question.

I escape my duties for exactly an hour at a local health club. Under normal conditions I view a two-mile run as a rather unpleasant chore, but with my present activities, it becomes the highlight of my day. Hey! I'm out of the house! And I'm not at soccer practice or a supermarket! I'm taking care of me!

While I'm panting on a treadmill, a woman parks a baby stroller across from the machine next to me. She starts it up and coos at her baby, who is positioned to watch her as she jogs. Since we're two mothers, the inevitable happens: We talk about kids. "Mine are all in school," I tell her.

"You're lucky," she says.

I smile and nod. She tells her friend on the StairMaster this.

"Oh, you must be thrilled," says her friend. "I can't wait. I have two more years to go."

Kyle and Bill come home at 3:30, while I'm finishing up the downstairs powder room. "Hey!" I yell at them as they stampede up the stairs. "Come down and get your laundry, guys. It's on the couch."

"Comin'," they say. They're not. I figure I'll nag them about this later, closer to dinner. I'm not running up those stairs again.

I catch myself falling into the parental trap of viewing my kids as dirt-making machines. I remind myself that they're also nice human beings with many fine redeeming qualities. It's just hard to think of any when they seem to destroy in five minutes the work of an entire day.

I check the list of sports practices. Bill, the youngest, has lacrosse practice at 4:30. "Bill!" I shout up the stairs at four. "Let's go. Lacrosse!" He clomps down the stairs in his gear and heads out to the car. Unless Bill is actually laughing, he looks for something to worry about.

"The gas gauge says E," he says as we pull out of the driveway. Bingo.

"It's fine. I'll fill it up on the way home. We don't have time right now."

"What if we run out of gas?"

"It's not really on E from where I'm sitting," I tell him. He cranes his head to check this out. He frets all the way to practice. "My coach is driving me home, so even if you run out of gas, I'll be okay," he says in the egocentric way of a nine-year-old.

"Thanks," I tell him. "I was worried about that."

I get home and start dinner. I can't imagine trying to accomplish all this and also work a nine-to-five job. "Juggling" is the term most often used to describe how working mothers balance the demands of home and work lives. Juggling? That fanciful skill we associate with mimes and circus performers? It would be closer to competing in a triathlon, with work being the twenty-six-mile marathon, and home the swimming and biking events directly afterward.

Kyle is watching cartoons in the kitchen and tossing his lacrosse ball around with his stick. The dogs think it's a game of keep-away, and are crashing around as they leap for the ball.

"Kyle!" I say over the barking. "Do that outside." Fred has forgotten he's been fixed and is now attempting to mount Celeste. Kyle tries to keep them apart with his lacrosse stick. I notice the filthy kitchen floor and remember that I mopped it only yesterday. The tiny area rug that I laundered this morning is a mass of dirty smudges again. I look at Kyle and point to the television, desperate to take attention away from the humping dogs. "Are you logging in these cartoons?" The kids are supposed to log in how many hours of reading they do outside of schoolwork to earn an equal amount of time for television viewing. Tom is the only one indifferent to the lure of the idiot box, and has accumulated so much reading time his dad jokes he must be saving up to watch a miniseries.

"Uh, no, I'm not really watching it," Kyle says. "I'm playing ball." I give him a look. He shuts it off and goes upstairs.

While I'm making dinner, I hear Tom come in and run up the stairs. A good-looking track star with his own car, Tom is rarely seen around the house unless he's eating or sleeping. I don't know when he finds time for all the reading he's supposed to be doing. "Tom!" I yell. "It's your turn to make the salad!"

I hear scrabbling on the linoleum behind me and see that the dogs are back at it again: Fred, tongue lolling demonically, is grinding away at a prone Celeste. She looks up at me with a bored expression, oblivious to Fred's carnal desires. This serves as a reminder to me that I'm going to be a stripper in my next job. At this point, I don't know whether to dread it or look forward to it. "Fred!" I clap my hands. He stops. "For God's sake!" I drag him to the opposite side of the room.

An argument breaks out upstairs. Something about the television log. Kyle's voice suddenly rises: "Why are you being such a little asshole?"

"I don't give a crap!" shouts Bill.

I hesitate for a moment in the meal preparation. Is a parental reprimand in order? Kyle's a good kid who rarely swears, and, who knows, maybe his brother was being a little asshole. I fall back on the maternal standby: Pretend I'm deaf. I think better of this and trot upstairs, wiping my hands on a dish towel. "It's okay to argue," I tell them, "but watch your language, guys." They fall back on the kid standby and pretend they're deaf. I trot back down to my dinner preparation. I hear Bob come home.

Tom reappears in the kitchen with wet hair. He's just showered. "I'm going out," he says.

"Did you notice the bathroom?"

"What about it?"

"It's clean!" I say. "Or it *was* clean." He shrugs. Kids don't notice a thing. It's a thankless job. "You're supposed to make the salad."

"Kyle said he'd do it," he says, peeling a banana.

"As long as someone does it. Kyle!" I shout. "Make the salad!" I see Tom's getting a jacket. "Where are you going?"

"I'm helping on the theater crew." The timer on the stove goes off. Time to flip the chicken.

"When will you be home?"

"Eleven o'clock, something like that."

"Where will you eat dinner?" I say as he leaves the room. I hear the front door slam and burn my wrist sliding the pan back into the oven. "Goddamn it!" I hope the kids didn't hear that. I stomp back over to the stairs. "Kyle! Salad!"

He comes down and throws a half a head of iceberg lettuce into a bowl along with a quartered tomato. He stands in the doorway of the kitchen. "Dinner's ready!" he hollers.

"Go in and tell your grandmother. I don't think she can hear you. And feed the dogs, please." Bill shows up so I hand him full plates to carry into the dining room. A dish he's carrying passes perilously close to Bob's shirts. I didn't have time to run them upstairs to his closet, so they're still hanging from the chinning bar.

"Careful, Bill," says Bob. "Lynn will kill you if you get sauce on those shirts."

"They're going to need to be washed and ironed again anyway," I say. "It's not like he's defacing a painting."

"Oh," says Bob with some amusement. "So whether the shirts need to be cleaned because he gets sauce on them or because they've been worn, it's all the same to you?"

I realize that it is. "Yes," I tell him, demoralized by the kitchen floor getting dirty again so fast. We sit down to dinner. Per Sally's instructions, I've rolled the chicken breasts in mustard and bread crumbs and baked them in the oven. I made broiled salmon last night, but since Eleanor doesn't eat fish I had to fry her a pork chop, and Bill won't eat salmon, so he chose fillet of sole. I felt like a short-order cook, an experience I'm not anxious to repeat.

Kyle says grace. Everyone takes turns, and you are encouraged to say something different each time, to make the thanks more meaningful and personal. "God is great, God is good, and we thank him for this food. Let's eat!" Bill and Kyle get the giggles.

"Kyle!" says Bob. "Try that again, please."

He murmurs some thanks.

"What?" says Eleanor. "I can never hear you!"

The chicken is consumed with some enthusiasm. It feels pathetic to crave a compliment on my cooking from a nine- and a thirteen-year-old. "Very good," says Bob. The kids nod in agreement. Or maybe they're just chewing.

I supervise the boys in their dishwashing duties, and Sally comes in to make tomorrow's list. My eyes are glazing over. I'm exhausted. I didn't finish all the laundry today, and no doubt more dirty laundry will be deposited on the floors of the bathrooms this evening, since the hampers are still in the garage.

"You know," she says, "most women build up to this gradually."

"But I walked into all the other jobs this same way," I tell her. "The problem with this job is that it's like Alice in *Through the Looking-Glass*: 'It takes all the running you can do to stay in the same place.' "

"You're absolutely right," she says. "And this is why housework is never looked at as real work because you never seem to accomplish anything! There's no progression, no advancement. My living room looks the same every day, so," she gestures around her, "what progress have I made?"

I set out some leftover chicken on a plate for Tom after Sally goes up to bed. If he's hungry when he comes in, he can heat it in the microwave.

It's eleven o'clock. I can hear the television in Eleanor's bedroom going at top volume. *"Good evening!"* it booms. *"The top story tonight . . ."* Fortunately, her room is on the ground floor, well away from the other bedrooms. I walk up the stairs for the twentieth and last time that day. I hear Tom come in just as I shut my eyes. I sleep and dream I've lost the keys to the car, which is filled with lacrosse equipment.

I wake up the next morning to the alarm, and, as usual, I delay getting up by methodically reading all the names of bands written on the window. This reminds me that Snake once told me he'd always wanted to name a band "Free Beer. That way you'd pack every place you played." This brings a sleepy smile to my lips, even as I contemplate carpooling and linen-changing day.

While I'm grabbing my quick cup of coffee before shouting for Kyle, Bob says, "I have an idea. Let's go out for dinner tonight." I perk up instantly.

"What?"

"There's a nice pizza place near here," says Bob. "How 'bout if I meet you and the kids there after work, say at seven-thirty?"

"Great!"

No defrosting! No meal preparations! No nagging about who sets the table and who makes the salad! Of course, I still have to finish the laundry, change all the linen in the house, and vacuum and dust—in between carpooling and sports practices. But, if I hurry, I might be able to actually catch up with my list.

I look in the linen closet. Let's see, striped sheets for Tom, the peach-colored king-size stuff is for the master bedroom, the Smurfs sheets must be for Bill . . . I hesitate between Star Wars and Superman for Kyle. Superman it is. I brace myself to enter the disaster areas that are boys' bedrooms.

The sports equipment I threw in here yesterday is undisturbed. I wade through the heaps of clothes and pull the linens off the beds. Kyle and Bill sleep on the top bunks of two bunk beds that lack ladders, so dealing with the linens requires quite a bit of hopping up and down. Once up on Bill's bed, I crawl about like a demented spider trying to tuck the top sheet in and arrange the comforter. I hop back down to grab the pillow, step on something slick, and crash to the floor. I wonder if Eleanor heard that over Rush Limbaugh. Apparently not. I lie still for a moment and see how narrowly I missed cracking my skull on the corner of a small worktable. I look at my foot. *What the . . .* I see white shavings ground into the rug. Ivory soap? Bill's making soap sculptures in his room? I leave him a note saying "Clean this up please! NOW!"

I just barely get everything done by 6:30. I fight Tom for the shower so I can spruce up for my big night out. I'm actually wearing clothes I don't want the dogs to slobber on. I dab on some perfume. I haven't felt this excited to be clean since I was a roadie.

We get a table for seven. The restaurant is fairly modest, but I couldn't be more excited when a waiter hands me a menu. I am being waited on! Not having to cook for this group is like hearing I've been spared from throwing an impromptu dinner party.

"You know," says Sally, who has joined us for dinner. "I've been thinking. It's the kids that make it worthwhile. *That's* where you see the advancement, the progression. Not in the housework."

"Forget about the history books and statues," says Bob. "What you really leave behind for the benefit or detriment of mankind—are your kids."

The following day, I pass by one of the blaring television sets that Eleanor has abandoned and see salmon leaping upstream. A nature program, not one of Eleanor's usual choices. I'm momentarily distracted by the determination of the fish to try to swim up waterfalls, so I sit down in an armchair, cradling the spray bottle of Fantastik in one arm. The announcer's voice is saying the fish are "driven by the desperate need to reproduce." That reminds me: The kids will be home from school

**183**

soon, and I've got to finish cleaning the kitchen before lacrosse practice.

That brief glimpse of fish leaping upstream haunts me the rest of the time I'm a housewife. The days pass and I perform the same tasks over and over: I stuff socks and T-shirts into the hamper, feed the cats, make dinner, drive to school. Salmon either make it to their spawning ground and reproduce or die trying. A fish can never opt out of this insane journey, so their entire lives are lived for this one moment of reproduction.

I begin to wonder if we're so different, despite our culture, our science, and our lofty dreams of technology. I remember for the first time in years a conversation I had with my mother when I was twelve. I decided I wanted to be a movie star (not an actress), because I wanted to be "immortal," I said. "I want to be remembered after I'm dead."

"I'm already immortal," said my mother. This took me by surprise. What had she ever done? "When I'm dead," she said, "you'll remember me."

On my last night, I make pizza, a real hit with the boys. I ask Bob if he feels any kinship with a salmon's life cycle.

"With salmon?" he says. He chuckles at first, and then raises his eyebrows in agreement. "It's not a bad analogy to all this," he says, sweeping his arm across the table in gesture that encompasses the boys. "Although the dying part happens at a much slower rate."

# 7

## Take It Off. Take It All Off.
## Then Put It Back On.
## Put It All Back On.

**M**y domestic routine at home now seems quaintly miniaturized, a quarter-inch scale model of what I was doing in Connecticut. I feel like a lady of leisure, curled up on the couch after dinner, peacefully watching television with my husband.

We're watching a comedy show, and a stand-up comedian is yelling back at a heckler. This prompts a fresh worry about my impending stripping career. The peaceful feeling vanishes.

"What if I'm booed off the stage?" I blurt out. I'm trying to keep these questions to a minimum, since Jeremy's grown tired of hearing about how his wife is about to dance naked for strangers. It's probably why we're bickering about little things lately.

"Lynn," he says, with some exasperation, "no woman, who is taking her clothes off, *ever gets booed off a stage!*"

This makes me laugh. I'm enormously relieved. He's right, of course.

At *least*, I hope *he's* right.

The prospect of taking my clothes off in front of strangers for money resulted in the endless replaying of a single thought: Surely my mother raised me better than *that*. Between my family, my teachers, and my friends, the message I received over the years was clear: It may be fine for some women to earn a living as strippers, but not for me. I had known only one stripper in my life, a twenty-seven-year-old college classmate with a ten-year-old son born out of wedlock. She dyed her hair jet black, wore lots of makeup, sported a couple of tattoos, and was known for a fondness for truckers. Now *that's* a stripper.

I planned to be drunk the first time I had to strip. I thought the first time would be the worst, but if I could somehow get through that, perhaps it would get easier. For months, every time I felt visually raped by a gang of construction workers hooting and whistling at me, I thought: That's how it's going to be when I'm a stripper, only a hundred times worse. I imagined standing offstage, feeling a bit queasy, conjuring up the same amount of bravery and leaping-off-the-cliff determination that I needed to stage-dive at a Skid Row concert the first time. As usual, I was wrong about everything.

Taking my clothes off in front of strangers turned out to be pretty easy to do. It's walking by a construction site that's a hundred times worse than disrobing in a strip joint. Men are much more cowed and intimidated in front of strippers than they are on the street. They're on our turf in a strip club, and they don't want to do something wrong or they'll be thrown out.

I was also surprised to notice that I've felt more judgmental stares directed at me when I've been on a beach in a bikini. Perhaps this is because women are on beaches, and they're far harder on themselves and each other than men are. Out on display in a strip club, I felt nothing but acceptance, approval, and appreciation. I never once was made to feel as if my body was lacking in any way—quite the novel experience.

Fortunately, I had a mentor on this job, a raven-haired twenty-year veteran named GiO, who is, as she will happily tell you, the premiere stripper of her generation. GiO started life thirty-seven years ago as Lisa Suarez, and was one of the stars of the 1984 documentary *Stripper*. She did her wild cowgirl act (that one involves a gun and a whip) for none other than movie director Oliver Stone at the wrap party for *JFK*, and so outraged actress Sissy Spacek that Spacek attempted to throw a jacket over her during her performance. Her non-stripping achievements include working on Jimmy Carter's 1976 election campaign and being a groupie for Led Zeppelin—which resulted in being the inspiration for their song "South Bound Saurez." GiO has a ring through one nipple, flames tattooed on her labia, and a degree in industrial design from Pratt Institute.

"Walk out there like you're going shopping," she says to me on my first night at the Bourbon Burlesque, a charmingly seedy joint on Bourbon Street in New Orleans, GiO's home when she's not on the road. She's repeating advice she got twenty years ago from a veteran stripper when she was about to walk the runway for the first time. "Walk out there like you know what you want, and you're gonna get it. Remember, *you're in charge.*" I walk into the curtained booth that contains the three steps up to the stage. The stage itself is shaped in a half circle, with a brass pole in the middle. The perennial stripper's prop—a wooden chair—is on one side of the stage, against the large mirrors. The stage itself is ringed by a narrow bar for the patrons who want the up-close-and-personal experience. I'm absolutely sober. The two drinks I gulped down an hour ago have worn off completely.

As I make my entrance, I try to imagine I'm in Bergdorf Goodman's and the men seated around the stage are the latest in footwear. It doesn't really work. I try the old public-speaking trick of imagining my audience naked, but that's too grotesque an image, so I convince myself that they're all a hallucination. I'm actually alone in my living room, dancing to a blues version of "Heartbreak Hotel" and the Clash's "Should I Stay or Should I Go" while dressed in black patent leather. This works. This is pretty easy. Then I see the Israeli merchant marine has just moved up to be closer to the stage.

This particular Israeli merchant marine and I had been chatting over drinks just a few minutes ago. I was lulled into the familiar territory of a-guy-buys-me-a-drink-in-a-bar, and after making the usual small talk for some minutes, I realize that despite all this verbal bobbing and weaving, despite the fact that I wasn't the least bit interested in him, he was nevertheless about to see me *naked!* I was eventually going to have to get up from the bar stool, saunter over to the stage, and strip down to a black G-string the size of a bookmark. And now here I am, wearing only the bookmark, and here he is, holding up two folded dollar bills. It is the weirdest experience I've ever had. I can hardly look at him.

"You've got to work on making eye contact," says GiO, over drinks at the end of the night at 2:30 A.M. I let out a groan. "I know it's hard," she says. "But it's the only way you make money." It turns out she's right. I try it and see that it also provides power and control, a feeling so intoxicating that eventually making eye contact is what I do best. As a stripper, if you can do that, everything else you do is icing on the cake.

I practice the icing in my hotel room during the day. Unfortunately, my room lacks a vertically positioned brass pole, but it does have a wooden chair. I shove aside the furniture, play my portable stereo, and, borrowing heavily from Bob Fosse's choreography in *Cabaret*, I try to think of seductive ways to position myself on the floor and the chair while I remove my clothes. GiO instructed me to buy five different outfits before I left New York. I made the interesting discovery that stores catering to transsexuals are the places to get stripper wear, as the clothing is so outrageous, campy, and such an exaggeration of female sexuality that most biological women wouldn't dare wear it outdoors. The clothing had to be easy to take off, so I looked for zippers, simple clasps, or places where I could sew in Velcro. I bought the shortest, tightest shorts, a wild fringed bikini, a bondage dress, black patent leather garter belts, G-strings, stockings of every description, and a black leather studded bra. This stuff isn't cheap. The bra alone cost over $100.

Now that I'm a stripper, my days inevitably include time at a gym. I mull over song and costume ideas while I'm running on a treadmill, lifting weights, and getting in a hundred sit-ups with a dedication previously undemonstrated: Nothing like knowing you'll be naked onstage to make you stick to an exercise plan. There are other self-imposed rules: I sleep until I wake up—not being a slave to the alarm clock is what I consider to be a major perk of the job—and after a huge lunch at three o'clock, no eating until I finish my shift in the wee hours of the morning. I have a weekly manicure and pedicure, forgoing my usual choice of pale, neutral polish for bright red. The term "skin care" takes on new meaning when it's not just my face people are looking at. I use vast quantities of moisturizers, balms, astringents, exfoliators, and razors.

When I tell people I'm a stripper, the first thing they ask is whether I strip *completely naked*. The answer is no, and I see I've either gained or lost an inch on their moral yardstick. Some people seem relieved that I'm not so tarty that I would strip down to nothing at all; others turn their noses up at my cowardice in hiding behind a G-string. "Oh," says this latter group, "so you're not *really* stripping. Not *totally*." Neither group seems to realize that whether I take it all off or not is determined by state law. In Louisiana, I can only strip down to a narrow, triangular piece of fabric that is held on by bits of string. Wearing a garment that is so small you could mail it with a first-class stamp requires such a thorough removal of pubic hair that I begin to wonder if I shouldn't just shave it all off and be done with it. So *do* I strip naked? You put that little scrap on and see how fully dressed *you* feel.

"I use Nair," says GiO, in answer to my inevitable question, which is regarding the best method for this near-constant pubic hair removal. While I use the common dressing room downstairs in the club during my shift, she generously permits me to share her private dressing room upstairs to stash my street clothes and put on my work clothes. She shows me how it's a real time saver if you put on your makeup while the Nair (Tropical Formula with Cocoa Butter is best) is fizzing quietly between your legs. You just have to sit funny in the chair.

The dressing room downstairs has a mirror, a small table, and several lockers. It's a place where strippers retreat periodically to stow cash, retouch makeup, spritz on perfume, and get dressed after being on stage. It's a small, cramped room that smells overwhelmingly of disinfectant and Ben-Gay, and perhaps some take-out Chinese food that someone is picking at. The dressing room is the strippers' equivalent of the office water cooler, where gossip, stories, and advice are passed along. Trish, a tall, thin Eurasian girl from Canada, says, "Number one: Shave under your arms every day. Two: Always point your toes onstage. And three: Always cut the string off your tampon."

Another bit of business that must be done in the dressing room is the mandatory application of what strippers call "tittie tape," and what the medical profession calls Micropore surgical tape. Strippers in many states, including Louisiana, must "cover" the center bit of their nipples somehow, whether it's with a thin coating of latex or this sheer tape. Tape is preferable to latex because you can cut two small strips and wrap the nipple in such a way as to ensure it remains in the perky, upright, gee-I'm-horny posture no matter what. I would often forget about removing the tape at night, and in the locker room at the gym the next day, women would stare uncomprehendingly at my nipples, which by now would have accumulated small bits of lint at the edges of the tape. Ironically, most guys in the club remain unaware that there's anything on your nipples at all.

"Well, you don't want to *stare*," is the usual answer as to why the average patron hadn't noticed. Put a woman out on the street minding her own business and guys walk into lampposts to get a better look, but let a woman do the naked limbo two feet from his face, and he doesn't want to be *rude*.

My co-workers are usually friendly, and at worst, slightly aloof; I encounter none of the outright hostility that I did from my fellow cocktail waitresses. There is, however, some competition when a likely looking customer walks in—"likely looking" meaning someone with a wallet. The race to see who can sit down with the guy first and get him to buy a table dance can mean that a few waitresses get knocked over.

Despite the name, a table dance is not performed on a table. A customer pays us $20 to strip while we stand on a little plywood box *next* to his table. This puts our crotch at his eye level. "Take your shoes off before you get on the box," says GiO when I ask her how a table dance should be performed. "It's basically posing, or moving slowly, rather than dancing. You're up there for one song." Twenty dollars for three minutes' work. This is where you really make your money. Your stage act, where you dance to two or three songs of your own choosing and get tipped mostly in singles, is your introductory offer.

While onstage, a stripper might slowly remove her clothing, writhe around, caress herself, crawl on all fours, wrap her legs around the pole, slide up and down on it, do the splits, put her legs behind her head. We look at the guys: Can you imagine this in your bed? What would it be like to do it like this? How about *this?* This is why a guy's date will look so stricken while watching us on stage. *He likes this,* is what she's thinking. *And I can't do it.*

Contrary to popular opinion, success in the stripping profession is more dependent upon good salesmanship than a good body; it's by no means the prettiest girls who make the most money. A guy can buy *Playboy* for a good body, but in a strip club, he wants personalized attention: The naked girl here can smile back. It's possible to sell a table dance to someone who doesn't really want one if you make him believe he'll be seeing something really special; in other words, you're selling the steak, but it must have some sizzle. He may buy another table dance if he thinks that you are smiling and staring while you gyrate because of his charm and charisma, rather than his $20. A good stripper can discover fairly quickly after she sits down if she's got a fish on the line or whether she should cut bait and move on.

I usually start with an introduction, and if I'm lucky I get some sort of conversation going before the carnivorous waitresses descend upon us and interrogate the customer: "Care to buy the lady a drink?"

"Uh, sure," he might say. The waitress disappears and reappears with what is laughingly called a "champagne cocktail." What it really is is some cranberry juice and a beverage called "nonalcoholic champagne" over ice. What it costs is $8 for a "single," $16 for a "double," and $24 for a "triple," and the wait-

If that chair could talk. Me and my mentor, GiO, pose onstage at the Bourbon Burlesque. (*John Chiasson*)

ress will bring whatever she thinks the market will bear. We're not allowed to drink anything else, and we must sell six drinks a night or we don't get paid our wage of $4 per hour. You *can* have the "alcoholic" version of a champagne cocktail, which also comes with ice and a splash of cranberry juice. It has very little alcohol in it, and manages to taste even worse than the horrid nonalcoholic version. Neither drink looks anything like champagne, unless you're color-blind and like your Perrier-Jouet on the rocks. When the price of the drink is announced, the customer must deal with his shock, cough up the money, and God help the guy who forgets to tip the waitress. "What about me?" is the standard threat.

The waitress's sharklike attitude is why the guy will blame *me* for the cost of the drink, as if I could have ordered a $4 beer but instead chose to fleece him. A cowboy with one clouded blue eye grabbed my drink, took a sip, and announced, "I just paid twenty-four dollars for a fuckin' *Cherry Sprite!*"

When a guy from New Jersey was told "That'll be sixteen dollars" when my drink arrived, he turned to me and said, "Don't fuckin' *pull this shit* with me!" He refused to pay, and his somewhat calmer bespectacled friend offered to buy my drink. "Go sit with him!" I'm told by the hothead.

I change seats and join the guy wearing glasses. He looks at my drink and says, "If you tell me that I just paid sixteen dollars for a *Campari and soda*," he pauses for emphasis, "I'll slap the shit out of you."

These unpleasant encounters are why I learn to warn the guy what he's getting into. I tell him the cost of the drink: "I'd love one, but my favorite drink is eight dollars," and under the advice from one stripper, add the psychologically damning "if you can afford it." After all, an angry customer is not going to buy a table dance, which is why I'm talking to him at all. I'm certainly not there for the conversation.

"Nostradamus predicted everything," says a guy who's a regular customer on Bourbon Street. He's a maître d' at a restaurant in the French Quarter. "He's been right about everything."

"Yeah, especially the part about restaurateurs being irresistibly drawn to strip clubs."

He looks at me as if I'm a precocious child. "You don't even know who Nostradamus is," he says. I was treated as if I didn't have a brain when I was a fashion model years ago, but I didn't know it would be worse as a stripper.

A British guy is telling me a positively riveting story about how many prawns he once ate. "It must have been about a kilo!" he says. "A kilo is two pounds," he adds.

"Actually, it's 2.2 pounds," I say.

He looks genuinely surprised: "How did you know that?"

Another guy from New Jersey raises his drink glass to me. "*Salud,*" he says.

"*Salud,*" I answer, toasting back.

"Oh, you don't even know what that means," he says.

"If I pretend I don't," I ask him, fed up with this sort of chat, "will that make you feel better?"

"So!" he says, ignoring my comment. "Tell me your real name."

Guys expend a lot of desperate energy trying to get you to tell them your real name. It's a more tantalizing secret than what's beneath your tiny strip of a G-string. My stage name is Dolores Haze, which happens to be Lolita's real name in the book by Vladimir Nabokov.

"If I tell you," I say, trying not to wince when I sip my drink, "I'll have to kill you."

GiO took her stage name from an Aldous Huxley story, but tells me that most strippers seem to get their names "from the cheap perfume department of a drugstore. 'Hi, I'm Ciara.' 'I'm Charlie.' 'I'm Tabu.' "

To our up-close-and-personal audience, a stripper's real name is something intimate, a password to the Real You. I walk into the dressing room to see one stripper crying. She's the one who wears a white bikini with ragged cutoff denim shorts and always dances rather furiously (and, it turns out, appropriately) to "I Hate Myself for Loving You." She looks up from the dressing room table. "My ex-boyfriend won't leave me alone," she says, sobbing in great gulps. "He came in and screamed *my real name* right across the bar!"

"Dolores Haze?" says a biker. "Like from *Lolita?*" It turns out he's a film buff and an aspiring screenwriter. Grabbing this tiny opening, I spin a story about NYU film school and how I'm working on a screenplay about strippers. This has the desired effect of him buying two table dances that I don't have to perform. "I don't like people to watch my private business," he says, pressing the bills into my hand, "but I'd like you to have the money."

"Lynn!" whispers GiO when I show her this easy cash. "You've learned to bullshit!"

This is a big improvement over my second night, when a guy kept handing me money just so I wouldn't leave his table. The evening ended with him begging me to have coffee with him in a public place for $450. I declined with a severe case of the creeps.

"You could have gotten so much more money out of him," says GiO, over breakfast at St. Ann's Deli at 3 A.M. I got $250. "You could have gotten five hundred, six hundred. What did he do for a living?"

"I have no idea," I say.

"You have *no idea* and you talked to this guy for how long?"

"Well, he went on and on ad nausem . . ."

"Ad nauseam. You see, if there's enough money involved, you don't feel sick. You have to look at it as a game. To see how much money you can get out of a guy."

"I felt drastically overcompensated as it was," I say meekly.

"No," GiO says emphatically. "You were drastically *under*-compensated. Remember," she says, "shrinks make sixty to a hundred dollars an hour." And like so many other guys, he really just wanted to talk. About himself, that is—it's a monologue. In the middle of telling you their girlfriend troubles guys will say, "I don't know why I'm telling you this . . . can I give you my number? Maybe you can call me. Just to talk . . ."

I eavesdrop on the other strippers as often as possible to study sales techniques. One stripper knows just when to take out her empty purse and pull out pictures of her kid (the hard-luck rap); one announces that she finds him wildly, wildly attractive, and would love to hook up with him, but she can't stop worrying about some overdue bills. I heard another not-so-attractive stripper who always gets plenty of tips telling two guys, "I moved here from Texas." She lets out a dirty laugh. "Ha ha! From Texas . . . ha ha! To the Big Easy! Ha ha ha!" They were on the edge of their seats. I guess it isn't what you say but how you say it.

I take as my rap my experiences as a teacher. "I haven't been stripping long," I say. Men like to hear this. It makes you seem wildly broad-minded but not exactly slutty—the classic center-fold fantasy. "Only about a month. I used to be a substitute high school teacher in Virginia, but I only earned forty-eight dollars a day—and taxes were taken out of that! So anyway, I moved down here and I'm waiting for a permanent teaching position for the fall. Until then, I'm working here as a dancer." *Dancer* sounds more demure than stripper.

"So do you like doing this?" he'll ask, shocked but titillated at the thought of a stripping teacher. I say I teach English or math, because it fits the prim part of the fantasy.

"It's fun," I say. "I like the performance part. I don't like having to bug the customers for a table dance, but [here's where I shrug modestly] it's where you really make your money."

This is when he caves in, and it's table dance time. When I tell a group of naval officers my little rap, they give me $60. "You don't have to dance," one says. "We know you have to work, but we're romantics. We'll pay you just to sit here and talk to us about math." When I do go up onstage to strip, the officers move ringside. One picks up my discarded bra and wears it dreamily on his head.

Since I only go onstage about once an hour, the nights are filled with this sort of hustling. I'm busily scanning the crowd looking for a docile victim when a guy at the bar grabs my arm. "Can I buy you a drink?" He's got a gold tooth and is presently being set upon by a stripper with the completely misleading name of Demure. ("It's kind of a Greenland/Iceland thing," explains GiO.) It's considered bad stripper form to horn in on a guy that a girl is already talking to, but if he makes the overture, all bets are off.

"It's not so exciting to see me drink," I say, for the twentieth time that night. "But it is exciting to see me dance. Why don't you buy me a table dance instead?"

"A table dance?" he says. "What's that?"

"That's where we go over there," I say, pointing to one area of the club with chairs nailed down to the floor a certain distance from plywood boxes also nailed down to the floor.

"You see *tits, ass*," says Demure.

"And I dance on one of those boxes *just for you.*"

You see it *all*, baby," says Demure, kissing his temple.

"It's only twenty dollars," I say, wishing Demure would both shut up and refrain from licking the customers, "and I dance for a whole song."

"Um, okay—which one of you dances?" he says, diplomatically, not wanting to do the wrong thing. He says it's the first time he's been in a place like this. ("Me too," is what I always say back. I hear this all the time.)

I glare at Demure, as I've already broached the subject.

"Dolores can, she brought it up," says Demure.

"Uh, do I have to take care of you?" he says to Demure, who stupidly misses an opportunity.

"Later, baby," she says in what she imagines to be a seductive way.

Of course, why anyone in their right mind would pay $20 for something they can see on stage for free is beyond me, but what he's paying for is the illusion that I'm dancing *for him,* and even though the D.J. keeps mentioning these *"personal, private, table dances,"* anyone in the club can glance over and see all of the proceedings as well. To help reinforce this charade of exclusivity, I make plenty of eye contact—with the idea of getting repeat business and/or a very nice tip.

Most men are even more subdued during a table dance than they are watching from the edge of the stage, as they're now isolated from the pack and are in the spotlight. They generally sit politely back and watch with the expression of a four-year-old watching Barney the dinosaur: mouth slightly agape, an expression of pleased wonder. There's usually nothing lascivious about their behavior, only mine.

Occasionally the attention gets to be too much for them. I was doing a table dance for a twenty-five-year-old guy from

Seattle who could hardly look at me at all, and every time he did he blushed. I put my hand on his shoulder to steady myself, and leaned in to ask, "Am I embarrassing you?"

"Uh, no," he says, blushing again. "But can you leave on your stockings and garters?" Some things never change, despite the advent of grunge.

GiO and I are the only two strippers in the club who wear garters and stockings. Most strippers find them to be too much trouble, and favor instead stretchy minidresses worn over a G-string. Taking stockings on and off all night may mean extra work but it also means extra money, since there are very few men immune to their charms. Two teenagers buy me a drink and admire my patent leather shorts and matching garter belt. "When I get married," says one of them, his voice wistful, "my wife is going to wear stockings and garters, like, every day."

I test out my theory that men are just as fascinated by watching women dress as undress. I notice that most strippers throw their clothes back on after a table dance, anxious to move on to the next paying customer. I experiment with talking and putting my clothes back on in an easy, deliberate way after a table dance, and I see it's usually good for about five extra dollars. I have to get dressed anyway, I might as well earn some money in the process.

After a week as a stripper, I started to hear the same questions over and over.

"What do you do during the day?" asks an orthopedic surgeon.

"Sleep," is the simple, obvious answer, but men have a fantasy that strippers have some other "straight" life where no one suspects that they're a stripper in the evening. Like we're all bored housewives, medical students looking for tuition money, and randy librarians. This is proof that men think that the plots of porno movies are based on real-life incidents. Further proof is when they ask, "Do you get excited onstage?"

The temptation is to look this weekend golfer and father of four in the eye and say, "Not unless I'm being handed really big bills." The *power* is exciting, and it's fun to dance well for an audience, but I didn't find it—nor did any other strippers I asked—sexually exciting. Still, a wise stripper feeds into his fantasy that we've chosen this line of work for the supposed sexual gratification, and not for the money involved. The party line to his question is "Oh sure! *Absolutely!*"

I found it interesting how many men become infuriated if there's any hint that we are viewing them strictly as money objects. We, however, are not supposed to mind being viewed strictly as sex objects. In fact, we're supposed to enjoy it so much we'll do it for free.

One guy was smiling at me the whole time I was onstage, but never came up to tip. After I finished I went over to him and asked if he enjoyed the show. "Yes, I deed," he says. Oh shit, he's French, I think. Bad tippers as a rule. "I like ze girls who smile."

"If you liked it, you should have given me a tip," I say.

"Ees zat why you were smiling at me?" he says indignantly. "To get *ze dollar?* Eez zat why you are doing zees? For ze *money?*"

Yes, you fucking moron.

In a similar vein, guys naively think that you're asking them to buy you a drink because you really want *a drink,* when what you want is to make your six-drink quota before the end of your shift, and this is part of your *job.* "We'll buy you a drink!" says one of two besotted UPS drivers. "But not here! Too expensive! Let's go someplace else and we'll buy you all the drinks you want!" A croaky-voiced biker with long blond hair also misses the point and offers, "We'll pay you fifty dollars to come have drinks with us at the Dungeon later. You won't even have to take your clothes off! We'll buy you all the drinks you want, *get you drunk*, listen to some good tunes!" Oh sure, that's *just* what I had in mind, let me get my coat.

Before I worked as a stripper, I heard they earned $1,500 to $3,000 a week. I usually heard this from strippers on the *Geraldo* show and on other stripper forums. "Honey, I don't take my clothes off for less than five hundred a night," says one stripper from another club who dropped in to check out our action. "How much do you make here?"

"About that," I lied. I suddenly understand why strippers might prevaricate about their income: It's embarrassing to say you take your clothes off for money and then admit that you don't earn all that much. I figure I make anywhere from $60 to $300 a night for six hours of work. This sounds paltry for a stripper, but it's by far the highest-paying job I'll have all year.

I could be earning much more, I scold myself, watching Kate, "Queen of the Table Dances," stuffing cash into her locker. Then again, I don't go for the businessmen as often as I should, and spend too much time cajoling broke college kids. Some nights the club is packed, but with people who refuse to part with money: Two panicky Englishmen briskly say, "No thank you!" every time I open my mouth, even when I ask, "What part of England are you from?" There are guys who think they're in love and throw money at you, but these types are few and far between. One thing, however, is obvious: This sure beats cocktail waitressing.

The reasons are numerous: I still depend on tips, but I don't have to remember anyone's blasted drink orders and how much they cost. I don't have to pacify a bartender. My shift is shorter, and not only can I sit down if I want to, I can take off my shoes.

And if I'm wearing a silly outfit, it's one of my own choosing. Men look at waitresses as servants, but a stripper is revered as a performer. Men in strip clubs prefer to believe I'm a nice girl who strips, but men in a casino are hoping to discover that I'm a slut who serves drinks. I am treated better as a stripper and I make more money. But despite the vast difference in the level and tolerance of sexual harrassment, most parents would think it's okay for their daughter to work as a cocktail waitress, but not as a stripper.

The one advantage cocktail waitressing has over stripping is that you're far more likely to have a good relationship with a man. The social stigma on stripping is more than most relationships, or prospective mothers-in-law, can stand. Because of its fringe standing, the stripping business also seems to attract women who feel shut out of the mainstream. Many were sexually abused as children, have a history of abusive relationships, and suffer from low self-esteem. Contrary to popular myth, most strippers are not well educated. Most of them feel they lack options and could not work anywhere else.

One kid who can't be more than seventeen asks me if I have a boyfriend. I tell him yes. (Even though I wear a wedding band, a lot of customers refuse to believe I'm married—it doesn't quite fit into their fantasy—and choose to believe I wear a ring "to ward off the jerks." *Then it's not working,* is my silent reply.) The seventeen-year-old pictures me prancing around the house in a scanty outfit and practicing my routines for my boyfriend all day long. "And he gets it all *for free!*" he says. He has an I.D. that says he's eighteen, which means he can only drink $4 sodas. He's trying desperately to make his few dollars last as long as possible in this living wet dream, so the idea of unlimited free access is making him a little giddy. "And you strip for him anytime! And he can, uh, you know, touch you! And everything else! *Man!*"

I decide not to tell him that this is not what happens if a man dates a stripper.

"I won't date a guy who's seen me perform," says Trish, when GiO and I meet her for lunch one day. "If you think I'd go out in public with you after you've seen me, forget it!"

"But what about guys you meet in other ways?" I ask. "Do they ever get to see you perform?"

"No. It's not a good idea. You put on a different face at work. As you know." She shrugs. "I've never been in a good relationship."

GiO warns me not to let my husband see me strip, an idea that set in after a certain amount of pride in my abilities took hold. "Bad idea," she says. "He doesn't need to see you bending over to get a dollar from some cheeseball. And anyway," she says, "they start to wonder." They, meaning male partners, wonder about what is real. *Is she enjoying herself now onstage or is it an act? Is she enjoying herself in bed with me, or is that the act?* Naturally, being so conflicted about what you do for a living dooms a relationship from the start. Strippers think there's something sleazy about a guy who approves of what they do, and it's impossible to continue to date a guy who doesn't. "You don't want to date someone you meet in a club anyway," says Trish. "Because *he's a guy who goes to tittie bars.*"

Suzette, the quintessential bimbo stripper with big hair who dances only to Pearl Jam and Nirvana and insists on angrily lip-synching like a demented drag queen, thought she was pregnant. She announces tonight that she finally got her period.

"Does she have a boyfriend?" I ask GiO.

"Yeah. He doesn't like what she does, says she's being a whore. Of course she's supporting him. That's fairly common.

I've been guilty of that myself," she says. Suzette won't go on unless she's high on pills. She's very good at simulating having rather violent sex onstage—and not enjoying it all that much. Seeing her unsuccessfully trying to reapply her lipstick, I ask her what she's taken. She looks up, smiles with her lips firmly shut, and finally slurs out, "Wouldn't you like to know."

Of course, the very thin, prima-ballerina-built Trish is just the opposite; she looks like she's having a ball. She starts out prancing around like a delicate glass unicorn, and then turns into Gumby on the floor, all long limbs that can bend and fold every which way, and she does it all with a beautiful smile.

"They're awful," she says of men in general. "You just haven't been doing it long enough. After a while you get kind of, like, you guys are all the same. You see men at their worst in this job." And then the girl who makes men swoon at the thought of her in bed mentions that she doesn't really like sex at all.

Most of the strippers I meet live in the type of apartments that look like they've been decorated with items that can be packed quickly. They're notoriously bad with money, unable to save, unable to plan for any sort of future, even the ones with children. GiO is an exception, as she's not only a college graduate, but also markets her own video and Mardi Gras poster. She's a homeowner and a landlady. This is in addition to headlining at the Bourbon Burlesque, which means she gets paid to do two or three twenty-minute shows a night and doesn't have to table-dance or hustle drinks. Being a "headliner" is what most strippers aspire to.

One stripper, a slightly chubby girl with long black hair, tells me she's been stripping for a year. "Before that," she says, "I was with a guy for about five years. I worked in a Chinese restaurant." She's so shy she can barely even come out of the dressing room, and hardly ever sits with guys or gets a table dance.

"I can't stand the rejection," she says. "I know they're going to say no, so why bother asking?"

She whispers to me about the new stripper in here tonight. "You didn't hear it from me," she says, "but she's seventeen. A runaway." I don't have to ask why—like so many other teenaged runaways, it's probably incest. The girl has a cute body, but has bad skin, which she hides with lots of makeup. A wildly energetic dancer who favors funky rap music, she hasn't yet learned to make time in her routine for the guys to respond by tipping. Of course, I can't help but think that what she should be doing is making out with guys in cars on dates, not learning about the best way to retrieve folded-up dollar bills.

I mention the girl's young age to Trish, who tells me she started stripping at seventeen. "I guess I was a 'bad girl,' " she says with a smile. "I had some friends who were doing it and they were earning a lot of money. I thought, I could do that." Now it's eleven years later. "This business breaks down your ego so much . . . you think you really can't do anything else." She says she wishes she could open a clothing wholesaling business with a girlfriend in Canada. "I've got no education. There's not a lot I can do. And there's nothing else I could do that would bring in this kind of money. I have so much admiration for strippers who get out of this business and do something else. The thought terrifies me! It's a big bad world out there."

"*Out there?*" I say. "I've got news for you; the 'big bad' part is in here."

"But this is safe," she says. "It's familiar."

Kate comes in to stuff more money into her locker. "Queen of the Table Dances," I say as she enters. "How do you do it?" I ask her. "How do you get so many table dances?"

"I don't know," she says, in a barely perceptible Irish accent, as she opens her purse. She looks to be in her twenties, and with her pert figure and short blond shag haircut she manages to convey a Goldie Hawn wholesomeness, even more so now that she's gained back the weight she lost when she was a junkie. She keeps the skull 'n' snake tattoo on her calf covered with leather boots. "I've been dancing for so long, I guess I just don't take no for an answer. I keep bugging them."

"So what do you want to do later?" I ask. "I mean, when you stop stripping. Any ideas?"

"I don't know. Marry a rich guy." She slams the locker shut and spins the combination lock. "I guess I should be saving my money."

I follow her out of the dressing room and am immediately stopped by two college kids. "Excuse me," one says, "but did we just get ripped off?"

"She just took all our money," the other one says, pointing at Kate, who's sitting down with another guy across the room.

"She charged us *each* twenty dollars and then danced for half a song, and now she won't even look at us! She won't even talk to us!" Once again, I see that my method of making guys feel as if they've spent their money wisely is far less efficient than Kate's slash-and-burn technique.

"So how much do you charge?" says one.

"It's twenty dollars," I say.

"For each of us?"

"Well," I say, not wanting to emphasize that Kate obviously charged what she correctly thought the market would bear, "you can avoid the extra charge if you don't both look at me at the same time."

"We have two dollars," says one.

"Do you take Visa?" says the other.

"Yes, we do!" I reply.

"How about Texaco, do you take that?" he says.

"Look, you can charge a table dance, no problem," I say.

"No, we can't do that, I'd get in trouble," he says.

"What can we get for two dollars?"

"How about the hell out?" I say sweetly.

I find that stripping to Chris Issak's mournful song "Wicked Game" is a real money-maker for me. It's slow and sad, evocative of lost love—the perfect backdrop for a strip joint. Men often sing along to the chorus. I meet their eyes, and that's when the dollar bills start flying out. I look up during this song to see the two college kids. They're handing me their two dollars.

I enjoy stripping for college students—even the high school students in here with fake I.D. cards. Younger men are cute, they smile a lot, they blush charmingly, and they have a lot of enthusiasm, so I don't mind that they're usually broke. They also lack the emotional baggage that older men can have, that palpable bitterness that comes from some woman wrecking their life, divorcing them, and keeping the kids, which leads them to view all women as scheming gold diggers or whores. Especially women in strip clubs.

Some businessmen can let go of this barely submerged hostility and be pretty good customers—that is, someone offering up plenty of money for tips. But anyone wearing a suit is likely to get lost in all your friendly attention, and once his ego—if nothing else—has puffed up he'll say, "How much for something extra back in my hotel room?" The trick as a stripper is to leave them wanting more, but getting them to pay for it whether they get it or not.

"Come on, we're not the police," say two laser manufacturers in town for a convention. They'd just finished telling me about the *Seinfeld* episode where it is discovered that "Dolores" rhymes with a part of the female anatomy. "Can't you come back to our room," one of them asks with a big smile, "and put on a private show for us there?"

I don't want to hear what they think is a private show, but I'm pretty sure it doesn't involve a G-string. "I'm a dancer, not a prostitute," is my standard reply to such requests. I try to look hurt, since that usually results in a tip just out of guilt. I wear my pained expression when I deliver this news to a French sailor, who asks me if there's some place we can go later for sex. Upon hearing my reply, he manages to look even more hurt than I do. "No, not for money," he says, shocked. "For . . . *l'amour.*" Yeah, those French guys really are cheap bastards.

I ask GiO if it's true that hookers never strip and strippers never hook. "Yes," she says. "Why would hookers want to work that hard?"

"But at closing time," says Veronica, an Australian who would love to be a gangster's moll, "you should see the guys out there, waiting in the street. It's, like, Trick City."

"That's different," says GiO, pressing her lips together into a thin line of disapproval. "Those girls are Bourbon Street whores."

While onstage, a stripper must entice her audience, but keep an eye out for the type of guy who tries to take liberties while he attempts to tuck a dollar bill in your G-string. Young guys prone to traveling in packs and wearing baseball caps backwards can be generous with tips, but are also the ones most likely to try and touch you. They wait motionless at the edge of the stage like tigers; when you get a little too close, they strike, choosing their moment so the bouncer doesn't see their hand swiping right up into your crotch. You eventually develop a sixth sense about this sort of guy, and learn to ignore him. Far better to lavish attention on the quiet nerd whose glasses are about to steam up. He's the type who will tip.

One guy identified as a record producer came in with a gang of his friends who balled up dollar bills and pelted dancers with them. "Fuckers," mutters Veronica, coming offstage with a handful of wadded tips. "A couple of those really hurt."

"At least they tipped," I point out. I can do without the Japanese businessmen who sit for hours with the same unchanging expressions, without tipping. Ditto the midwestern tourist couples who *never* tip.

And it's usually the businessmen who want to know if you can remove *everything*, as if their imagination is so limited they can't possibly imagine what's under that tiny scrap of fabric. The older, church-deacon types are the worst: One fiftysomething guy with a bad comb-over says, "I'd better not buy a table dance. I know I'll be a bad boy and misbehave with my hands." Another gray-haired man asks if he can have a "lap dance," which is where a dancer sits and grinds around in his (clothed) lap, in some approximation of dry humping. "They do it in Florida," he says with a leer.

"It's illegal here," I say.

"So then I'm going to get all excited, and what's going to happen? Nothing!"

"Don't you know that we're just in the arousal business?" I try to smile as sweetly as possible, but I keep hearing the voices of high school dates telling me they've got blue balls and I've got to do something about it. I knew back then that his erection was somehow my problem, but my pregnancy wouldn't be his problem. It occurs to me now that this geezer still thinks his erection is my problem, but that my rent isn't his problem.

I learn from GiO to wear at least three G-strings that get

progressively smaller, since it gives you more stuff to take off when guys think there's nothing else to remove. Of course, she likes to remove the penultimate G-string, dip the crotch into a guy's beer, and then wring it out into his open mouth.

I learned from GiO to execute some small stunt periodically when retrieving a tip: Do the splits, bend way over, drag the bill suggestively up my body. Guys may give you more money to see you do it again. GiO and I tip each other throughout the night to show the audience that something interesting may happen if money is proffered. It was while retrieving a tip that GiO unintentionally broke a guy's nose—with her crotch. She was working in Canada when a man leaned back and put his head on the stage with a dollar bill in his mouth. "I meant to do the splits over him and stop short right over his face," she says, "but I lost my footing, and *wham!* I slammed down right on his nose and just *broke* it! The first thing the guy said as he sat up with blood streaming down his face was, 'What am I going to tell my wife?' "

Canada is the promised land for strippers, where the clubs are plentiful, and "the dressing rooms are nicer," says Trish. "Some have a practice room with a brass pole, a gym, showers, everything. Usually, the club pays you to do a twenty-minute set for sixty dollars. I can usually cut it down to about sixteen minutes, if I pick short songs," she says proudly. "You work totally nude, table dancers are five dollars, and there's no tipping."

Well, no wonder Canadians are so stingy in Las Vegas.

"But sometimes you do the table dance," says Trish, "and the guys says, '*That's* not worth five dollars!' "

Trish, GiO, and I check out the Crescent Cabaret on our night off, a so-called classy strip joint in town that doesn't permit its dancers to (1) wear anything but white, (2) bend all the way over ("too slutty"), or (3) touch the floor with anything other than the soles of their feet. I see forty very similar-looking dancers milling from table to table, disco music blaring, businessmen agog. It's strictly giggle and jiggle, body parts on parade, with the girls paid to be barely animated pinups. One girl shakes her shoulders slowly at a guy and smiles with the tip of her tongue caught between her teeth. They could call this place Horny Stepford Wives. We know the drill here—we tip. I used to think that strippers didn't like women coming into a club. Now I know they just don't like non-tippers.

I find this assembly-line giggle-and-jiggle stuff much more objectifying than what we do at the down-and-dirty Bourbon Burlesque. Rather than selling body parts, we sell sex. At the Crescent Cabaret, the strippers all look alike. At the Bourbon Burlesque, for better or worse, each girl has her own style.

Alma, for example, has a belly dancer's technique and looks like Louise Brooks—if Louise Brooks had bright red hair and several tattoos. She compliments me on my writhing, snakelike dance to Jimi Hendrix's "Are You Experienced?"

"I thought it was beautiful," she says meaningfully. Another stripper admires the artificial flowers on her flapper dress.

"Thank you. I steal them," she says, and names a notions shop.

"Well, steal some for me next time."

Alma turns back to me. "I'm really a dressmaker. I do this so I don't have to make the dresses I don't really want to." She introduces me to another stripper, Miss Lucy, who is wearing a platinum blond wig styled into a short bob. Miss Lucy smiles and reveals actual fangs. She's had her incisors filed and capped to permanently mimic a vampire. I eventually tear my eyes away

from her teeth only to gaze at her pierced nipples. I realize I'm
the only stripper here without either a tattoo or a nipple ring.
Breast implants are much more common at the giggle-and-jiggle
clubs, although GiO had hers done a few years ago. "Best invest-
ment I ever made," she says, wiggling them violently around.
She stands in the doorway of the club and does this to draw in
customers. It works. "I did it because it gives me a longer shelf
life in this business."

"How do you do that?" I say, meaning making her breasts bob
independently around like they're about to leap out of her cor-
set.

"Practice flexing your pectoral muscles. See? It's like wiggling
your ears."

I look up from my chest to see a couple waving me over to
their table. I walk over and take a seat. They're from Tennessee
and look to be in their forties; he's a mechanic, she runs her own
nail salon. She says she wants me to do a table dance for her
husband. "Okay!" I say. Afterward, she instructs him to buy me
a drink. I tell her that sitting with couples is "pretty unusual for
me."

"My friends think I'm crazy," she says. "But we do this every
time we're on vacation. And you know what? You dance for him
here," she winks lasciviously, "but I reap the benefits later back
in the hotel."

There are other memorable customers. Some kind of carnival
freak show came in one night, a guy with a flipper for an arm, his
pinhead friend, and their lady dwarf dates. They cheered everyone on enthusiastically but never tipped. "They're poor," GiO
says, although I noticed they did give her a few dollars. The guy
with the flipper came back a week later—"Hel-lo Dolores!"—
and bought me a drink. Another night a whole table of lesbians

tipped me by dealing out a wad of bills like they were playing cards. They waited until I finished onstage and called me over. "This is for you," one said, laying out the bills in a fan.

Of course, there's always a guy in the club who wears a tense expression that reflects a grim determination not to become sexually excited, but mostly the customers are men who are chagrined and are sitting there looking dazed and goofy. And I now know how to walk over to the edge of the stage and look right into their eyes so their hand will inevitably crawl right over to their pocket to retrieve a dollar bill, and hand it to me.

"I don't know how you do that," says the chubby girl who won't leave the dressing room.

"Look at 'em like they're doing something wrong if they don't tip you," says Veronica. She likes to dance to Aretha Franklin's "You Make Me Feel Like a Natural Woman" in a floor-length satin gown and elbow-length opera gloves. "I mean, Christ. They know what to do! They're in a bloody strip club!"

I come in to work one night wearing my usual street clothes of jeans and a T-shirt. Since it's raining, I put on my Skid Row baseball cap. "You know those guys?" says Trish. She thinks I strip in New York City, so I nod as if I met them somewhere. "Me, too!" she says. "I went out on a date with Rachel," she says.

"Really! I don't know him very well," I say, which is true.

"He's really nice. We went out once together. I mean, nothing happened. I think he was lonely. We both were." She smiles a little. "I think he was missing his girlfriend."

"You look like her a little bit," I tell her, thinking of the tattoo on his arm of a girl's face.

"I've heard that," she says.

Later on in the dressing room, she tells me a story about a girl from Calgary who was always bragging about knowing Skid Row.

"Is she Asian with huge lips and giant breasts?" I ask, "but very short?"

"Sylvia!" she exclaims. "That's her! You know her?"

I remember her as a snotty, obnoxious groupie who got booted out of the dressing room. We had a brief encounter when she attempted to amuse the room by contrasting my filthy high-top sneakers with her bright pink pumps. "She's a stewardess for Air Canada, right?"

"No way. She's a stripper, honey." Such a small world, I think to myself, as I adjust the straps on my bondage dress. Taking a deep breath, I walk out into the club.

I sit down with a college student who says he's here with his pals, celebrating his friend's birthday. Kate sits down with the birthday boy and after about two minutes, moves away.

I lean over and tap this guy on the shoulder. "Can I ask you what she said to you?"

"She said I was really cute. Then she asked if I wanted a table dance, and I said no. I don't like blonds. Not my type."

Some minutes later, while I'm dancing for his friend, I see Kate giving Mr. I-Don't-Like-Blonds a table dance. "So how did she convince you?" I ask him later, hoping to at last discover Kate's secret.

"Well, she jiggled her tits at me."

"That's it?"

"And he made me!" he says pointing to another friend. "He said, 'Go for it, dude. You can afford it.' You know," he says morosely, "she didn't even wish me a happy birthday. And for twenty dollars, I think that should be part of the deal."

Later on in the night, I'm putting my clothes back on in the dressing room after I've been onstage again. A stripper named Cherie runs in. She had been sitting ringside with some guy who was tipping me very well while I danced.

**215**

"I have to ask you something," she says, a little breathlessly. She looks very similar to a young Sally Struthers, dimple in her chin and all. "Are you bi?"

"No."

"Can you pretend to be bi?" she says. "See, this doctor," she says, proudly waving his business card. Alleged doctor, I'm thinking. The card looks cheap and flimsy, like it was made in a Xerox shop. "He wants us to go back to his hotel room and do this bi scene for him for four hundred dollars. Two hundred for me and two hundred for you."

"No, I don't think so."

"Yeah, I thought so. I'm trying to think who's bi in the club who I can ask."

Cherie looks at another stripper in the dressing room, Anna, who dances as if she was trained in ballet. "What about you? He liked you. You want to just pretend we'll do it and sit with him and get him to buy us drinks and tip us? We'll just get as much money out of him as we can and then say we won't go to his hotel."

"Yeah, sure!" she says.

Some minutes later, I see Cherie alone. "So what happened to the doctor?"

"Oh, he got pissed off and left," she says. "But that's okay. I've got his card. I can fuck with his head anytime I want."

I watch her sit down at another table. The businessman she's joined has no idea that all she has on her mind is the content of his wallet. Like every other guy in here, he wants to be king for a day, to have beautiful women perform and undress for his pleasure. He thinks that this pretty girl with the blond ringlets finds him attractive, stimulating, funny, and wise. He believes he can tell when a woman is being sincere, and he knows that a woman

216

who shows her body so frankly would be incapable of hiding the truth when she speaks. What a sucker.

The man I'm sitting with says, "You know, a lot of women working in these places are putting themselves through college." Why do men think it's only women who fall for stupid lines?

"You're right," I tell him. "I'm a substitute teacher, but I'd really like to go back for my master's degree. I'm trying to save up a little money over the summer."

His eyes light up. I can feel the money in my hand already.

# 8

# RApe Is a Four-Letter Word

It was just before I became a publicist that I told my brother, Rob, and his wife, Kathy, about the jobs I was going to be taking. I paused after I said, "I'll be a stripper," since that's usually when people cut in with questions or expressions of surprise. This statement elicits no more than amused grins from them, but then I said, "Then I'll work as a rape crisis center counselor." The grins abruptly disappeared. They looked at my husband, Jeremy, for support in their shock. The four of us were having dinner in a restaurant in Richmond, Virginia. It was Christmastime.

"What?" said Rob, stunned.

"You're kidding," said Kathy.

"No," I said, instantly on the defensive. Nothing like family members to push all your buttons. "Why? What's the big deal? Lots of people do it."

Rob made a strangled noise of outrage. "You're going to counsel rape victims?" he said. "You're not qualified!"

Kathy was wearing a smile of incredulity. She's a family therapist, and my brother used to be a child abuse case worker. I'm *treading heavily on their turf here, but my indignation at the suggestion that I'm incapable or unsuitable prevents me from acknowledging this.*

"They train volunteers," I said, a nasty edge to my voice. "I'll get the training, Rob."

"What, you're just going to walk in there . . ."

"How are you going to keep the horror out of your head!" said Kathy. "You're going to be absorbing all of this horror, day after day!" She shook her head as if I'm talking about leaping out of an airplane without a parachute.

"It's different if you're a journalist," I said, feeling my defensiveness turning to resentment, and maybe to anger. A childish voice in my head said: My older brother never thinks I can do anything. "I hear horror stories all the time," I said. What am I, a war correspondent? "I'm used to it," I went on. "I can look at it objectively. It's not going to affect me at all."

Now Jeremy joined the loud chorus of dismay. Someone dropped a piece of silverware.

"Not going to affect you!"

"What?!"

"You don't know what you're talking about!"

"Stop picking on me!" I said to Rob, who looked surprised at my vehemence. I sounded like a nine-year-old, too proud to see their point. It's not easy taking these jobs. Everyone likes to enumerate the ways I can fail. Hot tears roll down my cheeks. Poor me.

"Lynn," said Rob, exasperated.

"Shut up." This unpleasant scene was my fault, but I was powerless to stop it. I sliced blindly at my food, my appetite gone. A waitress appeared in my peripheral vision.

"Is everything all right?" she said perkily.

"Hi," says the girl sitting cross-legged on the examining table in a hospital in Austin, Texas. "How's it goin'?" she asks me, smiling a little. Her skin is broken out, but she's wearing mascara and a little blush, her brown medium-length hair is clean and shiny. You'd think of her as someone between pretty and plain, a girl wearing a green long-sleeve thermal T-shirt, brown shorts, white socks and sneakers. She's scratching a mosquito bite on her shin. She's fourteen years old and was gang-raped by three men.

This is my first time to the hospital emergency room as an Austin Rape Crisis Center volunteer. I received rather accelerated training in order to become fully qualified as a volunteer in as short a time as possible. My week of studying videotapes, reading books, and private tutoring with some of the Center's therapists concluded with them assuring me that I would be just fine at the hospital. Now that I'm here with a rape victim, I feel a desperate need to run out of the room and quickly review some sections of my notes and the Austin Rape Crisis Center manual. This is not role-playing in the office, with a therapist pretending to be a victim, and correcting me when I say something inappropriate. This is the real thing.

When an area hospital admits a rape victim, she is asked if she'd like to talk to someone from the Rape Crisis Center. She almost always says yes. The hospital calls the Center's twenty-four-hour hotline, and the Center in turn contacts the beeper-wearing volunteer on duty. These calls are almost always in the middle of the night, although this one happens to be in the early evening.

The girl was raped almost twenty-four hours ago, and like so many victims, she delayed going to the hospital, and has already showered and changed clothes since the incident. When I walked into the emergency room, two Victim Services workers who were sipping coffee near the door stopped me. "You from the Rape Center?" said one of them, his photo I.D. card hanging from a cord around his neck. His walkie-talkie squawked in his back pocket. Victim Services workers usually deal with burglary or robbery victims or family members of a homicide. They're paid by the city, we're volunteers. "She's in that examining room over there. That's her mother." The woman he pointed out is sitting down chatting to two policemen. "She's fourteen," he says, meaning the victim, "a chronic runaway, sexually active."

I walked away, wondering what the phrase "sexually active" has to do with anything. Would a jury consider her "spoiled goods" and not convict a guy who raped a sexually active four teen-year-old?

When I knocked gently on the examining room door, and heard the girl say "Come in," I was expecting to see someone whose face was raw from crying or bruised from being beaten. I was expecting tears and hysteria, anger, sadness. What I am looking at is a girl who seems extremely calm and very matter-of-fact. She's picking at her chipped red nail polish. I'm thinking something I don't want to be thinking: *It's hard to believe she was raped.*

I'm thinking this even though my training manual says that "a prevailing myth about rape victims is that they are hysterical and tearful following a rape." Many victims "may come across as calm and controlled by masking, hiding feelings."

I introduce myself and ask her her name: Shannon. I resist the natural impulse to ask "What happened?" We're not supposed to make a judgment or get the details of the crime—that's something the police do—but "provide emotional support to the victim" and give her information regarding free counseling services.

"How are you feeling?" I ask, wondering if that sounds like a stupid question. My manual says, "Be a calm and safe presence for her."

"I guess I'm mad, a little bit," she says. Other than that, she can't really say how she feels. She was in here all alone—why isn't her mother in here with her? I decide it's a good thing she isn't, because we're told in training that it's a better idea if family members wait outside while we talk. Spouses or parents are dealing with their own reactions to the rape, and may unintentionally cause the victim to feel guilty "about all the trouble she's caused." It also puts the victim in the position of taking care of her family's emotions instead of her own.

The nurse comes in, one of the ones they call SANEs—Sexual Abuse Nurse Examiners, specially trained in evidence gathering and disease detection for rape cases. They always have a terrific bedside manner, something many doctors don't have time for.

"Go ahead and talk," the nurse says to me, preparing her little bottles and swabs. *About what?* is what I'm thinking. The police have already questioned her, and I can't ask her about the rape, and she seems to have said all she's going to say about her feelings.

"You know," I begin, "whatever happened . . . is not your fault. You do know that, don't you?"

This prompts her to speak. She tells me a few details about what happened. I listen and nod. She was raped by three guys she'd never seen before. "I've been raped twice before," she says. "So I'm thinkin', Why me? Do all the dudes out there say, 'Six months! Time for Shannon to get raped again!' " She lost her virginity the first time she was raped—by a friend of her brother's—the second time it was "kind of a boyfriend." Her mother's reaction, she says, to her present predicament is,

"You're always getting raped." This is why she's not in the room.

The nurse leaves for a moment. "This is confidential, right? You won't tell the police? I knew those guys." She accepted a ride home with friends late at night, and they all piled into one car. "We were dropping everyone off, and I guess I dozed off, because then it was just me and these three guys." She doesn't want to prosecute because she fears reprisal. When her mother discovered she was raped and called the police, Shannon decided she had to lie about their identities to protect herself. That taken care of, her biggest worry at the moment is that her reputation in the neighborhood as "respectable" is ruined, that these guys will brag about having sex with her. "They don't think they raped me. Because they do this to girls all the time," she says. "I don't know if it should be called rape. This is when a guy forces you to have sex."

"What do you think rape is?" I ask her, trying to restrain my incredulity.

"When you don't know the dude, I guess. I don't know."

After we talk about this for a while, I remember I'm supposed to "give the victim options, restore their decision-making power." Rape removes choice, and many family members unwittingly reinforce this by insisting on making all the decisions for the victim.

"You don't have to do anything you don't want to do," I tell her. The words feel hollow, but the manual assures me they have meaning. "You don't have to tell the police anything until you feel ready. You don't have to tell your friends or family anything. *You* choose who you tell."

The nurse returns for the dreaded pelvic exam. "Do you want me to stay or leave?" I ask Shannon.

"Stay."

"Do you want to hold my hand or would you rather I stand over here?" This is called "providing options, make her feel like she has control."

"I want to hold your hand."

The nurse inserts the speculum as gently as possible. Shannon tries not to scream. She wrenches my hand, her ragged fingernails dig into my palm. "They entered dry," she gasps, "so it really, really hurt."

Swabs for semen are taken from her mouth and vagina, even though she's showered and brushed her teeth. Pubic hair and head hair are combed and loose strands are placed in an envelope, in the event they are the perpetrators', and a few hairs from both sites are yanked out by the roots for comparison purposes. "Yeow!" Shannon yelps.

"That's the end of the hairdressing service," the nurse jokes good-naturedly. "Now's the manicure. Which one of your nails can I take a little bit of with these clippers?" Shannon proffers one. "Now I need to scrape under your nails to see if you managed to get any skin under them." More envelopes are filled and sealed. The evidence gathering finished, we move on to disease and pregnancy prevention as she's given two spermicidal tablets to insert. The nurse leaves again and returns with a can of Sprite and several antibiotics for treatment of possible STDs, along with a high dose of Ovral as a "morning-after pill." She gently explains how to go about getting tested for exposure to the AIDS virus.

Shannon gets dressed. We sit and wait in the examining room for the swabs and specimens to come back from the lab. I tell her about the Center and the services we provide. "If you just want to talk—anytime—call the number. Your family and friends may tell you that you need to put this behind you and forget about it, but not dealing with it can cause a lot of problems later. In the weeks and months ahead, you may get some bad dreams, have trouble sleeping or eating, you might become fearful. You might find yourself afraid of things you weren't afraid of before." I go through the list of typical secondary reactions. She listens attentively.

We continue to chat until the lab results come back; she tells me about home, school, boyfriends, clothes. Shannon goes to the ladies' room while I walk out to the reception area to wait for her. The nurse hands the two policemen the sealed evidence kit. I look at them and feel guilty. *I know something they don't know.* An officer's large, clumsy hands are holding the taped box. They're working with false information, I think helplessly. It's a waste of their time. This feels very strange.

"We got sperm," the nurse says.

"Did you test for cocaine?" says the cop. Suddenly I'm not so guilt-ridden. This question implies that cocaine would be a mitigating factor in the perpetrators' culpability.

"That's not part of the rape exam," says the nurse diplomatically.

I say goodbye to Shannon, urge her again to call, and watch her leave. She and her mother do not touch on the way to the car. I'd been with her for three hours.

I had heard a few years ago that hospitals sometimes use trained volunteers as a kind of buffer between rape victims and the police. I thought a job like that would be the closest I could get to law enforcement and the criminal justice system. I imagined Texas as a place where outdated sexual stereotypes are still dusted off and proudly displayed.

I arrived in Austin seven days before I met Shannon in an emergency room. I was surprised to see that the Austin Rape Crisis Center is in a modern four-story office building just off

Interstate 35. I don't know what I was expecting. A sanctuary? A private home? I knew that it's a nonprofit organization, and that all of the ARCC services are free of charge and available twenty-four hours a day. I have literature that says the Center is funded by the city of Austin, United Way, Travis County, the Texas Department of Health, private donations, and fund-raisers, and it's staffed with 225 administrators, therapists, and volunteers. I am now one of them. Normally, volunteers are on call a couple of nights a month. For maximum exposure, I ask to be on call every night for three weeks.

I wasn't wrong in my assumptions about Texas: Austin has the distinction of being the city of the "condom rape case." A woman pleaded with a knife-wielding stranger who broke into her house to wear a condom before raping her. The rapist was not indicted because the grand jury believed the sex must have been consensual if he used a condom, regardless of the fact that he broke in, woke her up, and threatened her with a knife. After a firestorm of national controversy mirroring the initial Rodney King verdict, a second grand jury indicted him and a jury found him guilty. He was sentenced to forty years in prison.

"Did he use a condom?" is one of the questions the nurse examiner must ask a victim. In about a third of the cases I witnessed, the victims said yes. This is a good-news/bad-news scenario. The good news is that men finally seem to be willing to use them even when not asked, possibly sparing the victim pregnancy, AIDS, and many other sexually transmitted diseases. The bad news is that for a rapist, using a condom is the equivalent of a burglar wearing gloves—there's no identifying semen left behind. Further, rapists who heard about the condom rape case think that wearing a condom is a way to beat the rap.

I had initially imagined that counseling rape victims would be like talking a jumper down from a building—a lot of intensely emotional experiences, a lot of hysteria. I thought I'd see horribly beaten women, and uncaring, uneducated policemen. I wondered if the women I'd work with at the Center would be not just staunch feminists, but man-haters owing to the accumulated bitterness, rage, and injustice. These stereotypes describe the rare exceptions.

"Have you been raped?" is the first question everyone asked when I said I was going to work in a rape crisis center. "If you haven't been raped, how will you be able to help anyone? You won't know what they're going through."

"It's called *empathy*," says Kat Hammer, a therapist at the Center. Possessing empathy is how counselors, whether they've been raped or not, help victims. Kat's the tall blond owner of the truck out front with the bumper stickers "Poverty Is Violence" and "Don't Mess with Texas Women." She's a therapist in her mid-twenties and has been working at the Center for two years, and while working on getting her master's degree, she's an amateur boxer.

The assumption that we must be rape survivors also arises out of the belief that being raped—and having an ax to grind—is the only reason why someone would choose to work in such a presumably depressing place. I found working in a casino—and watching people lose money they can't afford to lose—far more depressing than working here. Even though women come to us because of a tragic incident, the Center is ultimately about helping people who appreciate our help very much.

I was surprised to discover that there are male volunteers. Their reasons for donating their time to the Center are very similar to those of the female volunteers; they want to "do some good," to "give something back to the community," to "help right some cultural wrongs." Far from being anti-male, the Center welcomes men as workers and administrators, but when a male volunteer is on duty, a female must also be on as a backup, in case a victim would prefer to talk to a woman. "I *never* get to go to the hospital," says one male volunteer when he hears how many times I've been. While his intentions and ability as a counselor are good, I can't say that I would be interested in having a man—any man—hold my hand during a pelvic exam after I was raped.

Rita Garza, the volunteer coordinator, says the question of whether or not she has been raped comes up all the time when she gives talks to local high schools about sexual assault. "If I have been," she tells the students, "isn't it insensitive of you to ask about it?" Yet it's a question that most people ask in the same way of determining marital status. We counsel victims that this is a personal question, and one they needn't answer—whom they tell is their own business, something the media aren't as respectful of as they should be when they print a victim's name in the paper.

Kat points out that while there are very good therapists and volunteers who happen to be rape survivors, being a rape survivor is no guarantee that you'd be able to counsel others effectively. "You might have unresolved issues of your own to deal with," she says, referring to a "savior mentality. You want to save everyone else as a kind of denial of your own issues."

During the day, I work in a little cubicle and answer the hotline phone. I watch Jhaki Gonsalvez, a therapist who is pregnant with her first child, take a few calls before I feel sufficiently confident to take one on my own. There are two forms to be filled out while you talk to the caller; one is a questionnaire with the victim's name, address, and pertinent facts, the other is a confidential form for statistical purposes only. Sometimes an hour can go by without a call, and then two come in at the same moment, requiring a free therapist to take the second call. I kill time by reviewing the 300-page manual devised by the Center: Xeroxed notes and reprints of texts bound together in an un-wieldy loose-leaf notebook.

A staff meeting is called, and I'm introduced to all the thera-pists and administrators. Even though I was just told that Lynn Thompson-Haas is the executive director, I don't get any sense of a pecking order, the way I did at the advertising agency. The big topic of discussion today is how best to address people in power—senators, legislators, lawyers—without trying to placate them and accept their hostile and/or patronizing behavior. Suggestions are thrown out as to how to handle the sexism, rac-ism, or homophobia that is often a factor in these encounters without alienating the offending sexist, racist, or homophobe. We spend thirty minutes trying to balance the need to correct and educate people without appearing to be pushy man-hating women. It's unlike any discussion that a group of businessmen would have.

This is one of the reasons the Center feels so far away from the male-oriented business world. Another, apparent to any visi-tor, is the abandonment of the "Dress for Success"code. The women here come to work in loose sundresses, cotton pants, oversize shirts, just-above-the-knee-length shorts. There are no high heels, no pantyhose in mid-summer. The one exception is Rita; her silk-and-pearls business wardrobe gives away the fact that, until recently, she worked for a department store. Most workers and therapists try for casual without being sloppy, cool without trying to look sexy. Volunteers are also reminded not to visit the hospital "dressed inappropriately"—meaning short dresses, revealing clothing, midriff tops. I keep a denim jacket in the trunk of my car in case I'm beeped while out in a tank top.

After working for a few days on the hotline I see that women who have been raped recently make up a very small percentage of callers. A fairly typical call is this one: A thirty-year-old woman says she was raped ten years ago by an acquaintance. "I wouldn't really call it a date," she says. "I'm having a lot of nightmares about it." She's in Overeaters Anonymous and has battled drug problems. "I never reported it to the police," she says. The initial decision of rape victims to "forget about it" often means they call a rape hotline years later, with a history of failed marriages and possibly drug and alcohol abuse. They're thinking about the rape more and more often, and wonder if they shouldn't talk to someone about it. I make an appointment with her to come in for an "intake," an evaluation with a therapist to determine the kind of therapy (group or individual) that might be best.

A lot of calls are from adult survivors of incest. This is such an issue that the Center currently has five incest survivor groups meeting for therapy, compared to two rape survivor groups. I begin to notice how often callers will mention incest in addition to talking about a rape—or several rapes. One incest survivor tells me how she was "gang-raped by three guys in school, while a junior." Then she was raped by "a fat guy," then "this other guy," then "a friend of the family," and was "gang-raped again by three guys." She only reported one rape to the police. I listen, but all I can think is *How can all this happen to one woman? What is she doing?*

"I feel like I'm getting very close to blaming the victim," I tell Vicki, a therapist, after I hang up. "When I find myself wondering why certain women are raped several times. I mean, most of us think that one time is colossal bad luck, but not your fault.

Even twice isn't your fault. But when it gets to five or six . . . how can you not ask yourself why this keeps happening to her?"

"It's common for some incest survivors to lack boundaries," Vicki says. "Because they learned early on that their body is not their own property, they don't set limits or boundaries with other people." In addition to this, "Incest survivors often seek to re-create abusive relationships, figuring that if they can change this person, it'll somehow fix everything that went on before." In other words, some women consistently pick the wrong men to be around. It's a depressing thought.

I sit in on an intake with a therapist and a woman in her early thirties who comes in with a toddler, a little girl who is the by-product of a rape. The therapist holds the questionnaire that the hotline volunteer filled out when this woman called. As the therapist reviews her answers, more and more tragedy emerges. She was raised in an orphanage and was raped when she was nineteen. "I found out I was pregnant," the visitor says, "and under the advice of other people, terminated the pregnancy. I don't want to talk about that, it's too painful," she says, watching her daughter crawl around the room. We're sitting in a play-room used for therapy for children who have been molested. "I was raped again by a man two weeks after the abortion." She mentions that "I was tortured by my husband. He forced a gun into my mouth. He, uh . . . I know people don't believe this, because we were married, but he raped me then too." This qualifier refers to people who believe that it's not rape if a husband forces his wife to have sex. She goes on to say that, after her divorce, "a good friend of mine, a guy who's married," drugged her drink and had sex with her when she passed out. The toddler on the floor is his daughter. He is still married to his wife and wants nothing to do with this woman or his child. She says she's feeling "very depressed."

"What do you remember from your childhood?" the therapist asks. "Do you have any early memories?"

This question is designed to uncover child abuse. "Oh, I remember stuff from when I was in my crib," says the woman in a matter-of-fact way. "I have a memory from when I was two years old."

"What do you remember?"

She looks up, pale and startled as a deer, her brown bangs falling into her eyes. She's in the middle of picking up toys from the floor.

"That's when my father . . ." She stops, unable to finish the sentence.

"That's okay," says the therapist. "You don't have to talk about it if it's too painful."

"I was told I have a *victim's mentality*," she says, her voice a bit louder. She's on the brink of tears, but is forcing them back with anger. "And I don't want that anymore! If you're strong, people don't prey on you, but if you're vulnerable . . ."

"Do you find yourself unable to account for long periods of time?" says the therapist. "Do you experience blackouts?" This line of questioning is to determine whether she suffers from multiple personality disorder, sometimes a factor in adults who were sexually abused as children. A blackout occurs when an "alter" or other personalities kick in. If she does have MPD, we may not admit her into therapy. ("MPDs often require more intervention than we can provide," explains Kat, later.)

The woman is puzzled. "The day sure goes by quickly sometimes, that's for sure."

"But do you remember everything that happened?"

"Yes," she says, a bit confused, as if we know something she doesn't. She doesn't have MPD.

One other question concerns whether there's been any involvement with satanic cults. If the answer is yes, we can't admit them, as they require extensive therapy, and are also typically suffering from MPD.

Back in my hotel room, I sit with the television on, my beeper clipped to my belt, and my manual open to the "Satanic Cults" section. I read case after case, detail after detail. "Cult survivors often have a missing finger to the first joint . . ." I think about how Texas is really creep central: *The Texas Chainsaw Massacre*, David Koresh's Messiah audition in Waco, rumors of a thriving snuff film industry in Houston, cults, and satanic activity so rife it's probably going on right in this hotel. It certainly seems like it could go on in the spooky parking garage . . . I look up when I hear a scream and see that a vampire movie is on television. I quickly grab the remote and change it to a *Mary Tyler Moore Show* rerun. I used to love horror movies. It used to frustrate me that my sister-in-law, Kathy, has such a low tolerance for them. Now I get it.

I notice that whenever I'm outside, whether I'm in the aforementioned parking garage, in a bar, or walking down a street, I begin to think about how it would "look" to the police and to the general public if I were raped at that moment. I work over the details I would have to give at the hospital: It's midnight, I've had two drinks, and I'm walking back to my hotel wearing tight blue jeans . . . would someone think I'm "asking for it"? Never mind the juries, I think about the statements rapists give to the police: "You weren't there. You don't know," they insist. "She wanted it!" Even when a rapist stabs a woman, beats her senseless, he insists she really wanted to have sex with him. I hear a volunteer tell a victim, "I guarantee he'll have a different story," referring to the perpetrator. "They always do," she says, and tells the victim to be prepared to hear some "whopping lies."

It's three in the morning and someone pulled the fire alarm in my hotel. I throw on a pair of pants and a sweatshirt and hurry to the fire exit. A man startles me in the stairwell. Does he think—and would a jury think—that I "want it"?

On another night, I go out with Kat to a bar and look at a man on a bar stool and start to wonder: Is he the guy who likes to torture women, the one who pokes them with a knife while he rapes them? Austin is a party town with a thriving music scene, but I found myself watching a musician and wondering: Is he the one who rapes girls in the park? I can't wait until I'm in New York City, where I don't know as much about all the rapists who haven't been caught.

This line of work does give you a warped point of view regarding the evil that lurks in the hearts of men. Or maybe—and this is where the creeping paranoia sets in—I'm seeing for the first time how things really are, and to believe otherwise is to have the warped point of view. One of the Center's therapists remarks on this occupational hazard: "So I hear a girl in a bar talking to her friend about some guy she just met. 'Should I go home with him? I just met him. Does he seem nice to you? What do you think I should do?' I cut in and said, 'Honey, I work at the Rape Crisis Center, and if you knew what I know, you wouldn't do it.'"

A week ago, I would have thought that was an extreme statement. I mean, you have to trust your judgment and follow your heart sometimes, and not all men are rapists.

My beeper goes off at 2 A.M. A woman was raped. I meet her at the hospital, where she tells me that she'd been playing pool with a guy in a bar who suggested they go out to his car to get high. They drove to a park, smoked a joint, and he raped her. He seemed like "a nice guy," she said. This was why, just prior to the rape, she gave him her business card, which has her home address and phone number on it.

This is not something all of Austin knows this morning, because not one of the rapes I heard about was ever reported in the newspaper. We hear statistics about how only one in ten rapes is reported to the police, but if all the ones that were reported to the police were written up in the paper, there wouldn't be much room for any other news. In this world I now occupy, rapes are everywhere. And it's not just the ones in the Center or at the hospital.

"You work at the Rape Crisis Center?" asks a woman I've just met. "I was raped when I first got out of college." She chuckles slightly. "Oh, it was about ten years ago. My friend and I were in this bar in Bakersfield, California, and had way too many margaritas. *Way too many.* And all of a sudden, I don't know where my friend went, but all of these *guys,* these *migrant workers,* came out of the woodwork! They bundled me into a van and four of them raped me."

I'm aghast. "Did you ever seek counseling for this?"

"What? Naw. I just sort of dealt with it myself."

Another woman taps me on the arm in the hospital waiting room when the person I'm counseling has gone to the bathroom. "I was raped once," she says. She apparently heard a nurse tell someone I was with the Center. "By a neighbor. I didn't tell anyone."

I have a bizarre urge to tell her, "Look, one rape at a time, okay? That's all I can handle at the moment." Instead, I urge her to call our hotline, and maybe arrange to come in and see a counselor. I'm thinking of seeing one myself first thing in the morning.

I seek out Nancy Tartt, a therapist and the director of client services at the Center, and ask if I can speak to her. "I need to process," I say, in the jargon of therapy meaning "Let's talk." Volunteers and Center workers often say this when they have to talk over something that just happened. An African-American woman from New York City, Nancy exudes a soothing combination of serenity and practicality. I need to hear from her that what I'm going through is normal. She tells me it is; rape center workers hear rape stories from, well, just about everyone.

"People react in different ways when they hear where you work," she says. "It can be a real conversation stopper at a party. Faces just fall. They might say 'Oh,' or 'That's interesting,' and run away. Or they may take it as a signal that you want to hear their personal problems."

"Sometimes you can't get your checkbook out at the supermarket without someone telling you they were raped," says Kat. "Or saying something incredibly stupid about rape. It gets to the point where you don't want to tell people where you work. Not out of shame, but because people can be so ignorant, and you don't always have time to deal with that. I either give them my standard monologue about it, or I give them the raised eyebrow." This is where Kat gives off a stare like twin laser beams, with one eyebrow up. Any further discussion is immediately halted.

Knowing how to stop people from unloading these personal tales of horror and degradation onto you at every turn is invaluable if you want to escape secondary post-traumatic stress syndrome, another occupational hazard for volunteers. Here I am in Austin, Texas, and I'm more fearful, more paranoid than I ever have been in New York City. When I was a cocktail waitress in Vegas, I often wandered about reviewing which drinks are garnished with limes, which with cherries. Taking your work home with you at night when you're a rape crisis worker is a different story. Okay, so Rob and Kathy were right.

My low-grade level of personal dread turns into outright panic one evening at my hotel. After parking my car in the basement garage, I walk briskly, as is my nervous habit, to the elevator. I press my floor number and the Door Close button. The door does not close, and I can hear approaching footsteps in the distance. I pound the Door Close button rapidly, I hold it down, but still the door is wide open, and the footsteps are getting louder. A man appears wearing a raincoat. I'm bug-eyed with terror. He gets in the elevator—the door finally closes behind him—and he presses a floor above mine. My heart pounding, I press the button for the lobby, and we ride the one floor up in silence. The door opens and I run to the desk clerks and demand to see the manager. I scream at everyone who will listen that I could have been attacked because their Door Close buttons don't work. It is explained to me that the doors have a built-in delay because the hotel caters to disabled guests. "Why don't you park your car out front?" says a desk clerk.

"Because there are never any spaces!" I say, hysterical with anger.

"You can valet park it," they suggest. Oh sure, and how easy will it be to rustle up a valet parker in the deserted lobby when I'm beeped at three in the morning?

"If the buttons don't work, you're removing my choice to shut the door," I tell them. I step outside of my anger for a moment to marvel *I sound just like a therapist!* "Look," I tell them, "just fix the Door Close buttons, okay?" They don't get fixed, and it is a constant source of irritation.

For months afterward, I receive letters from the hotel corporate headquarters assuring me that they've fixed the door-closing buttons. These letters only serve to remind me how completely unglued I became in that job. While working as a housewife, a cocktail waitress, and a roadie, I felt close to being overwhelmed by the work, and struggled to keep my head above the rising tide of duties. At the Austin Rape Crisis Center, it was as if a giant wave had risen up, knocked me down, and swept me out to sea.

Kat tells me of other traps volunteers can fall into. "There's the crisis junkie," who is not unlike the pyromaniac who works as a volunteer fire fighter in order to have a legitimate excuse to be near fires. I'd heard about a woman who works in Victim Services who showed up—unnecessarily—at the hospital when a rape case came in that mentioned sexual torture. "As soon as she hears torture," says the volunteer who handled the case, "man, she's right there."

"They get real desensitized to what they see and hear," says Kat, "and then talk about it with their friends at dinner parties for shock value."

I feel a pang when she says this. My friends are intensely curious about what I'm hearing, and I'm dying to tell them. They want to hear the real stuff, the front-line war stories. Here I am, elbow-deep in human depravity! Am I telling them stories for their own good, because the newspapers won't? Or is this the ghoul in me rearing its storytelling head? "True crisis junkies," clarifies Kat, "will tell you every gory detail possible."

I feel relieved—I have a way to go yet. Still, this intense curiosity is more than human nature or tabloid consciousness. As a speaker at a volunteer lecture pointed out: "Questions to victims like 'What were you wearing?' or 'What were you doing?' is our misguided effort to convince ourselves that we're not at risk, that we're not vulnerable to rape. So we try to figure out what they did wrong to get themselves into such a terrible situation." I admit that I sometimes go to the hospital, counsel a victim, and silently search for one tiny reason why this would never have happened to me. I have to look pretty hard.

One woman, Suzannah, was awakened by a rapist in her loft bed. She's a college student who lives with two other roommates. The rapist was a co-worker of one of her roommates, and was supposed to be sleeping on the couch downstairs. Suzannah awoke to find him inside her. Seeing her panic, he put his hand over her mouth. "Do you want me to stop?" he asked, removing his hand. "Yes!" she said. Before leaving, the guy explained that he must have "gotten the wrong impression." He had heard about a party the roommates held the previous weekend, there was a keg and people played Twister. This was apparently enough to convince him that a woman involved in such a party would not object to a stranger attacking her while she slept.

After the rape exam, I accompanied Suzannah to the police station, where she gave her statement. "Maybe he was confused," she said to the police, about the rapist. I look at her with a pleading expression. *Why is she saying this?*

These unfortunate statements are quite common, and come from the victim's need to understand why it happened and also to "trivialize the event," as a way of making it seem less terrible and easier to cope with. I heard victims say, "He didn't mean to really hurt me" (when the rapist had actually stabbed them) and "It wasn't so bad. I could have been beaten or killed." This is exacerbated when there isn't an available examining room for the victim to wait in, and we're forced to witness the parade of trauma that comes into every emergency room. Gunshot wounds, broken limbs, a guy whose car radiator exploded in his face, burning his eyes with antifreeze. The victim sits there, watches this, and thinks, See, I'm not so bad off. When there are no visible physical injuries, a victim will often believe there are no psychological injuries either.

Suzannah looks at five mug shots the cop has laid out on his desk. "That's him," she says, pointing at one of them. He looks like a college kid—short brown hair, a strong jaw. The cop nods and types this into his computer. They got the perpetrator's name and address from the roommate, but haven't yet gone to pick him up. For the Sex Crimes Unit to have a mug shot of him means he's been arrested for this before. The victim hasn't made this connection yet.

The cop reassures her that this was a "good rape," meaning she wasn't culpable in any way, and that the perpetrator should certainly do jail time. "Some girls we see," says the cop, "they haven't shown very good judgment. You want to turn the light bulb on in their head."

He meant well, but we always walk the fine line of blaming the victim. You never hear about the man not showing very good judgment when he rapes a woman. Apparently, any man is expected to rape a woman if the circumstances are right. If I were a man, I'd resent this universal assumption that I'm an animal, incapable of choice or reason.

One rape that, by this cop's standards, was not a "good rape" was the rape of a woman in the park. She was roaring drunk when the police brought her to the hospital. She was so out of it, she couldn't decide if she wanted a rape exam, and became fixated on "who's going to pay for it! I don't have health insurance!" I tell her the Austin police will pay if she agrees to press charges.

"No they won't!" she screams. "They said they wouldn't! They treated me like a fucking criminal!"

I go out to the waiting room to talk to the officer who brought her in. He's sitting down, squeezing his hat brim in his hands. He looks very young, and very uncomfortable to have this duty. It's not why he became a cop.

"She tried to get out of the car when we were going fifty-five miles an hour," he says, incredulous. "So I stopped and locked her in! She was so drunk . . . she kept saying how she wouldn't ride in an ambulance because she couldn't afford it, so I took her here. I didn't want her to get hurt. Any worse than she already is."

The SANE nurse tries to get the victim to agree to the exam if only for her own personal safety. The victim won't hear of it. She calls a friend of hers. I wait until the friend shows up, and make sure she has our hotline number. Sometimes, this is all you can do.

The next day, while I'm on the hotline, a hospital calls the Center. A free therapist is dispatched. When she returns, she tells me about the case.

The victim, like many other people in Austin, left her front door unlocked, and was raped by a man for two hours. He prodded her with a knife, shaved off all her public hair, and photographed her. "He made her pose," the therapist says in a flat tone of voice, the professional's objective mien. Meanwhile, my mind is racing—I'm frozen in my chair trying to put these degradations in order of outrage. It's not easy. I silently remind myself to stop picturing myself as the victim. "He kept a blanket over her face," she goes on. "He kept saying, 'See what happens when you leave your door unlocked? This'll teach you a lesson!'"

"What was she like at the hospital?"

"She was very shut down. It's like you said: You'd never know what happened to this person just by looking at her. But that's something we try and educate the public and grand juries about—that the person you see in court as the victim, who appears to be very calm and untroubled and not upset by what has happened, is not the person inside that victim. Same thing with the offender. There he is with his suit on and his most solemn face; you almost feel sorry for him! That's not who he is inside either."

The rapist wore gloves and a mask, and was very calm and methodical, an indication that he's done this before. "Gloves are unusual," she says. "He sounded psychopathic. That's not your typical rapist. Rapists are generally your everyday type of guy." The victim noticed that her driver's license was missing after the rapist left.

"Why did he take that?" I ask her. "He already knows where she lives. Do Texas driver's licenses have your Social Security number on them?"

"He probably took it as a souvenir. A memento." Serial killers are often caught and convicted by the fact that they've got a little collection of driver's licenses, bits of clothing, or other memorabilia. Serial rapists are sometimes the same way.

The victim, in trying to trivialize the event, also told the police that she didn't think the rapist wanted to hurt her. This was because he was careful when he shaved her, and he only poked her in the chest a couple of times with a knife "to let me know he was still there."

Some might believe that on this particular evening a rapist crept around a neighborhood looking for unlocked doors. Research shows, however, that women who've been stranger-raped have often been stalked for weeks. In the old days, a Peeping Tom was thought to be a harmless voyeur. Now police departments are realizing that they should tell women who report one to get bars for ground-floor windows, a deadbolt for the door.

My manual also states, "It is not sexual arousal but the arousal of anger or fear that leads to rape." A rapist is typically a man who has bought into the Rambo/James Bond type of male stereotype. He believes a man should be dominant, tough, and always right. When he finds he can't measure up to such an unattainable standard, he acts out, due to feelings of extreme inadequacy. But he's not going to pick a barroom fight with someone who can kick his butt. He wants a victim he can successfully attack and humiliate, an act that will bring back his lost feelings of power. "Rape is a pattern of sexual behavior," says my manual, "that is concerned much more with status, hostility, control and dominance than with sexual pleasure or sexual satisfaction. It is sexual behavior in the service of non-sexual needs." This is why that sweet eighty-year-old grandmother is raped by a guy who worked as her handyman. It wasn't because she was wearing a particularly sexy housedress that day.

I take a call on the hotline from a man. Since it seems very hard for him to speak, I wonder if he's been raped; male rape victims are by far the most uncommon calls. Usually a male caller is the loved one of a woman who has been raped, and is calling to sort out feelings of his own regarding the incident. The center has several support groups for loved ones of a rape or incest survivor.

"Can you tell me your name?" I ask him.

"I'm wanted by the FBI," he finally says. His ex-wife got custody of their young son, and on a visit, he kidnapped his child and transported him across state lines.

"Is there something I can call you for the purposes of conversation?"

"Uh . . . Sonny," he says. He and his twelve-year-old son have been on the run for six years. His son recently revealed that he was molested by a friend of his father's five years ago. "I'm a cab driver, and the guy was a regular customer. He broke his leg and couldn't drive. I left my son with this guy maybe fifteen or twenty minutes. I play it over and over in my mind," he says. It sounds like he's at a pay phone out on a highway. I hear trucks going by. "I can see the manipulations. I'm suffering a lot of guilt. My stupidity about pedophiles."

I'm jotting down notes while he speaks in order to organize my thoughts. I'm rather stunned to realize that, for the first time, counseling someone on the hotline feels natural. I used to depend on just being a good listener. It's taken me two weeks, but now I actually know what to *say*.

"Does your son want to press charges against this man?" I ask.

"Yeah, we talked about reporting it to the police. He's willing. I was wondering . . . Is there any way to prosecute without giving the details of the legal custody of my son?"

"Realistically?" I ask him. "No." I tell him that he and his son have got to decide whether putting this guy behind bars is worth his losing custody. That the event happened while the child was in his father's care does not help his case.

"I know that," he says. "I've seen this guy, this pedophile, on the street. I thought about revenge, various things . . ."

"I can't advise you to take this into your own hands. But you should know that the average number of victims for a pedophile is *nine*. Your son isn't the only one this guy molested." We talk for a while. He seems relieved to be able to discuss his situation, but never loses the panic of a guy wanted by the law. "You and your son should really get some counseling," I tell him. "Whatever you decide to do."

"Yeah," he says. "Thanks. I just . . . thanks for all your help. I'll do some thinking and call you back." I wonder if he will.

I look up after the call and see Diana, an intern in the office.

She sits in the cubicle opposite mine. A former aerobics instructor with teenaged kids, she's studying for her master's in social work. Right now she's telling Kat about a call on the hotline. "This woman said, 'I need to find a place to send my daughter, because she's sleeping with her stepfather and it's *her fault!*' Her daughter is ten."

The phone rings again. I pick it up. A male voice asks me my name.

"This is Lynn," I tell him.

"Liz," he says, "I'm feeling lost and confused."

"Yes," I say, deciding to ignore the Liz part.

"Liz, I'm seeing an older woman," he says. "She's recently divorced. I'm very sexually attracted to her. Do you think it's okay for a younger man to be with an older woman?"

*What?* My forehead screws up involuntarily, but I remain silent.

"Liz, I want to tell you what we did together recently. What happened to me."

"Wait," I tell him. "Let's back up." A tiny voice in the back of my head is reminding me that rape victims often want to talk about their feelings. They want to talk about anything else but a blow-by-blow account of the rape. Another tiny voice is telling me that it sounds like he's masturbating. "You were saying you're feeling lost and confused?" In the event that I'm horribly wrong about him, I try to get him to talk about his feelings rather than the sexual details.

Diana looks up when I say this, and swivels her chair around. She looks at me wide-eyed. I write down "crank call?" on a piece of paper and hold it up to her. She nods vigorously, quickly handing me a Xerox detailing chronic crank callers to the hotline. She reaches over and underlines "He says he feels mixed-up and confused."

Oh, great. A crank caller to a rape hotline. Beautiful. I read off the suggested response: "I will talk to you about how you are feeling, if you feel you've been violated. I will not talk to you about graphic details." He hangs up.

Diana tells me about another hotline call from a woman who is an adult survivor of incest. She's not from Austin, which unfortunately means we can't help her, but she says there are no similar organizations for rape victims in her town. Her story is this: She tried to commit suicide and was admitted to a hospital for depression. While she was a patient, she was raped by another patient, a manic-depressive who threatened to find her as soon as he was released. The hospital, for reasons of self-protection, is covering up the crime. I wonder how you'd ever recover from something like that.

On my last night as a volunteer, my beeper goes off at 3 A.M. A homeless twenty-year-old woman was raped. Unlike the other women I've counseled, who've all been white, she is African-American. When I see her in the hospital waiting room wearing a sweatshirt and terry-cloth shorts, I think the rapist beat her up. It turns out the bruise on her face is from a bad fall a week ago.

She sits in silence next to the policeman who brought her in. I introduce myself quietly, and ask the admitting nurse if there's an empty examining room where we can wait instead. This provides privacy and it also spares her seeing gruesome hospital admissions.

As usual, I'm careful not to ask what happened, but she provides a few details. She was raped in a car. I assume it was by someone who offered her a ride. The police were called by neighbors across the street who witnessed the struggle in the car. "They shined a flashlight on his ass," she says, referring to how the perpetrator was caught. She has a very high voice. "He wasn't wearing nothin' but sneakers and a rubber." She smiles in spite of herself.

When I first started speaking to her, she was very agitated and upset. "Where am I going to go tonight?" she says, on the brink of tears. She says she lost her home four weeks ago. Victims often shift all of their anxiety from the event itself to an ancillary problem or issue. For example, a married woman I counseled could only focus on the idea that she may be pregnant with the rapist's child, and wouldn't talk about anything else. Since this homeless woman is upset about where she will go when the exam is over, I ask her if she would like me to see what I can do. She nods yes.

I go back out to the waiting room and ask the officer who brought her in what he thinks could be done. The Austin Police Department will pay for a woman to stay in a hotel for a night if she is pressing charges and was raped in her home. But what if she's homeless?

"No, not in that case," he says. "How about the Battered Women's Shelter?" he suggests. She doesn't really fit that category either, so we call the Salvation Army. They say she's free to come in as long as she hasn't been there in the last ninety days. I tell them her name, which is Darla, and to make sure she can shower when she gets there.

I pass the vending machines on my way back to the examining room and wonder if she's eaten anything recently. I buy a package of Hostess chocolate cupcakes. The cafeteria is closed, and this is the closest thing to real food in any of the machines. I knock gently before coming back in. The nurse is there with her.

"I thought you might be hungry," I tell her. She nods vigorously and reaches out, childlike, for the cupcakes. Since the nurse has already taken a swab from her mouth, she can eat them right away.

"After we finish here . . . if you want," I add hastily, giving her the choice, "the Salvation Army said they'd be very happy to have you stay with them." I was trying to think of a way to say this that sounded like good news rather than the prospect of a homeless shelter. Never mind—she's relieved to hear it. The nurse is telling her that, unfortunately, she has to give up her clothes as part of evidence gathering—she's wearing the clothes she was raped in—which means she'll have to go to the Salvation Army in disposable surgical scrubs and booties. The Center tries to get area hospitals to store a box of clothing for just this purpose, but hospital storage space is at a premium.

The nurse leaves with the specimens, and Darla finishes her cupcakes, swinging her legs on the examining table. I tell her she looks just like a doctor. She smiles and lies down, pulling an examining smock over her.

"Would you like me to find you a blanket?"

She shakes her head no.

"Do you want to sleep a little? We may be here a while. I can turn out the lights and sit outside the door, or I can wait in here with you."

She doesn't speak for a while. "I love to sleep in hospitals," she says. "Where we lived before, I used to go with my mom to the hospital. She was a nurse. They used to fix up a little room for me there where I could sleep."

"Where's your mom now? Do you get along with her?"

"My mom died when I was ten," she says softly. She falls asleep in a few minutes.

When the lab results come back forty-five minutes later, I wake her up. The nurse gives the evidence kit to the officer, who promises to deliver her to the Salvation Army and see that they let her shower—if she wants to. I watch her get into the squad car. She waves goodbye.

I drive to my hotel, and get back into bed. I toss and turn for a while, and finally admit defeat and turn on the light. I pick up my manual, which is on the bedside table next to my beeper. A newspaper clipping I saved falls out.

"According to the FBI," it says, "only 2 percent of rape victims see their attacker caught, tried or jailed. Almost half of all convicted rapists serve jail terms of a year or less; 25 percent never go to prison; another 25 percent serve 11 months in a local jail. A rape case is twice as likely as a murder to be dismissed."

I think about a bumper sticker on Kat's truck: *Stopping rape is men's work*. When I first read that, I reflexively wrote down a joke response in my notes: *But it's cheaper to hire women to stop it*. Now that I'm at the end of my time here, I see the bumper sticker as being too true to be part of a joke anymore. Making women the sexual police is like making a rabbit guard a hen-house.

# 9

# Early to Bed and Early to Rise Means You Work in a Factory

**M**y five-month job hunt for factory work reached a crescendo of hysteria four days before I was finally hired. I was hoping for work in a chocolate factory, but my last-minute desperation was such that I faxed my plea to just about everyone on the eastern seaboard—from cough drop companies to car battery manufacturers.

I look at my list of recipients and call Sunsweet Growers.

"Everything's automated," says the woman in charge of hiring. "I mean, maybe you could drive a fork lift," she says, with a little chuckle.

"Why not?" I say. "Can I? Can I have a job driving a fork lift?"

"Do you know how?"

"No, but I'm a fast learner, you really wouldn't believe some of the things I've learned how to do." I pause. She hasn't cut me off, so I plunge on again. "Please let me. You don't even have to pay me! And if I don't learn everything about fork lifts in one hour, I'll give you twenty dollars. How's that?" I hear the crazy edge to my voice. She laughs.

"No. I'm sorry," she says.

I hang up. This is insane. Eight successful hires and now I'm offering to pay someone to give me a job. I put an X next to Sunsweet and call the Goldenberg Candy Company in Philadelphia.

"We'd love to hire you," says the owner, a nice guy named David.

"Terrific! Oh my God! I'm thrilled!"

"But we're closed down. We don't go into operations again for another six weeks." How cruel of him to say those sentences in that order. "I'm really sorry," he says. "Good luck."

I hang up and the phone rings a second later.

"Hello?" I say. Please let this be someone with a factory job. This is a wish I never thought I'd have.

"Hey kid." It's my dad. I tell him about my rotten morning. A writer's life is supposed to be filled with rejection, but that's nothing compared to someone looking for factory work.

"Oh, what do they know," says my dad. "Don't sweat it. You'll get a job." Easy for him to say; he's held lots of jobs, and is consequently never afraid to quit them, usually with the announcement, "Life's too short." He still can't get over the fact that his brother, who took an early retirement from Pepperidge Farm, couldn't get me a factory job at any of their plants. My dad thinks that working for the same company your whole life should mean you can get your niece a minimum-wage, dead-end job with that company. I agree, and dial a small candy company.

"Look," I tell the man in charge, "if you hire me, or if you can tell me where I can get hired, I'll give you a hundred dollars the day I start work."

There's silence on the line for maybe six seconds. He hangs up without saying another word. Maybe he thought I was part of an *anti-corruption task force for candymakers. Either that or I named a bribe so low I insulted him. What is the correct bribe for an unskilled-labor position?*

*I never get to figure that out, since I get the call I've been waiting for: I have a job at a chocolate factory. With any luck, it'll be just like that* I Love Lucy *episode where Lucy works on an assembly line and ends up eating half of what she makes.*

It has taken me eight jobs to see the pattern: Before getting hired, I worry about something that I'm sure is a big part of the job. Then I get hired, and I see that whatever I was worried about turns out to be a complete non-issue, and I discover something else that was far more deserving of fretful attention late in the night.

Before I was a roadie, I worried about the logistics of sharing a bathroom on the bus with so many other people. Once on the job, I saw that if I'd only worried about something sensible, like the disgusting locker rooms, I might have packed something useful, such as rubber shower shoes. I was consumed with doubt over whether I remembered certain subjects well enough to teach them in high school, when I should have been boning up on crowd-control techniques. At the Austin Rape Crisis Center, I was worried about becoming traumatized at *seeing* blood and carnage. I should have wondered about the long-term effects of *hearing about* rapists, and how I would get the disturbing stories out of my head.

When I started worrying about how I was going to overcome the crushing boredom and mindless repetition of a factory job, I told myself I was undoubtedly missing the point once again. But now that I've worked as a hand-molder at a chocolate candy factory in a bleak little New England town, I see that the pattern has finally been broken. My worries concerning the boredom and repetition were right on the money.

I had, however, incorrectly assumed it would also be too noisy to talk, listen to a Walkman, or even think. I suppose I should be grateful I was wrong about this, but what I had to listen to in the relative silence was the relentlessly inane, depressing, or misinformed chatter of fellow factory workers as we went about the swift completion of our incredibly boring tasks.

"We went to Kentucky Fried Chicken's all-you-can-eat buffet for $4.99. Very good! I ate so much I thought I was gonna just blow up."

"You know what's good? Tuna Helper on broccoli. My kids love it."

". . . and I got Tropicana orange juice for ninety-nine cents! Which is a really good price, you know, for Tropicana."

"Yeah. I go to Waldbaum's with their coupons and my coupons."

"Me and my husband, together, us both workin' full-time jobs, our combined income is twenty-five thousand. Which is not very much . . ."

"My sons say they wanted roast beef sandwiches for lunch. So I bought six slices, and it's two dollars! So they each got two slices. One of them says, 'Ma, I want more beef!' and I says, 'Not on my budget! You get two slices, not three!' "

"The collection agency calls again, and I realize that this guy who'd been givin' me all this grief is, like, nineteen years old! I tell him I'll pay whenever."

"So why don't you file for bankruptcy?"

"I thought about it, but I found out it costs six hundred dollars to do it! Shit, if I had six hundred dollars I could pay off my bills!"

My main co-workers are Grace, Laurie, and Susan. Grace is sixty years old and has been working here for twenty years. Laurie is in her forties, a devout Catholic who, aside from being married with four children, could easily be mistaken for a nun. She's been working here for almost fifteen years. Susan is the baby of the group at twenty-nine, but has been married for twelve years and has three kids. Other workers pass in and out of our orbit, the guy who adds to the vats of chocolate, a few supervisors, other workers sneaking past on unofficial cigarette breaks. Everyone stops to chat.

Money is a big topic of conversation when you don't have any. The average worker here earns $200 a week and takes home $161.70. But since blue-collar workers live by the clock rather than the calendar, they say they earn "five bucks an hour." If a worker wants health insurance, an additional $29.75 is deducted from the check, leaving $131.95 a week to fritter away on food and shelter. A married person who opts for family health coverage would see a deduction of $75 a week, leaving a take-home pay that is under $100.

On the half-hour lunch break on Fridays, there's a mad dash out of the parking lot, with workers frantic to get to the bank where they can cash their paychecks. No one ever seems to deposit anything. If you wish, the company will deduct an additional sum out of your tiny check to be put aside in a savings account for you. I'm surprised to hear that so many workers opt for this, apparently recognizing that they would never have the willpower to save it themselves. "If I don't see it," says one worker on this plan, "I won't spend it."

Lining up at 7 A.M. to punch the clock, I look at the crowds of people waiting to work an eight-and-a-half-hour shift. Men, women, Hispanic, white, young, old. We stand just outside, on the small cement staircase at the employees' entrance. We park in a lot down the hill, on the side of the building near the loading docks. The administrators, the white-collar workers, park right in front of the building. All of their cars are parked facing in—the mark of an executive who is eager to get to work and stay there as long as necessary. Down the hill, we back into our parking spaces, each car facing out, ready to spring from its spot at quitting time like horses leaving the starting gate. The differences in parking styles mark the essential differences in attitude between the white-collar and blue-collar worker. There's none of that dawdling after work here the way white-collar workers do to impress their bosses. Now that I'm blue-collar, I can predict within two minutes exactly when I'll arrive home at the end of the day. If I'm later than that, there's a little something extra in my paycheck at the end of the week. It's called overtime, something a salaried white-collar worker rarely gets.

Workers greet each other while the last cigarettes that can be smoked before the first ten-minute break at 9:30 are being savored and stubbed out. I'm one of the few workers who show up already wearing the tan work smock—most workers carry theirs and throw it on at the last minute as we clock in. I relish the fact that I don't have to worry about what I wear to work, but they're taking those precious few minutes before work to show their coworkers how nice they look, to express their individuality before they become just another worker bee. Once inside the building all hair must be covered with a hairnet that looks like a white shower cap. Men with beards must wear beard guards that resemble surgical masks.

I'm staying at a hotel with a small kitchen in my room. I get up at 6 A.M., run a brush through my hair, put on jeans, sneakers, and a T-shirt, and have a cup of coffee while I pack my lunch. Before leaving, I grab a clean work smock that has drip-dried in the shower overnight. I bathe when I get home. Most female workers are not this blasé about their appearance. Even though Susan has to get three kids off to school, she gets up early to wash, set, and style her hair into an elaborate French braid that no one sees unless she's on a break. She says she'd never come to work without makeup. I count not having to wear makeup as a perk, but after a few months of this, I too would probably view lipstick and eyeliner as necessary morale boosters.

I see a worker in the line shyly eyeing me. He's got hair past his shoulders and a beard, and he's got on blue jeans and construction boots. It's the beginning of summer, but he wears a leather jacket. He nods as he stubs out a cigarette. I nod back without enthusiasm. Susan walks up and says hello to him and some of her other friends who are Hispanic. That she is white and has friends outside of her racial group marks her as unique in this place. She tells me she gets grief about being "too friendly" from some of the other workers—the limp code of racism.

We open the doors and the cloying smell of chocolate washes over us in a wave. Even though I love chocolate, this is definitely too much of a good thing. My stomach, empty except for some coffee, does a slow flip. It's only my second day, but I wrestle with the urge to march back down the hill, get in my car, and drive back to New York City and consider myself done with the whole escapade.

The factory looks like a large warehouse from the road, which is a quiet side street lined with small single-family homes. The company makes chocolate candy of its own, but also makes novelty chocolates for other companies, such as Fannie May and Hershey's. These include such perennials as chocolate Santas on a stick, valentine hearts, and Easter bunnies, and non-perennials such as chocolate golf balls. There are machines that can do everything from melting and molding the chocolate to wrapping the finished product in foil, but there are plenty of jobs that require the human touch. Easter bunnies, for example, must be hand-foiled. Bows must be hand-tied, and eyes painted on. And if the company takes on an order that's too small to make it worth changing over a production line, it passes the work over to the hand-molders. Even though we're much slower than the machines, we're cheaper for a small order.

"Hey, you're back!" says Grace, who showed me how to hand-mold yesterday. "My sister-in-law got a job here, and went out for her first ten-minute break and never came back! A lot of people can't handle it." I nod and shrug.

Here's what I learn about making molded chocolate candy: Like making a good mud pie, it's all in the consistency of your materials. The chocolate can't be too thick, too thin, too hot, too cold. We temper it with our hands. This means that our hands, and most of our forearms, are covered in chocolate all day. And here's the interesting part—we're not wearing any gloves. We're forbidden to wear false nails, nail polish, or any jewelry other than a wedding band. We wash our hands, roll up the sleeves of our smocks, and dive, bare-fisted, right into the sugary brown muck.

I work from a shallow pan filled with chocolate. The plastic heart-shaped molds with "Be My Valentine" written on the front are about five inches across. When filled, they form one half of a hollow-body heart. I hold the mold in my left hand and dip my right in chocolate. I rub the gooey stuff into all the crevices, then I scoop up a handful and overfill the mold. Then I tip the mold vertically and pour some chocolate out, helping shape the hollowness in the center with my index finger. Now I put it aside to "set." Once it does—and there's a very small window of opportunity when this happens—I take a putty knife and scrape

Why is this woman smiling?

the overflow of chocolate off the mold and clean the edges of the heart. If you wait too long, it's like chiseling cement; too soon, it's still runny and you can't get a clean edge.

When ten heart halves are completed, I slide the full tray into a large refrigerator, pull out a tray that's done, carry it to the counter, and pop out the hearts. The heart halves are assembled later, whether by hand or machine, I have no idea. Like other factory workers, once the product leaves my section, it's not my problem anymore.

I stack the heart halves into my bin, mark each completed layer with a small dot of chocolate on the wall above, knock and scrape off any excess chocolate from the molds, carry the empty molds over to the tray of chocolate, and begin again. By this time, the chocolate in the pan is too thick and cool, so I dump most of it into a heated vat and scoop up some warm thin stuff.

The tempering process begins again: the batting, squishing, and stirring. Over this repeating cycle, the conversations go on.

"Kids today!" says Grace, primed to add another barroom generality that is at the root of all conversations at the factory. When two people speak, it's very often two alternating monologues, rather than a dialogue. "When they get to be my age," she says, "they'll all be deaf because of loud music, and bald from washin' their hair so much and puttin' the gels and mousses in it all the time." I think this is a veiled comment about Susan.

"All men are dogs," says Susan. Non sequiturs are the rule here rather than the exception. "Trust me. I know."

"The news media is sick!" says Grace. "I won't watch the news anymore because it's all bad."

"Yeah, me too," says Laurie. "And when my husband says, 'Don't you want to know what goes on in the world?' I tell him we talk about what's goin' on at work, and that's enough."

I raise my head from the molds. The only current events I ever hear discussed in great detail are taken from the plots of each Movie of the Week. But since they're usually based on some real-life incident, I guess this qualifies as news to Laurie.

Susan mentions last night's movie, which was apparently about abortion rights. "If you can live with murdering your baby," she says, "and *that's what it is*, you should have an abortion. That's what I believe. It's up to each person to decide."

Another worker passes by and senses a political discussion is under way. "William Kennedy Smith," she says, apropos of nothing. "That girl was askin' for it. She was askin' to be raped."

I keep my head down, my hands in my chocolate. I'm supposed to be an unemployed teacher, not someone fresh out of a rape crisis center. I had initially worried that no one would believe my cover story, but the scary part is that these workers know better than anyone how bad the economy is, and it doesn't surprise them a bit that a teacher might be forced to take a job in a factory.

It takes more than a week, however, before anyone asks what my husband does for a living. It occurs to me then that they've probably assumed that he's unemployed, in jail, or gone altogether. "He's a free-lance artist," I say as vaguely as possible. He's actually a production designer and art director for films and television, but I can't say that without everyone wondering why on earth I'm working here.

"Oh," says Laurie. The expression on her face says it all. I've apparently just said I'm supporting a bum who is never going to get a real job.

At 9:25 A.M., we stop work and go out to the big industrial sink and wash our arms and hands. You need lots of hot soapy water to cut through the greasy film of chocolate.

"Make sure you let hot water run under your nails real good," cautions Laurie, who is washing her hands next to me. "When you're scoopin' your chocolate around, a hard piece of chocolate can get up in there and give you an infected nail."

"What happens then?"

"Your nail swells up with pus," she says. "It hurts real bad. When that happens, I'll tell you what to do," she says, wiping her hands on a paper towel so she can demonstrate. "After your hands have been in water, you know, like after you do the dishes? You take a needle and stick it under the nail," she says, miming the action, "and squeeze it all out. It heals pretty fast then."

I'm sure I've gone a bit pale.

"This happens a lot?" I manage to say.

"Well, sometimes," she says. "You can't hand-mold if you have an infection."

"What do you do instead?"

"If there's nothing here for you to do, you stay home until you're better. A girl was out two weeks once with an infected nail."

That's two weeks without pay. There's no such thing as a paid sick day here. Those of you who worry about whether the people who make your chocolate wash their hands often enough can find something else to worry about.

I have been experimenting during break times with finding a suitable clique to hang out with. Yesterday I took a break in the room upstairs that's home to the vending machines, and I was introduced to a college student working here for the summer. The introductions were made by her mother.

"She's a teacher," says the mother, referring to me. She heard this on the factory grapevine. The mother thinks we have something in common, perhaps because she's assuming I went to college. The daughter's tiny eyes flicker over me as we grunt hello. *Was* a teacher, is what she's thinking. *Now she works in a factory.*

"Where do you go to school?" I ask her as she rips open a bag of pretzels.

"Yukon," she says. She says this in a tone of voice that means she's ending the conversation. We sit in silence and watch her mother play cards with some other workers, a clique that I think of as the Old Biddy Mafia, a group of older chain-smoking women who've been here since Paleolithic times. It hits me later that this girl was referring to the University of Connecticut, and said "U. Conn.," not "Yukon." I find myself grateful that I didn't ask her how she liked Alaska. I felt a big enough idiot as it was.

On breaks and during lunch, Laurie has the strange preference of sitting alone and reading romance novels in a tiny cloakroom off the bathroom. I opt for some fresh air and decide to camp out at the front entrance on the steps. The workers who hang out here are mostly Hispanic. I close my eyes and listen to the Spanish being spoken around me and enjoy the nonchocolate-scented air, the warmth of the sun. I have to remind myself at work to sit on the tall stool provided for me when I fill the molds. At other times in the cycle I'm on my feet. But unlike being a cocktail waitress, at least I can wear sneakers with good arch supports.

At the end of the break, everyone stands up at once; they know ten minutes are up without consulting a watch. I tuck my hair back under my hairnet, plop a brown company-approved baseball cap over it to keep the draft from the air-conditioning vent off my neck, and head back inside.

I'm filling molds when I hear Grace let out a short gasp. She works at the station behind me. "I cut myself," she says. "This damned scraper." She examines her hand.

"Time for a midget condom?" says Susan, a little louder than necessary. She's got Michael Bolton on her Walkman.

"It's my knuckle," says Grace.

"If you cut your finger," explains Laurie, for my benefit, "they make you wear a little protective sleeve on it." She starts to giggle. "It looks like," she says, really laughing now, "like a condom *for a midget*." Laurie is always breaking herself up like this.

"Pain in the you-know-where," says Grace, about the condoms.

"Then," says Laurie, calming down somewhat, "you gotta mold with your other hand, which is real hard."

About an hour later, Grace says, "I don't believe this. I cut myself again."

The problem with cuts, I'm told, is that the chocolate gets in them and causes infection very quickly. "These cuts burn like fire," says Grace, keeping up her production even so. Because we don't get paid for sick days, workers hide injuries such as these from supervisors who might send them home.

Lunchtime. Everyone lines up again at the time clock, holding brown-bagged lunches, Thermos jugs, and small insulated packs. Since we don't get paid for that half hour, we must clock out. If you forget to bring something, you can run to the McDonald's down the street or scavenge chips, pretzels, and sodas from the vending machines in the deserted loft space upstairs.

I sit outside on the front steps and unpack my lunch, which includes a small bottle of Evian water. "What's that?" says a young guy fresh from San Juan, Puerto Rico. "Vodka?" he guesses. I smile and wink.

Some sparrows that live in the buildings' eaves know it's lunchtime too, and fly down to hop expectantly around a few feet away. A worker tosses a few grains of rice at them from his rice and beans. The birds gobble this up. I ball up a small nugget of bread. A sparrow hops over to me, eats it, and waits for more. I toss him another small piece.

"You shouldn't feed wild animals," says the long-haired worker, who is sitting a few feet away.

"You're right," I tell him. "But this is a bird. It's okay to feed birds."

"They won't know how to find food on their own," he says, eating his sandwich.

The bird, dissatisfied with my response time, moves on to another worker. I peel an orange. I stare at its beautiful lush color, all the more vivid against the brilliant blue of my jeans. Colors seem almost supernaturally bright after staring at brown chocolate and dull stainless steel all day.

Everyone seated around me knows without asking that I work in the hand-molding room; we're the ones with chocolate smeared and spattered all over the fronts of our smocks. Some workers look down on us for this, they point to our smocks and laugh, or say "Have an accident?" Lots of workers—such as the ones who must feed and tend the machines—who are asked to work as hand-molders turn down the opportunity because they don't want to get so messy. I notice the sun is melting the hard bits of chocolate stuck to the tan polyester. A brown rivulet is threatening to run onto my jeans. I move my legs so it can drip on the asphalt. It looks like carnage, like the guts of the candies we've been making. *The hog butchers of the chocolate factory.*

Grace has noticed that I didn't return to the card-play-ing enclave upstairs, and asks where I ate my lunch. "Outside. To enjoy the fresh air."

"Not me," she says, preferring the deserted loft space with its painted-over windows and the smoke of about twenty cigarettes going at once. "If I went outside, I'd never come back."

While we work, Susan fills me in on the gossip of the factory. "It's like one giant soap opera," she says. She tells me about a husband and wife who work here. "He had a girlfriend here too," she says. "Everyone knew about it." Eventually, the company fired the girlfriend, because, she says, "they liked the wife bet-ter." Now the couple is back together, but there are some people who think he's scum for what he did. "His wife forgave him," says Susan, lowering her voice, "why can't they?"

Most of the workers see things in terms of black and white, and consider the ability to see the shades of gray an affliction, or, at best, an unnecessary distraction. "I'll tell you what's wrong with this city," says one worker on a break, sounding exactly like Archie Bunker. "In a word, *low-income housing.*"

The racism and prejudice between whites and people of color in the factory are easily apparent, if only because the two groups take pains to ignore each other as completely as possible. "I admit it, I'm prejudiced," says one white worker. "Because they're all on welfare." The term "they" in this setting always refers to Hispanics. "I see 'em sittin' on their porches every day, hangin' out, havin' babies."

After a couple of beers in a bar I might be stupid enough to put the question that begs to be asked—"But why do you hate the ones who work here? They're not on welfare"—and I would have my front teeth knocked out as an answer. Since we're in a factory, I say nothing and know the answer is: Everyone needs someone to look down on. Satisfying this overriding need becomes the second most popular topic of conversation.

If you're going to be polite here, you use the word "colored," instead of "nigger" or "spic." The words "Puerto Rican" are said in such a way that it renders it a derogatory expression. One white hand-molder responsible for directing the silent Hispanic man working the chocolate melter continually addresses him as if he's mentally retarded rather than someone who speaks English as a second language. This condescension irritates Susan. "He speaks good English," she whispers to me. No one says "black" or "Hispanic," and the odds of anyone saying "African-American" are about on par with anyone saying "Native-American" or referring to the "girls" in the hand-molding room as "women," even though, with one exception, we're all over thirty. The notion of being politically correct is a luxury of the upper classes.

Jeffrey Dahmer worked in a chocolate factory, and his co-workers said that the cannibal serial killer constantly muttered about "niggers." I try not to think about that too often.

Since that chocolate smell first thing in the morning isn't getting any easier to stomach, I think about transferring to the shift that works from 3:30 P.M. to 11 P.M. "Not unless you want to be the only English-speaking person in the whole place," says a supervisor. "Even the bosses are Spanish." No one wants to work the night shift: You don't have any time with your family and the pay isn't any better. The day shift is particularly appealing to women because of the overlap with school hours.

This is why Grace ended up working here twenty years ago, when her three kids were small. It was her husband's idea. She still longs for her previous job as a waitress. "I loved that job," she says, slinging out valentine hearts at a furious clip. "I was very good at it. It was at Long John Silver, a nice restaurant. On Wednesdays, we had the Rotary Club in. One night one guy asked me what a bug was doing in his chicken salad. I said," she stops to laugh a bit, " 'It looks to me like he's tryin' to get out!' I got along great with all the customers. And I made more on a Saturday night than I do here in forty hours. But my husband made me come and work in this dump, and I've never forgiven him for it." She swirls her chocolate around while she muses on this statement. It was nice, she says, when the kids were small, to have a job that allowed her to send her kids off to school and also be there when they came home. She thought working here was a temporary measure. "I thought at one point I'd go back to school," she says, "but my husband got sick, and that was it." He had two heart attacks and is now on disability. Grace never thought she'd be working here into her sixties.

Everyone talks about their kids. It's the bright spot in their lives, the reason they've worked in this place all these years. "All my kids work here in the summer," one grizzled worker tells me between puffs on her cigarette. "Then they know what we go through. And it makes them stay in school."

"Yeah, all mine worked here," another agrees. "And they all graduated college. One earns twenty-eight dollars an hour as a systems analyst. With computers."

At the end of the day, we're responsible for washing out our pans and scrapers in the big sink. The machine workers must wash the chocolate off certain metal parts of their machines at the end of their shift, and they also fight for sink space. I get to the sink at the same time as one of the college kids who's working here for the summer. We throw our stuff in the sink, and spray it down with hot water.

"Sometimes I don't know what to clean up first," I say in the clouds of steam. "Me or these tools." He cuts a glance at me and my chocolate-covered smock, gathers the bits and pieces from the sink, and walks off without a word. I get the same treatment from the other college boys. I keep giving them second and third chances for conversation, but they make it clear that they think they're better than I am. They're not ending up with some factory girl, not even as a friend. If they've heard I'm a teacher, they can probably guess that I must have screwed up pretty badly to end up here. They look at me as if I've got a big "L" branded on my forehead: L for Loser.

The next day at work, I hear Grace raving about me to Gail, one of the supervisors. Recently promoted from the ranks of the tan smocks, Gail preens a bit in her new blue supervisor's smock, smoothing the pockets. "She caught on real quick," Grace says, pointing out that I'm up to 300 hearts a day. Susan's had two months' practice and churns out 370.

"Have you worked in clay before or something?" says Gail.

"Yeah," I say. Agree with anything is my get-along motto in here.

"You took to this like a duck to water," says Grace. "You must have done this in a former life."

"God, I hope not," I blurt out, profoundly depressed at the very suggestion. This has the unexpected effect of cracking up the whole room.

Soon after this, a supervisor named Kevin comes in and announces we're to start on something new: Fannie May dinosaurs. He shows us a mold for a giant hollow egg, and nesting inside will be a tiny solid chocolate dinosaur, made from another mold.

"A triceratops!" I say with excitement. The room stares at me.

"A what?" says Susan.

"Triceratops," I say, faltering a bit. "My nephew is nuts about dinosaurs," I explain.

"Let's see," says Kevin, surveying the work orders. "Grace will start on eggs, and Lynn, you start on the . . . uh, the dinosaurs." Other workers will join in during the week.

Laurie passes on some techniques for making solid-body chocolates. "You fill both sides of the mold, then quickly press them together real tight." The molds have small notches and raised knobs that fit together.

I get both hands completely goopy trying to work this out. Popping the dinosaurs out of the mold means that there are often a few ragged bits of chocolate sticking out that must be shaved off with a putty knife. Any imperfect ones go into a separate bin for "good" scrap chocolate—stuff that hasn't fallen on the floor—and it all gets melted down again.

I think about the looks I received when I knew the species of dinosaur. It's the summer of *Jurassic Park*, it's not exactly an obscure subject at the moment. I make other gaffs: On my break I sit next to a woman in her forties who tells me that she has a fear of driving over bridges.

"What, visions of Chappaquiddick?" I joke.

"Uh," she says, puzzled. "I just think about the car going in the water and me *drownding*." I manage also to resist the urge to tell her there's only one "d" in "drowning."

With evidence such as this, it's hard not to make the sweeping generalization that factory workers are uneducated and ignorant. They do, however, take a bizarre pride in their situation, putting down educated people as being "stuck up," and general knowledge as "brainwashing." This is all part of needing someone or something to look down on.

"You been brainwashed!" says one worker, when I tell him I don't smoke after he offers me a cigarette. "You believe all that crap about smokin', don't you?"

I know I'm on dangerous ground here, so I just shrug. He continues anyway.

"Let me tell you something," he says. "My parents both smoked for fifty years and nothing's wrong with them! My mom's eighty years old and my dad died of a heart attack three years ago! This crap about cancer is just a load of crap! Ain't nothin' wrong with smokin'."

It's more than pure ignorance, it's an entirely different value system. For example, Laurie's and Grace's speech—like everyone else's here—is peppered with double negatives, along with other classic examples of bad English. "Isn't" is never used when "ain't" will serve, "don't" replaces "doesn't," "good" is confused with "well." The two of them, however, will not tolerate any swearing in the chocolate room because it's "low class." This is explained to me right after Laurie came in and announced a fellow worker's absence by telling a supervisor, "She ain't comin' in today, she don't feel so good." But me blurting out "Shit!" when I drop a perfect dinosaur right out of the mold is cause for raised eyebrows and great consternation.

The entire group confesses that they really don't hold with fancy restaurants, French cuisine, or anything "gourmet," a word that's said with all possible scorn. "Dressin' up for dinner?" says one woman passing through. "For *what?* I go out in my sweatpants."

"I don't go anywhere where there's more than one fork on the table," says one guy wearing a beard guard.

I remain silent and feel like an insufferable snob. I'm thinking about a French restaurant in New Orleans that invites high school French classes to come in during the day. The French owner was telling me they teach them about different utensils, stemware, and how to order from a menu. "Their parents take them to McDonald's all their life," he says, "and they don't know these things, and are afraid to go to real restaurants. If I don't do this, I won't have any customers in ten years."

"My husband don't like any of that gourmet stuff," Laurie says. "Meat loaf is his favorite."

If you're earning minimum wage, a good meal out is one where a salad and a choice of potato and vegetable are included with the entrée, or else it's got to be an all-you-can-eat place. Since no one here can afford to eat out in slightly more upmarket restaurants, it's much easier to denigrate them. "Yeah," says one guy, "I had a meal in a French restaurant and the salad cost extra! And the main dish! It was this small!"

There's a seafood place in town that's talked about in glowing terms, as it's acknowledged to be the place to go on a really special occasion. This is for that once-a-year celebration when your folks can babysit and you have a little money set aside. Laurie promises to bring in a menu from this place, since it's talked about so often.

One day, when we're finishing up the tidying of the chocolate room, Laurie remembers that she brought it in. She comes out of the cloakroom with it—it's a paper menu that doubles as a placemat. She says she asked the waiter for a clean one as a memento from when she and her husband went there recently on their wedding anniversary. I make the appropriate noises of envy, and I'm careful not to brush it against my dirty smock.

I walk out with Susan to stand in line to clock out. We're not supposed to get in line until 3:26, so we walk slowly. At 3:28, one member of the Old Biddy Brigade cuts to the front of the line. She works tying ribbon all day, sitting on a chair plumped up with big fluffy pillows brought from home. She's the Queen of the Clock, and holds her time card just over the slot in order to prevent anyone from clocking out so much as thirty seconds early. When the sweep second hand gets to the dot of 3:30, her card goes in, and we can all follow suit.

"She drives me nuts," murmurs Susan.

"How can she cut in line like that?" I say, instinctively knowing that it's very bad factory etiquette to cut in line at the clock.

"She does it every day. It's stupid. We've got a three-minute grace period either way before we get docked."

The next day, Susan finds me in the line. She's got a mischievous smile on her face. "Why don't we go up and clock out right now? In front of her? It's 3:28."

I smile back. After working like a robot all day, this tiny act of rebellion feels like biting down on a good steak.

I follow Susan up to the time cards. We smile at the Old Lady Mafia and Queen of Clocks. We're cutting in line, *and* clocking out early. She reluctantly removes her card, apoplectic with shock. We punch out and walk down the hill to our cars, laughing. The expression of outrage on her face made my day.

"You can't clock out early," says one of the Old Biddies the next morning to me. "You and Susan. You're not supposed to do that."

"Yeah, okay," I say. It's too early in the morning for a lecture. I've got a headache from the chocolate smell as it is.

I see Susan when we write up our work cards. This is where we account for everything we do during the day—breaks taken, how many candies we made, how many are good, how many are rejects, at what time we clean up, and so forth.

"Did anyone say anything to you?" I ask her as we fill out today's date and our names.

"Oh, yeah," she says. "I got an earful."

Grace comes over. She's technically part of the Old Lady Mafia. "You girls can't clock out early," she says. I find it interesting that none of the supervisors has said anything to us. And why should they? The Old Biddies make sure that no one leaves hell until they say so.

"We got a three-minute grace period," says Susan.

"Not all the time," Grace says. "What if everyone did that? No one would be here at 3:30. You can't take it every day, or they'll dock your pay."

*What does it matter to you?* I wanted to ask her, but I see it's the crab-pot syndrome. Crabs in a pot that see another crab trying to climb up and escape will pull him back down so he can be miserable along with everyone else.

The conversations go on and our transgression is forgotten. One worker comes by and complains that her husband buys her lingerie. "So I look at the garter belt and I thinks it's a bra! An' I say, this'll never fit! He says, it ain't a bra, it's a garter belt, you dope! And I says, what can I say, that's what happens when you marry a young girl!"

"Oh I remember garter belts," says Grace.

I know about garter belts too, but I keep my head down, my hands in the chocolate.

Later on that day, after our second ten-minute break at two o'clock, Susan comes back to work in a state of high indignation. She mentions the name of a young worker, a seventeen-year-old kid. "He offered me cocaine!" she says. "He thinks I'm wild, that I like to party," she says, scandalized. "Just because I'm friendly!"

"Did he really have any?" I say, amazed that anyone here could afford such a thing. And why anyone would want to do cocaine in a factory is beyond me. "Maybe he was trying to impress you in a stupid way."

"Oh you'd be surprised," she says. "Sometime drug dealers take jobs like this because they need a job to show to the government, you know? As a cover for how they really earn their money." Still, considering what a successful drug dealer makes, the government must think he can really stretch a dollar if he works here.

"Hey, everyone!" says Grace, coming in with a dinner-plate-size brick of chocolate. "I got some good stuff!" She chisels chunks off and passes them around. This is chocolate that hasn't been melted down repeatedly, which eventually diminishes the taste.

Chocolate is the last thing I'm interested in eating no matter how hungry I get, but I take a small nibble. It's okay, I guess, but I'm craving bread, oatmeal, anything starchy and bland to counteract smelling sugar and chocolate all day. I get jittery just inhaling it.

"Isn't it great?" says one of the workers. I'm apparently alone in my aversion to chocolate.

Richard, the big boss, makes a tour through and sees us sampling the chocolate. Apparently, this is fine—workers can eat as much chocolate as they want on the premises, but they can't take it home. "If they could, people'd be selling' the stuff like crazy," explains Susan. "The place'd be cleaned out."

"This is good," acknowledges Richard, who tastes a chunk. "This is a mix with a little more cocoa butter in it."

"Hey, isn't it a little early," I ask him, "for us to be making all these valentine hearts?"

"Chocolate can last indefinitely," he says with a big smile. He takes another bite.

"What about that white stuff that Hershey's Kisses get when they've been sitting on my coffee table a couple of months?"

Richard shakes his head and swallows the contents of his mouth. "It has to be stored properly. That happens when it's at too high a temperature with too much humidity for too long a period of time."

"Hershey's chocolate stinks," mutters Susan.

"What? I love Hershey's," I tell her.

"I'll take you to a part of the plant on our next break," she says, "Where they're doin' Hershey's stuff. You'll see. It smells different than what you're thinkin'. When we do Hershey's in here, my kids won't hug me when I come home. They say, 'Mom, you stink!' "

We walk over to some machines turning out Hershey's candies. I take a deep breath. Bad goat cheese springs to mind. "See?" says Susan. "Like someone's smelly sneakers."

At least the Fannie May chocolate smells good, I remind myself as I crank out more dinosaurs. I refer to these chocolate creatures as "the little bastards," even though my language offends Laurie and Grace. Fannie May has a fudgier smell than the regular factory blend we were using for the valentine hearts.

At home, I feel like Lady Macbeth, compulsively washing my hands. Are they really scented with chocolate or is the smell, as

Susan suggests, just "in my nose"? I wash my smock in scented bubble bath—anything to kill that chocolate smell in my room.

Susan comes in from lunch all excited. A supervisor told her there's overtime work at the foiling machines if she wanted it. "Yes, yes, yes!" she says. Susan's husband also works in a factory and was sick with a twenty-four-hour bug that he passed on to his wife. "So both of us lost a day this past week," she says. Even though she was still weak and wobbly, she came back to work the following day because they couldn't afford otherwise. "Do you want to get a little overtime?" she asks me. "You come in at three A.M., work at a foiler until seven A.M., then you come in here and work your regular shift."

"What is that, time and a half from three to seven?"

"Yeah!" she says.

"I don't think I can get up at two A.M. to get to work," I tell her.

"I can do it for a week," she says. "I just have to go to bed when the kids do. If I do it, we can go camping at the lake next weekend." She smiles for the rest of the afternoon.

One of our refrigerators is malfunctioning, so a repairman shows up. He seems unusually embarrassed that he has to wear a white, shower-cap-style hairnet while he works. "They don't get it," says another worker. "We all wear 'em, we don't even notice! But they think everyone's lookin' at 'em."

The male workers seem much more vain about the hairnets than the women do, and bend the rules as much as possible. This means they pull the hairnet up so it covers only as much hair as the baseball cap they wear over it. The only time people wearing these hairnets look funny to workers is if they also happen to be wearing a business suit. A few of us giggle when Richard takes a few businessmen on a tour through the chocolate room. They look ridiculous, undignified, even emasculated. They might as well be wearing lipstick. Besides, it's fun to see people who make more money than you do look stupid.

Despite these welcome distractions, the boredom of the work is overwhelming. We break the monotony with conversation, but when the conversation turns to rehashing plots of a TV movie, I zone out and retreat to private thoughts until I notice someone is speaking to me. I make a game out of streamlining my tasks, eliminating extra steps, seeing how many dinosaurs I can make in an hour.

"How many of these do I have to make?" was one of the first questions I asked.

"As many as you can" was the answer.

"What if I only make twenty in a day?" I asked Grace when the supervisors left the room.

"They'd give you time to improve, and if you didn't, out you go."

Some departments are also paid for piecework, which can raise their salary considerably. A supervisor tells me that a really fast hand-foiler makes $30,000 a year.

"That's bullshit," says a hand-molder. "They get more, but not *that much* more." One of the reasons we don't get paid for piecework is because our supervisor, Rose, who died unexpectedly a few weeks ago after thirty years on the job, didn't go to bat for her workers over this the way other supervisors have.

"Has a union ever tried to organize this place?" I ask the room.

"They tried somethin' a few years ago, but nothin' happened," says Grace. "We would have gotten more benefits, basically. You don't really get much."

The image is of factory workers going off at the end of the day to a bar to drink pitchers of beer, but this happens only when wages are up over the $8- or $10-an-hour level, as with union auto workers. No one here can afford to drink in a bar; if your family budget allows it, beer is purchased by the six-pack and consumed at home.

"You hear about the concert tomorrow night?" says the long-haired worker at lunch. "It's a tribute to The Doors. Outside in the park. You goin'?"

"I hadn't thought about it," I tell him. He eats his sandwich for a while. I have the feeling he was trying to ask me out on a date. He either hasn't noticed my wedding ring or has heard my husband is "unemployed" and thinks I might be ready for a change. Asking someone if they're already going to a free concert certainly removes any possibility of a financial commitment.

"I like music," he says. "You like music?"

I nod.

"I was laid off for a while last year. This is a shit job, but I'm glad they hired me back." He works a foiling machine that he says is "always jamming." He mentions he lives with a roommate. "I'm thinkin' of goin' back to school."

"Oh really?" I say. "Where?"

"For welding," he says. "Be a welder, somethin' like that. I like to go out at night, and I can't afford to do it as much as I'd like to workin' here."

"Welding's a good idea," I tell him as we all stand up to go back inside.

"Yeah, I gotta get out of this place."


Rose's sudden death caught a lot of people by surprise. It happened just over a month ago, and is a major source of conversations around here. Most of all, everyone fears dropping dead one of these fine Friday mornings. "Wouldn't cha know?" says one woman. "Rose died on a Friday! She didn't even get to enjoy the weekend!"

Rose's passing has hit Grace particularly hard, since the two were almost the same age. "She put all this money away for retirement, and dies at sixty-two," she says, angrily. "She was goin' to move to Florida." She slides a tray in the fridge. "This job killed her. All the stress. I've got stress in my life, too."

A lot of workers who reminisce about Rose eventually take on a tight, worried expression. There's got to be a reward for working in this place. Some kind of life where you don't have to punch a clock, where you can finally do all the things you've been promising yourself. "What am I waitin' for?" says one worker, a big burly guy built like a bear. "When do I start living? Hell, I'm eight years younger than Rose. I could drop dead tomorrow!" He scratches his palm nervously. "I'll tell ya, it gets ya thinkin'."

It had me thinking, too. On my last day at the factory, I arrive at work with my bags in the trunk. In joyful anticipation of my imminent getaway, I make 111 perfect dinosaurs, a new personal best. I pack three of them into my lunch pail as souvenirs—with any luck, someone will see me doing this and I'll get fired before quitting time. But no—I work the full shift.

I scrub my hands at the sink at the end of the day, and smile as the melted chocolate swirls down the drain. *I never have to do this again!* I clock out and hand my filthy smock to a supervisor: "It's my last day," I tell her, "I quit." I drive back to New York City as if I'm being chased by chocolate dinosaurs.

I walk into my apartment, drop my bags, and take out a bottle of champagne from the refrigerator that's been saved especially for this occasion. As I peel away the foil, a thought intrudes: *Someone worked at a machine that wrapped this.* I pop the cork and drink the entire bottle myself.

# Epilogue:
# How I Got All Those Jobs

For those of you who believe there is more to getting nine jobs in a year than what was outlined in the introduction with my Five Basic Rules of Successful Job Hunting, you're right. There's more to the story because the hiring systems in this country make no sense at all.

For example, it was fairly easy to get the paperwork together to become legally qualified to teach high school, but incredibly complicated to get credentials to serve cocktails to gamblers in Las Vegas. The rock band Skid Row let me work as an explosives expert without so much as a second thought, but chocolate companies across the land refused to hire me as a factory line worker because of the liability risk. Confectioners were also strangely worried about my possible access to sensitive candymaking information, even though an advertising agency let me in on several highly secret ad campaigns, and the Austin Rape Crisis Center allowed me to work closely with both rape victims and the police.

What became immediately obvious is that it's easier to get a job almost anywhere other than a chocolate factory. I guess Jeffrey Dahmer, the serial killer who worked at the Ambrosia Chocolate Company factory in Milwaukee while indulging in some extremely nasty hobbies, has made everyone in that business a little skittish about new employees.

Over the past year, I developed what is perhaps the dangerous opinion that I could learn how to do anything—an offshoot of the accumulated confidence from the many strange little talents I had successfully mastered. My stint as a pyrotechnician caused me to believe I could custom-build a fluorescent light fixture for my aquarium, a project I would have never attempted before. Aside from encountering rampant sexism in hardware stores from clerks who refused to believe I knew what I was talking about, I learned that the world of electronics is not nearly as mysterious as I'd previously imagined. Or had been led to believe by sexist hardware-store clerks.

Being a roadie also showed me that my hair actually looks better if I—like other roadies—never blow it dry and barely brush it. This technique of streamlining of all activities comes in handy to this day, but was particularly useful on early-morning jobs such as schoolteacher, factory worker, and housewife.

As a former copywriter, when I see a terrible ad on television I no longer think, What idiot wrote that? Now I shake my head, damning the focus-group testing and the insecurity of the client. No waitress ever gets less than a 20 percent tip, I'm feeling a little kinder toward publicists if they give me a bad time, and I feel great bursts of irritation when I hear the phrase "she's just a housewife." And while it's somewhat comforting to know what to do and what will happen after being raped, it's knowledge I hope I never get to use.

While knowing how to do a professional striptease has a somewhat limited application in real life, working as a stripper brought two unexpected long-term benefits: One is that I'm no longer shy about changing in a locker room. The other is that the experience stopped a recurring dream that I've had since childhood, where I'm naked or in my underwear in public. Now that I've done it for real, it doesn't seem so terrifying, shameful, and embarrassing a situation. Unfortunately, my psyche has come up with new, even more humiliating scenarios for my nighttime enjoyment.

Being a former factory worker brings me new appreciation for Upton Sinclair's novel *The Jungle,* and effectively cured me of ever eating chocolate bars again. I confess that I still enjoy eating Hershey's Kisses, even though I know how terrible the raw chocolate smells. Of course, I would have never learned any of this had I not gotten the jobs in the first place. Here then, are some of the fine details.

The first job I went after was as a roadie—my stint in the most male-dominated field I could think of. I chose the heavy metal arena, since my impressions of this larger-than-life genre were based largely on Rob Reiner's "rockumentary" of a fictional heavy metal band, *This Is Spinal Tap,* along with actual heavy metal videos I'd seen on MTV—the latter seeming, at times, virtually indistinguishable from the satirical former. The music is very, very loud; the performers favor long hair, bare chests, tight pants, and macho posturing; and the typical concert takes place in a giant arena and features lots of explosions onstage. Of all the heavy metal bands, I chose Skid Row for three reasons: One was that they were actually touring; two was that while they have the adoration of angry male suburban teenagers, their appeal as pinups to the Clearasil set means there's a lot of gibbering, fainting females as well; and three, when they performed on *Saturday Night Live,* they seemed to have a sense

of humor. This is something I always look for in potential traveling companions. I had no idea that one side effect of this job
would be that I'd become a big fan of their music.

Knowing that the few women roadies that there are tend to be
"wardrobe mistresses," I asked their record company if I could
replace the one they had for a few weeks. My numerous faxed
requests eventually resulted in their handing me off to Skid
Row's management offices. Weeks of unreturned phone calls
led me to camp out in their offices, in a desperate attempt to
have an audience with Scott McGhee, their manager. After two
days of this, I finally managed to pitch my case in thirty-second
intervals between the breaks in Scott's incoming phone calls.

Eventually, Scott and the band agreed to let me join up with
them. The deal was that I wasn't going to get paid, and since
their wardrobe mistress had so little to do she was helping out
the production manager, I would be put to work doing whatever
most needed to be done. It turned out their pyrotechnician
needed an assistant. When I heard this, I thought they were trying to scare me away or have me killed. "Pack like you're going
camping," Scott advised me. "You know, work boots, nothing
fancy. Don't bring a lot of stuff."

A month later, I went directly from the late-night, all-night
grimy rock-and-roll world to the clean, conservative, nine-to-five
corporate realm of the advertising business. I got the job the
old-fashioned way, by knowing someone (Rule 4): The president
of a major advertising agency is a friend of a friend. Again, the
deal was no salary (yes, Rule 5 really works), no one in the company would know I was essentially a fraud with no experience
whatsoever, and I was also obliged to sign a confidentiality
agreement stating I would not reveal the name of the agency or
of any clients. The president felt that since they weren't paying

me, there was nothing to lose if I didn't come up with an ad, and there might be something to be gained if I did. I did come up with two ads that actually ran, but they weren't exactly award winning, ground breaking, or even memorable. In other words, they were much like the commercials most of us see and hear every day.

To be a substitute high school teacher in Virginia Beach, Virginia, all I needed to qualify was proof of a college degree, a doctor's note regarding the negative results of a TB test, a notarized statement allowing investigation into my criminal records in the state of Virginia (of course, my record in New York would be the one they should really be interested in, but this is obviously another argument for a nationalized records check), plus a list of five references. Attendance at an orientation day is required in order to process your paperwork. Being in a room full of prospective substitutes is to revisit memories of all the weird misfits that paraded through the classrooms of your youth, as the same types are still applying: the guys with the plastic pocket protectors, nerdy glasses, and bits of spittle collecting in the corners of their mouths, and the twentysomething women who can easily pass for Miss Jane on *The Beverly Hillbillies*. Since I was applying like anyone else, the good news was I was actually going to get paid. The bad news was finding out what teachers earn.

Of course, this little taste of bureaucracy was nothing compared to the Orwellian nightmare that is Las Vegas. As almost all of the casinos are unionized, I had to first contact the Culinary Workers Union, of which cocktail waitresses are members, to ask if they could grant me temporary union status. I was actually expecting them to laugh and hang up, but (Rule 1) I had the good fortune of stating my case to Local 226's own Johnny LaVoie. He thought my working undercover in a casino sounded like a great idea, so he and a dispatcher named Sandy Turner promised—and delivered—secrecy, full union support, and help looking for a job.

I was expecting my next position, that of a Los Angeles publicist to the stars, to be extremely difficult to arrange. I imagined I'd encounter a lot of resistance concerning the issue of client privacy, but it turned out to be the easiest job to get out of the whole bunch. I called the first firm on my list, Baker Winokur Ryder, located in Beverly Hills, and spoke to Angela Cabel, their office manager. I explained my project, and asked if I could work in their office for three or four weeks—without pay, of course. The answer was yes (it must be that magical Rule 5 again), with no conditions. Even when I was actually working there, I kept expecting someone to come to his or her senses and throw me out, but that never happened. I often think that most of the employees were sufficiently self-absorbed as to believe I was simply a new publicist, and the memo that went out announcing the meaning of my presence went the way of most memos: read and quickly forgotten, or ignored entirely.

The glamour of attending the Golden Globes was quickly replaced by the drudgery of cleaning toilets when I worked as a suburban housewife in Darien, Connecticut. I asked everyone I knew (Rule 4) if they could recommend a medium-sized family—no babies or toddlers—who wouldn't mind if I replaced the mother for a week or two. (It would be my briefest stint, but I couldn't imagine having this particular twenty-four-hour-a-day job longer than that.) I had imagined that perhaps dozens of families would beg me to come in and work for them, but I encountered resistance from a surprising number of mothers and a ten-year-old daughter, before I found a family that agreed to take me in. Since I was looking for the most realistic, suburban, married-with-kids experience possible, I explained that of course that would mean there would be no sex whatsoever between me and the husband.

For my next job as a stripper, I thought I needed a teacher, guide, and perhaps protector, in what I imagined to be the sleazy, venal workings of this demimonde. I remembered a New Orleans–based stripper named GiO from the 1984 documentary *Stripper*, a woman who also tours the country promoting her video *How to Strip for Your Man*. I contacted her management and was thrilled to hear that GiO was willing to be my mentor. After practicing the moves outlined in her video, I joined her in New Orleans, where she arranged for me to work at the club where she headlined, the Bourbon Burlesque. GiO told the management that I was an old friend and experienced stripper from New York. (Well, if you call stripping alone in my living room *experience*.) With this glowing recommendation, GiO was the only reference I needed. After I signed a paper saying that I understood that it was my responsibility to pay taxes, a Xerox was made of my driver's license—and *voilà*, I was officially a stripper. Perhaps not so surprisingly, this was the highest-paying job I had.

The following job as a volunteer in the Austin Rape Crisis Center in Texas began with the sensation that I had landed in an advanced psychology course a week before the final exam. Volunteers who cover the hotline and counsel rape victims at the area's hospital emergency rooms undergo forty hours of training in a classroom setting. But since the classes are video-taped, I was allowed to take a crash course by watching the tapes, studying the manual, and undergoing intensive private tutoring with Nancy Tartt and Kat Hammer, two of the Center's therapists. I quickly "graduated" and was issued my official I.D. card and a beeper.

My last job, as a chocolate factory worker, was, as I mentioned, surprisingly difficult to get. I had considered applying like anyone else, but I foresaw two problems, one being that most factories regularly lay off workers and rehire from that list when a job opens up, and the other was that no matter what my cover story was, I knew I wouldn't strike anyone as the type to stay in a factory for the next ten years, which is exactly who they're interested in hiring and training. I started my job hunt for factory work in February, well in advance, I thought, of when I needed to start work in June. By the time I was begging Sunsweet to let me drive a fork lift, I was contacting companies with my bags already packed.

The first of dozens of companies I contacted for employment was Pepperidge Farm. As I mentioned, my uncle was a longtime employee, and when I was eight years old, he showed me around a plant that made Goldfish crackers. My cousins and I ate them hot off the assembly line, and to a kid, it seemed a magical place to work. Pepperidge Farm, however, wasn't particularly moved to let me see whether an adult would feel the same way. Unbeknownst to me, I contacted them for employment when they were settling a class-action suit brought by their factory workers regarding repetitive-action injuries. This is undoubtedly why they found my interest in repetitive-action work rather suspicious, and declined.

As the months went by and the rejections from candymakers mounted up, I found the most common reason for refusal was my potential "access to proprietary information." I discovered this not only involved secret chocolate ingredients, but the layout of machinery and the machines themselves. I asked one chocolate company why they don't worry about their own employees selling secrets, and the response was that "they're too stupid to know what to do with the information"; in addition, "they really need their jobs."

The Palmer Chocolate Company of Reading, Pennsylvania, said they'd hire me to make hollow chocolate bunnies, but two months after they agreed, and two days before I was to report to their employment office to get my required drug test, dexterity test, and a complete physical (rather extreme requirements for a minimum-wage job, I thought), I was informed by mail that they'd changed their minds. Palmer was going to be experimenting with some new products ("something to launch us into the big time," the letter said rather ominously), and it was strictly top secret in the factory. I began to wonder if I shouldn't get a job in a defense plant or the Pentagon, where people aren't as paranoid.

Rule 4 kicked in when an associate remembered a childhood buddy who, he assured me, is "very big in the fudge industry." His friend, Mark Wurzel, approached ten factory owners in two days before finding a willing party: a family-owned chocolate factory in New England that manufactures chocolate novelties for such companies as Hershey's. Hershey's was another company that didn't want me in their factory, although they did say I was welcome to work in their theme park, Chocolate World. I declined.

I kept Hershey's rejection to myself when I met with Richard, the owner of the factory, who said I could start work as a hand-molder in the chocolate room the following week. The deal was that none of the workers would know my real story, I would conceal the name of the factory to protect the workers, and while I would be issued a time card, I wouldn't receive any pay. At this point, working in a factory for free sounded a little too good to be true, so I told Richard that if he changed his mind, I'd be back with a gun.

Fortunately for both of us, he didn't change his mind.